Market Sense and Nonsense

Other Books by Jack D. Schwager

Hedge Fund Market Wizards: How Winning Traders Win

Market Wizards: Interviews with Top Traders

The New Market Wizards: Conversations with America's Top Traders

Stock Market Wizards: Interviews with America's Top Stock Traders

Schwager on Futures: Technical Analysis

Schwager on Futures: Fundamental Analysis

Schwager on Futures: Managed Trading: Myths & Truths

Getting Started in Technical Analysis

A Complete Guide to the Futures Markets: Fundamental Analysis, Technical Analysis, Trading, Spreads, and Options

Study Guide to Accompany Fundamental Analysis (with Steven C. Turner)

Study Guide to Accompany Technical Analysis (with Thomas A. Bierovic and Steven C. Turner)

Market Sense and Nonsense

How the Markets Really Work (And How They Don't)

Jack D. Schwager

John Wiley & Sons, Inc.

Cover design: John Wiley & Sons, Inc.

Published by John Wiley & Sons, Inc., Hoboken, New Jersey.
Published simultaneously in Canada.

Library of Congress Cataloging-in-Publication Data

Schwager, Jack D., 1948-
Market sense and nonsense : how the markets really work (and how they don't) / Jack D. Schwager.
p. cm.
Includes index.
ISBN 978-1-118-49456-1 (cloth); 978-1-118-50934-0 (ebk); 978-1-118-50943-2 (ebk); 978-1-118-52316-2 (ebk)
1. Investment analysis. 2. Risk management. 3. Investments. I. Title.
HG4529.S387 2013
332.6—dc23

2012030901

Printed in the United States of America

10 9 8 7 6 5 4 3 2

No matter how hard you throw a dead fish in the water, it still won't swim.

—Congolese proverb

With love to my children and our times together:
To Daniel and whitewater rafting in Maine (although
I could do without the emergency room visit next time)
To Zachary and the Costa Rican rainforest,
crater hole roads, and the march of the crabs
To Samantha and the hills and restaurants of
Lugano on a special weekend
I hope these memories make you smile
as much as they do me.

With love to my wife, Jo Ann, for so many shared times:
5,000 BTU × 2, cashless honeymoon, Thanksgiving snow
in Bolton, Minnewaska and Mohonk, Mexican volcanoes,
the Mettlehorn, wheeling in Nova Scotia and PEI, weekends
at our Geissler retreat, the Escarpment, Big Indian,
Yellowstone in winter, Long Point and Net Result.

Contents

Foreword

I was initially flattered when Jack asked me to consider writing the Foreword for his new book. So, at this point, it seems ungrateful for me to start off with a complaint. But here goes. I wish Jack had written this book sooner.

It would have been great to have had it as a resource when I was in MBA school back in the late 1970s. There, I was learning things about the efficient market theory (things that are still taught in MBA school to this day) that made absolutely no sense to me. Well, at least they made no sense if I opened my eyes and observed how the real world appeared to work outside of my business school classroom. I sure wish that back then I'd had Jack's simple, commonsense explanation and refutation of efficient markets laid out right in front of me to help direct my studies and to put my mind at ease.

It would have been nice as a young portfolio manager to have a better understanding of how to think about portfolio risk in a framework that considered all different aspects of risk, not just the narrow framework that I had been taught in school or the one I used intuitively (a combination of fear of loss and hoping for the best).

I wish I'd had this book to give to my clients to help them judge me and their other managers not just by recent returns, or volatility, or correlation, or drawdowns, or outperformance, but by a longer perspective and deeper understanding of all of those concepts.

I wish, as a business school professor, I could have given this book to my MBA students so that the myths and misinformation they had already been taught or read about could be debunked before institutionalized nonsense and fuzzy thinking set them on the wrong path.

I wish I'd had this book to help me on all the investment committees I've sat on over the years. How to think about short-term track records, long-term track records, risk metrics, correlations, benchmarks, indexes, and portfolio management certainly would have come in handy! (Jack, where were you?)

Perhaps, most important, for friends and family it would have been great to hand them this book to help them gain the lifelong benefits of understanding how the markets really work (and how they don't).

So, thanks to Jack for writing this incredibly simple, clear, and commonsense guide to the market. Better late than never. I will recommend it to everyone I know. *Market Sense and Nonsense* is now required reading for every investor (and the *sooner* they read it, the better).

Joel Greenblatt
August 2012

Prologue*

Many years ago when I worked as a research director for one of the major Wall Street brokerage firms, one of my job responsibilities included evaluating commodity trading advisors (CTAs).[1] One of the statistics that CTAs were required by the regulatory authorities to report was the percentage of client accounts that closed with a profit. I made the striking discovery that the majority of closed accounts showed a net loss for virtually all the CTAs I reviewed—even those who had no losing years! The obvious implication was that investors were so bad in timing their investment entries and exits that most of them lost money—*even when they chose a consistently winning CTA!* This poor timing reflects the common investor tendency to commit to an investment after it has done well and to liquidate an investment after it has done poorly. Although these types of

---

*Some of the text in the first two paragraphs has been adapted from Jack D. Schwager, *Managed Trading: Myths & Truths* (New York: John Wiley & Sons, 1996).

[1]Commodity trading advisor (CTA) is the official designation of regulated managers who trade the futures markets.

investment decisions may sound perfectly natural, even instinctive, they are also generally wrong.

Investors are truly their own worst enemy. The natural instincts of most investors lead them to do exactly the wrong thing with uncanny persistence. The famous quote from Walt Kelly's cartoon strip, *Pogo*, "We have met the enemy, and it is us," could serve as a fitting universal motto for investors.

Investment errors are hardly the exclusive domain of novice investors. Investment professionals commit their own share of routine errors. One common error that manifests itself in many different forms is the tendency to draw conclusions based on insufficient or irrelevant data. The housing bubble of the early 2000s provided a classic example. One of the ingredients that made the bubble possible was the development of elaborate mathematical models to price complex mortgage-backed securitizations. The problem was that there was no relevant data to feed into these models. At the time, mortgages were being issued to subprime borrowers without requiring any down payment or verification of job, income, or assets. There was no precedence for such poor-quality mortgages, and hence no relevant historical data. The sophisticated mathematical models failed disastrously because conclusions were being derived based on data that was irrelevant to the present circumstances.[2] Despite the absence of relevant data, the models served as justification for attaching high ratings to risk-laden subprime-mortgage-linked debt securitizations. Investors lost over a trillion dollars.

Drawing conclusions based on insufficient or inappropriate data is commonplace in the investment field. The mathematics of portfolio allocation provides another pervasive example. The standard portfolio optimization model uses historical returns, volatilities, and correlations of assets to derive an optimal portfolio—that is, the combination of assets that will deliver the highest return for any given level of volatility. The question that fails to be asked, however, is whether the historical returns, volatilities, and correlations being used in the analysis are likely to

[2]Although the most widely used model to price mortgage-backed securitizations used credit default swaps (CDSs) rather than default rates as a proxy for default risk, CDS prices would have been heavily influenced by historical default rates that were based on irrelevant mortgage default data.

be at all indicative of future levels. Very frequently they are not, and the mathematical model delivers results that precisely fit the past data but are worthless, or even misleading, as guidelines for the future—and the future, of course, is what is relevant to investors.

Market models and theories of investment are often based on mathematical convenience rather than empirical evidence. A whole edifice of investment theory has been built on the assumption that market prices are normally distributed. The normal distribution is very handy for analysts because it allows for precise probability-based assumptions. Every few years, one or more global markets experience a price move that many portfolio managers insist should occur only "once in a thousand years" or "once in a million years" (or even much rarer intervals). Where do these probabilities come from? They are the probabilities of such magnitude price moves occurring, *assuming prices adhere to a normal distribution*. One might think that the repeated occurrence of events that should be a rarity would lead to the obvious conclusion that the price model being used does not fit the real world of markets. But for a large part of the academic and financial establishment, it has not led to this conclusion. Convenience trumps reality.

The simple fact is that many widely held investment models and assumptions are simply wrong—that is, if we insist they work in the real world. In addition, investors bring along their own sets of biases and unsubstantiated beliefs that lead to misguided conclusions and flawed investment decisions. In this book, we will question the conventional wisdom applied to the various aspects of the investment process, including selection of assets, risk management, performance measurement, and portfolio allocation. Frequently, accepted truths about investment prove to be unfounded assumptions when exposed to the harsh light of the facts.

Part One

MARKETS, RETURN, AND RISK

Chapter 1

Expert Advice

Comedy Central versus CNBC

On March 4, 2009, Jon Stewart, the host of *The Daily Show*, a satirical news program, lambasted CNBC for a string of poor prognostications. The catalyst for the segment was Rick Santelli's famous rant from the floor of the Chicago Mercantile Exchange, in which he railed against subsidizing "losers' mortgages," a clip that went viral and is widely credited with igniting the Tea Party movement. Stewart's point was that while Santelli was criticizing irresponsible homeowners who missed all the signs, CNBC was in no position to be sitting in judgment.

Stewart then proceeded to play a sequence of CNBC clips highlighting some of the most embarrassingly erroneous forecasts and advice made by multiple CNBC commentators, each followed by a white type on black screen update. The segments included:

- Jim Cramer, the host of *Mad Money*, answering a viewer's question by emphatically declaring, "Bear Stearns is fine! Keep your money where it is." A black screen followed: "Bear Stearns went under six days later."

- A *Power Lunch* commentator extolling the financial strength of Lehman Brothers saying, "Lehman is no Bear Stearns." Black screen: "Lehman Brothers went under three months later."
- Jim Cramer on October 4, 2007, enthusiastically recommending, "Bank of America is going to $60 in a heartbeat." Black screen: "Today Bank of America trades under $4."
- Charlie Gasparino saying that American International Group (AIG) as the biggest insurance company was obviously not going bankrupt, which was followed by a black screen listing the staggeringly large AIG bailout installments to date and counting.
- Jim Cramer's late 2007 bullish assessment, "You should be buying things. Accept that they are overvalued. . . . I know that sounds irresponsible, but that's how you make the money." The black screen followed: "October 31, 2007, Dow 13,930."
- Larry Kudlow exclaiming, "The worst of this subprime business is over." Black screen: "April 16, 2008, Dow 12,619."
- Jim Cramer again in mid-2008 exhorting, "It's time to buy, buy, buy!" Black screen: "June 13, 2008, Dow 12,307."
- A final clip from *Fast Money* talking about "people starting to get their confidence back" was followed by a final black screen message: "November 4, 2008, Dow 9,625."

Stewart concluded, "If I had only followed CNBC's advice, I'd have a $1 million today—provided I started with $100 million."

Stewart's clear target was the network, CNBC, which, while promoting its financial expertise under the slogan "knowledge is power," was clueless in spotting the signs of the impending greatest financial crisis in nearly a century. Although Stewart did not personalize his satiric barrage, Jim Cramer, whose frenetic presentation style makes late-night infomercial promoters appear sedated in comparison, seemed to come in for a disproportionate share of the ridicule. A widely publicized media exchange ensued between Cramer and Stewart in the following days, with each responding to the other, both on their own shows and as guests on other programs, and culminating with Cramer's appearance as an interview guest on *The Daily Show* on March 12. Stewart was on the attack for most of the interview, primarily chastising CNBC for taking corporate representatives at their word rather than doing any investigative reporting—in effect, for acting like corporate shills rather than reporters. Cramer did not try to defend against the charge, saying that company CEOs had openly lied to him, which was something he too regretted and wished he'd had the power to prevent.

The program unleashed an avalanche of media coverage, with most writers and commentators seeming to focus on the question of who won the "debate." (The broad consensus was Stewart.) What interests us here is not the substance or outcome of the so-called debate, but rather Stewart's original insinuation that Cramer and other financial pundits at CNBC had provided the public with poor financial advice. Is this criticism valid? Although the sequence of clips Stewart played on his March 4 program was damning, Cramer had made thousands of recommendations on his *Mad Money* program. Anyone making that many recommendations could be made to look horrendously inept by cherry-picking the worst forecasts or advice. To be fair, one would have to examine the entire record, not just a handful of samples chosen for their maximum comedic impact.

That is exactly what three academic researchers did. In their study, Joseph Engelberg, Caroline Sasseville, and Jared Williams (ESW) surveyed and analyzed the accuracy and impact of 1,149 first-time buy recommendations made by Cramer on *Mad Money*.[1] Their analysis covered the period from July 28, 2005 (about four months after the program's launch) through February 9, 2009—an end date that conveniently was just three weeks prior to *The Daily Show* episode mocking CNBC's market calls.

ESW began by examining a portfolio formed by the stocks recommended on *Mad Money*, assuming each stock was entered on the close before the evening airing of the program on which it was recommended—a point in time deliberately chosen to reflect the market's valuation prior to the program's price impact. They assumed an equal dollar allocation among recommended stocks and tested the results

---

[1]Engelberg, Joseph, Caroline Sasseville, and Jared Williams, *Market Madness? The Case of* Mad Money (October 20, 2010). Available at SSRN: http://ssrn.com/abstract=870498.

for a variety of holding periods, ranging from 50 to 250 trading days. The differences in returns between these recommendation-based portfolios and the market were statistically insignificant across all holding periods and net negative for most.

ESW then looked at the overnight price impact (percentage change from previous close to next day's open) of Cramer's recommendations and found an extremely large 2.4 percent average abnormal return—that is, return in excess of the average price change of similar stocks for the same overnight interval. As might be expected based on the mediocre results of existing investors in the same stocks and the large overnight influence of Cramer's recommendations, using entries on the day after the program, the recommendation-based portfolios underperformed the market across all the holding periods. The annualized underperformance was substantial, ranging from 3 percent to 10 percent. The worst performance was for the shortest holding period (50 days), suggesting a strong bias for stocks to surrender their "Cramer bump" in the ensuing period. The bottom line seems to be that investors would be better off buying and holding an index than buying the *Mad Money* recommendations—although, admittedly, there is much less entertainment value in buying an index.

I don't mean to pick on Cramer. There is no intention to paint Cramer as a showman with no investment skill. On the contrary, according to an October 2005 *BusinessWeek* article, Cramer achieved a 24 percent net compounded return during his 14-year tenure as a hedge fund manager—a very impressive performance record. But regardless of Cramer's investment skills and considerable market knowledge, the fact remains that, on average, viewers following his recommendations would have been better off throwing darts to pick stocks.

The Elves Index

The study that examined the *Mad Money* recommendations represented the track record of only a single market expert for a four-year time period. Next we examine an index that was based on the input of 10 experts and was reported for a period of over 12 years.

The most famous, longest-running, and most widely watched stock-market-focused program ever was *Wall Street Week* with Louis

Rukeyser, which aired for over 30 years. One feature of the show was the Elves Index. The Elves Index was launched in 1989 and was based on the net market opinion of 10 expert market analysts selected by Rukeyser. Each analyst opinion was scored as +1 for bullish, 0 for neutral, and –1 for bearish. The index had a theoretical range from –10 (all analysts bearish) to +10 (all analysts bullish). The concept was that when a significant majority of these experts were bullish, the market was a buy (+5 was the official buy signal), and if there was a bearish consensus, the market was a sell (–5 was the official sell signal). That is not how it worked out, though.

In October 1990 the Elves Index reached its most negative level since its launch, a –4 reading, which was just shy of an official sell signal. This bearish consensus coincided with a major market bottom and the start of an extended bull market. The index then registered lows of –6 in April 1994 and –5 in November 1994, coinciding with the relative lows of the major bottom pattern formed in 1994. The index subsequently reached a bullish extreme of +6 in May 1996 right near a major relative high. The index again reached +6 in July 1998 shortly before a 19 percent plunge in the S&P 500 index. A sequence of the highest readings ever recorded for the index occurred in the late 1999 to early 2000 period, with the index reaching an all-time high (up to then) of +8 in December 1999. The Elves Index remained at high levels as the equity indexes peaked in the first quarter of 2000 and then plunged. At one point, still early in the bear market, the Elves Index even reached an all-time high of +9. Rukeyser finally retired the index shortly after 9/11, when presumably, if kept intact, it would have provided a strong sell signal.[2]

Rukeyser no doubt terminated the Elves Index as an embarrassment. Although he didn't comment on the timing of the decision, it is reasonable to assume he couldn't tolerate another major sell signal in the index coinciding with what would probably prove to be a relative low

[2]"Louis Rukeyser Shelves Elves Missed Market Trends Tinkering Didn't Improve Index's Track Record for Calling Market's Direction (MUTUAL FUNDS)," *Investor's Business Daily*, November 1, 2001. Retrieved March 29, 2011, from AccessMyLibrary: www.accessmylibrary.com/article-1G2.106006432/louis-rukeyser-shelves-elves.html.

(as it was). Although the Elves Index had compiled a terrible record—never right, but often wrong—its demise was deeply regretted by many market observers. The index was so bad that many had come to view it as a useful contrarian indicator. In other words, listening to the consensus of the experts as reflected by the index was useful—as long as you were willing to do the exact opposite.

Paid Advice

In this final section, we expand our analysis to encompass a group that includes hundreds of market experts. If there is one group of experts that might be expected to generate recommendations that beat the market averages, it is those who earn a living selling their advice—that is, financial newsletter writers. After all, if a newsletter's advice failed to generate any excess return, presumably it would find it difficult to attract and retain readers willing to pay for subscriptions.

Do the financial newsletters do better than a market index? To find the answer, I sought out the data compiled by the *Hulbert Financial Digest*, a publication that has been tracking financial newsletter recommendations for over 30 years. In 1979, the editor, Mark Hulbert, attended a financial conference and heard many presentations in which investment advisers claimed their recommendations earned over 100 percent a year, and in some cases much more. Hulbert was skeptical about these claims and decided to track the recommendations of some of these advisers in real time. He found the reality to be far removed from the hype. This realization led to the launch of the *Hulbert Financial Digest* with a mission of objectively tracking financial newsletter recommendations and translating them into implied returns. Since its launch in 1981, the publication has tracked over 400 financial newsletters.

Hulbert calculates an average annual return for each newsletter based on their recommendations. Table 1.1 compares the average annual return of all newsletters tracked by Hulbert versus the S&P 500 for three 10-year intervals and the entire 30-year period. (The newsletter return for any given year is the average return of all the newsletters tracked by

Table 1.1 Average Annual Return: S&P 500 versus Average of Financial Newsletters

Time Period	S&P 500	Average of Financial Newsletters	Newsletters Minus S&P 500
1981–1990	14.5%	9.0%	–5.5%
1991–2000	18.2	10.0	–8.2
2001–2010	3.5	6.3	2.8
All Years (1981–2010)	**12.1**	**8.4**	**–3.7**

Source: Raw data on investment newsletter performance from the *Hulbert Financial Digest.*

Table 1.2 Average Annual Return: S&P 500 versus Average of Financial Newsletters in Top and Bottom Deciles in Prior Three-Year Periods

Time Period	S&P 500	Average of Top Decile	Average of Bottom Decile	Top Decile Minus S&P 500	Bottom Decile Minus S&P 500
1984–1990	15.2%	8.2%	5.0%	–7.0%	–10.2%
1991–2000	18.2	16.7	–0.7	–1.5	–18.9
2001–2010	3.5	3.4	6.1	–0.1	2.6
All Years (1984–2010)	**12.0**	**9.6**	**3.3**	**–2.4**	**–8.7**

Source: Raw data on investment newsletter performance from the *Hulbert Financial Digest.*

Hulbert in that year.) As a group, the financial newsletters significantly underperformed the S&P 500 during 1981–1990 and 1991–2000 and did moderately better than the S&P 500 during 2001–2010. For the entire 30-year period, the newsletters lagged the S&P 500 by an average of 3.7 percent per annum.

Perhaps if the choice of newsletters were restricted to those that performed best in the recent past, this more select group would do much better than the group as whole. To examine this possibility, we focus on the returns generated by the top-decile performers in prior three-year periods. Thus, for example, the 1994 returns would be based on the average of only those newsletters that had top-decile performance for the 1991–1993 period. Table 1.2 compares the performance of these past better-performing newsletters with the S&P 500 and also includes comparison returns for the past worst-decile-return group. Choosing

Table 1.3 Average Annual Return: S&P 500 versus Average of Financial Newsletters in Top and Bottom Deciles in Prior Five-Year Periods

Time Period	S&P 500	Average of Top Decile	Average of Bottom Decile	Top Decile Minus S&P 500	Bottom Decile Minus S&P 500
1986–1990	13.9%	1.7%	6.7%	−12.2%	−7.2%
1991–2000	18.2	15.6	−4.9	−2.6	−23.1
2001–2010	3.5	5.7	6.4	2.2	2.9
All Years (1986–2010)	**11.5**	**8.9**	**2.0**	**−2.6**	**−9.5**

Source: Raw data on investment newsletter performance from the *Hulbert Financial Digest.*

from among the best past performers doesn't seem to make much difference. The past top-decile-return newsletters still lag the S&P 500. Although picking the best prior performers doesn't seem to provide much of an edge, it does seem advisable to avoid the worst prior performers, which for the period as a whole did much worse than the average of all newsletters.

Perhaps three years is a look-back period of insufficient length to establish superior performance. To examine this possibility, Table 1.3 duplicates the same analysis comparing the past five-year top- and bottom-decile performers with the S&P 500. The relative performance results are strikingly similar to the three-year look-back analysis. For the period as a whole, the past top-decile performers lagged the S&P 500 by 2.6 percent (versus 2.4 percent in the three-year look-back analysis), and the bottom-decile group lagged by a substantive 9.5 percent (versus 8.7 percent in the prior analysis). The conclusion is the same: Picking the best past performers doesn't seem to provide any edge over the S&P 500, but avoiding the worst past performers appears to be a good idea.

Some of the newsletters tracked by Hulbert did indeed add value, delivering market-beating recommendations over the long term. Picking these superior newsletters ahead of time, however, is no easy task. The complicating factor is that while some superior past performers continue to do well, others don't. Simply selecting from the best past performers is not sufficient to identify the newsletters whose advice is likely to beat the market in a coming year.

Investment Misconception

Investment Misconception 1: The average investor can benefit by listening to the recommendations made by the financial experts.

Reality: The amazing thing about expert advice is how consistently it fails to do better than a coin toss. In fact, even that assessment is overly generous, as the preponderance of empirical evidence suggests that the experts do worse than random. Yes, that means the chimpanzee throwing darts at the stock quote page will not merely do as well as the experts—the chimpanzee will do better!

Investment Insights

Many investors seek guidance from the advice of financial experts available through both broadcast and print media. Is this advice beneficial? In this chapter, we have examined three cases of financial expert advice, ranging from the recommendation-based record of a popular financial program host to an index based on the directional calls of 10 market experts and finally to the financial newsletter industry. Although this limited sample does not rise to the level of a persuasive proof, the results are entirely consistent with the available academic research on the subject. The general conclusion appears to be that the advice of the financial experts may sometimes trigger an immediate price move as the public responds to their recommendations (a price move that is impossible to capture), but no longer-term net benefit.

My advice to equity investors is either buy an index fund (but not after a period of extreme gains—see Chapter 3) or, if you have sufficient interest and motivation, devote the time and energy to develop your own investment or trading methodology. Neither of these approaches involves listening to the recommendations of the experts. Michael Marcus, a phenomenally successful trader, offered some sage advice on the matter: "You have to follow your own light. . . . As long as you stick to your own style, you get the good and the bad in your own approach. When you try to incorporate someone else's style, you often wind up with the worst of both styles."[3]

[3]Jack D. Schwager, *Market Wizards* (New York: New York Institute of Finance, 1989).

Chapter 2

The Deficient Market Hypothesis

The most basic investment question is: Can the markets be beat? The efficient market hypothesis provides an unambiguous answer: No, unless you count those who are lucky.

The efficient market hypothesis, a theory explaining how market prices are determined and the implications of the process, has been the foundation of much of the academic research on markets and investing during the past half century. The theory underlies virtually every important aspect of investing, including risk measurement, portfolio optimization, index investing, and option pricing. The efficient market hypothesis can be summarized as follows:

- Prices of traded assets already reflect all known information.
- Asset prices instantly change to reflect new information.

Therefore,

- Market prices are true and accurate.
- It is impossible to consistently outperform the market by using any information that the market already knows.

The efficient market hypothesis comes in three basic flavors:

1. **Weak efficiency.** This form of the efficient market hypothesis states that past market price data cannot be used to beat the market. Translation: Technical analysis is a waste of time.
2. **Semistrong efficiency** (presumably named by a politician). This form of the efficient market hypothesis contends that you can't beat the market using any publicly available information. Translation: Fundamental analysis is also a waste of time.
3. **Strong efficiency.** This form of the efficient market hypothesis argues that even private information can't be used to beat the market. Translation: The enforcement of insider trading rules is a waste of time.

The Efficient Market Hypothesis and Empirical Evidence

It should be clear that if the efficient market hypothesis were true, markets would be impossible to beat except by luck. Efficient market hypothesis proponents have compiled a vast amount of evidence that markets are extremely difficult to beat. For example, there have been many studies that show that professional mutual fund managers consistently underperform benchmark stock indexes, which is the result one would expect if the efficient market hypothesis were true. Why underperform? Because if the efficient market hypothesis were true, the professionals should do no better than the proverbial monkey throwing darts at a list of stock prices or a random process, which on average should lead to an approximate index result if there were no costs involved. However, there are costs involved: commissions, transaction slippage (bid/asked differences), and investor fees. Therefore, on average, the professional managers should do somewhat worse than the indexes, which they do. The efficient market hypothesis proponents point to the empirical evidence of the conformity of investment results to that implied by the theory as evidence that the theory either is correct or provides a close approximation of reality.

There is, however, a logical flaw in empirical proofs of the efficient market hypothesis, which can be summarized as follows:

- If A is true (e.g., the efficient market hypothesis is true),
- and A implies B (e.g., markets are difficult to beat),
- then the converse (B implies A) is also true (if markets are difficult to beat, then the efficient market hypothesis is true).

The logical flaw is that the converse of a true statement is not necessarily true. Consider the following simple example:

- All polar bears are white mammals.
- But clearly, not all white mammals are polar bears.

While empirical evidence can't prove the efficient market hypothesis, it can disprove it if one can find events that contradict the theory. There is no shortage of such events. We will look at four types of empirical evidence that clearly seem to contradict the efficient market hypothesis:

1. Prices that are demonstrably imperfect.
2. Large price changes unaccompanied by significant changes in fundamentals.
3. Price moves that lag the fundamentals.
4. Track records that are too good to be explained by luck if the efficient market hypothesis were true.

The Price Is Not Always Right

A cornerstone principle underlying the efficient market hypothesis is that market prices are perfect. Viewed in the light of actual market examples, this assumption seems nothing short of preposterous. We consider only a few out of a multitude of possible illustrative examples.

Pets.com and the Dot-Com Mania

Pets.com is a reasonable poster child for the Internet bubble. As its name implies, Pets.com's business model was selling pet supplies over the

Internet. One particular problem with this model was that core products, such as pet food and cat litter, were low-margin items, as well as heavy and bulky, which made them expensive to ship. Also, these were not exactly the types of products for which there was any apparent advantage to online delivery. On the contrary, if you were out of dog food or cat litter, waiting for delivery of an online order was not a practical alternative. Given these realities, Pets.com had to price its products, including shipping, competitively. In fact, given the large shipping cost, the only way the company could sell product was to set prices at levels below its own total cost. This led to the bizarre situation in which the more product Pets.com sold, the more money it lost. Despite these rather bleak fundamental realities, Pets.com had a market capitalization in excess of $300 million following its initial public offering (IPO). The company did not survive even a full year after its IPO. Ironically, Pets.com could have lasted longer if it could just have cut sales, which were killing the company.

Pets.com was hardly alone, but is emblematic of the dot-com mania. From 1998 to early 2000, the market experienced a speculative mania in technology stocks and especially Internet stocks. During this period, there were numerous successful IPO launches for companies with negative cash flows and no reasonable near-term prospects for turning a profit. Because it was impossible to justify the valuation of these companies, or for that matter even any positive valuation, by any traditional metrics (that is, those related to earnings and assets), this era saw equity analysts invent such far-fetched metrics as the number of clicks or "eyeballs" per website with talk of a "new paradigm" in equity valuation. Many of these companies, which reached valuations of hundreds of millions or even billions of dollars, crashed and burned within one or two years of their launch. *Burn* is the appropriate word, as the timing of the demise of these tenuous companies was linked to their so-called burn rate—the rate at which their negative cash flow consumed cash.

Figure 2.1 shows the AMEX Internet Index during the 1998–2002 period. From late 1998 to the March 2000 peak, the index increased an incredible sevenfold in the space of 17 months. The index then surrendered the entire gain, falling 86 percent in the next 18 months. The efficient market hypothesis not only requires believing that the fundamentals improved sufficiently between October 1998 and March 2000

Figure 2.1 AMEX Internet Index (IIX), 1998–2002
SOURCE: moneycentral.msn.com.

to justify a 600 percent increase in this short time span, but that the fundamentals then deteriorated sufficiently for prices to fall 86 percent by September 2001. A far more plausible explanation is that the giant rally in Internet stocks from late 1998 to early 2000 was unwarranted by the fundamentals, and therefore the ensuing collapse represented a return of prices to levels more consistent with prevailing fundamentals. Such an explanation, however, contradicts the efficient market hypothesis, which would require new fundamental developments to explain both the rally and the collapse phases.

A Subprime Investment[1]

A subprime mortgage bond combines multiple individual subprime mortgages into a security that pays investors interest income based on the proceeds from mortgage payments. These bonds typically employ a structure in which multiple tranches (or classes) are created from the same pool of mortgages. The highest-rated class, AAA, gets paid off in full first; then the next highest-rated class (AA) is paid off, and so on. The

[1]For a lucid and colorful depiction of the subprime securities fiasco, see Michael Lewis, *The Big Short* (New York: W.W. Norton, 2010). This section has been excerpted from Jack Schwager, *Hedge Fund Market Wizards* (Hoboken, NJ: John Wiley & Sons, 2012).

higher the class, the lower the risk, and hence the lower the interest rate the tranche receives. The so-called equity tranche, which is not rated, typically absorbs the first 3 percent of losses and is wiped out if this loss level is reached. The lower-rated tranches are the first to absorb default risk, for which they are paid a higher rate of interest. For example, a typical BBB tranche, the lowest-rated tranche, would begin to be impaired if losses due to defaulted repayments reached 3 percent, and investors would lose all their money if losses reached 7 percent. Each higher tranche would be protected in full until losses surpassed the upper threshold of the next lower tranche. The lowest-rated tranche (i.e., BBB), however, is always exposed to a significant risk of at least some impairment.

During the housing bubble of the mid-2000s, the risks associated with the BBB tranches of subprime bonds, which were high to start, increased dramatically. There was a significant deterioration in the quality of loans, as loan originators were able to pass on the risk by selling their mortgages for use in bond securitizations. The more mortgages they issued and sold off, the greater the fees they collected. Effectively, mortgage originators were freed from any concern about whether the mortgages they issued would actually be repaid. Instead, they were incentivized to issue as many mortgages as possible, which was exactly what they did. The lower they set the bar for borrowers, the more mortgages they could create. Ultimately, in fact, there was no bar at all, as subprime mortgages were being issued with the following characteristics:

- No down payment.
- No income, job, or asset verification (the so-called infamous NINJA loans).
- Adjustable-rate mortgage (ARM) structures in which low teaser rates adjusted to much higher levels after a year or two.

There was no historical precedent for such low-quality mortgages. It is easy to see how the BBB tranche of a bond formed from these low-quality mortgages would be extremely vulnerable to a complete loss.

The story, however, does not end there. Not surprisingly, the BBB tranches were difficult to sell. Wall Street alchemists came up with a solution that magically transformed the BBB tranches into AAA. They created a new securitization called a collateralized debt obligation (CDO) that consisted entirely of the BBB tranches of many mortgage bonds.[2] The CDOs also employed a tranche structure. Typically, the upper 80 percent of a CDO, consisting of 100 percent BBB tranches, was rated AAA.

Although the CDO tranche structure was similar to that employed by subprime mortgage bonds consisting of individual mortgages, there was an important difference. In a properly diversified pool of mortgages, there was at least some reason to assume there would be limited correlation in default risk among individual mortgages. Different individuals would not necessarily come under financial stress at the same time, and different geographic areas could witness divergent economic conditions. In contrast, all the individual elements of the CDOs were clones—they all represented the lowest tier of a pool of subprime mortgages. If economic conditions were sufficiently unfavorable for the BBB tranche of one mortgage bond pool to be wiped out, the odds were very high that BBB tranches in other pools would also be wiped out or at least severely impaired.[3] The AAA tranche needed a 20 percent loss to begin being impaired, which sounds like a safe number, until one considers that all the holdings are highly correlated. The BBB tranches were like a group of people in close quarters contaminated by a highly contagious flu. If one person is infected, the odds that many will be infected increase dramatically. In this context, the 20 percent cushion of the AAA class sounds more like a tissue paper layer.

How could bonds consisting of only BBB tranches be rated AAA? There are three interconnected explanations.

1. Pricing models implicitly reflected historical data on mortgage defaults. Historical mortgages in which the lender actually cared whether repayments were made and required down payments and verification bore no resemblance to the more recently minted

[2]CDOs were a general type of securitization that were also built from many other types of instruments besides mortgage bonds, but these other constructions are not germane to this discussion.

[3]Although correlations for individual mortgages could also be significant during severe economic downturns, the degree of correlation would still not be nearly as extreme as the correlations between different BBB tranches.

no-down-payment, no-verification loans. Therefore, historical mortgage default data would grossly understate the risk of more recent mortgages defaulting.[4]

2. The correlation assumptions were unrealistically low. They failed to adequately account for the sharply increased probability of BBB tranches failing if other BBB tranches failed.
3. The credit rating agencies had a clear conflict of interest: They were paid by the CDO manufacturers. If they were too harsh (read: realistic) in their ratings, they would lose the business. They were effectively incentivized to be as lax as possible in their ratings. Is this to say the credit rating agencies deliberately mismarked bonds? No, the mismarkings might have been subconscious. Although the AAA ratings for tranches of individual mortgages could be defended to some extent, it is difficult to make the same claim for the AAA ratings of CDO tranches consisting of only the BBB tranches of mortgage bonds. In regard to the CDO ratings, either the credit rating agencies were conflicted or they were incompetent.

If you are an investor, how much of an interest premium over a 10-year Treasury note would you request for investing in a AAA-rated CDO consisting entirely of BBB subprime mortgage tranches? How does ¼ of 1 percent sound? Ridiculous? Why would anyone buy a bond consisting entirely of the worst subprime assets for such a minuscule premium? Well, people did. In what universe does this pricing make sense? The efficient market hypothesis would by definition contend that these bonds consisting of BBB tranches constructed from no-verification, ARM subprime mortgages were correctly priced in paying only ¼ of 1 percent over U.S. Treasuries. Of course, the buyers of these complex securities had no idea of the inherent risk and were merely relying on

[4]To be precise, the Gaussian copula formula, which was widely used to price CDOs, used credit default swaps (CDSs) on mortgage-backed securitizations (MBSs) as a proxy for default risk. However, CDS prices would have been heavily influenced by historical default rates that were based on irrelevant data. Moreover, the historical period for which CDS data existed was characterized by steadily rising housing prices and low default rates, thereby implying misleadingly low correlation among defaults in different securitizations and grossly understating the risk in CDOs, which were constructed by combining MBSs.

the credit rating agencies. According to the efficient market hypothesis, however, knowledgeable market participants should have brought prices into line. This line of reasoning highlights another basic flaw in the efficient market hypothesis: It doesn't allow for the actions of the ignorant masses to outweigh the actions of the well informed—at least for a while—and this is exactly what happened.

Negative Value Assets—The Palm/3Com Episode[5]

Although it would seem extremely difficult to justify Internet company prices at their peak in 2000 or the AAA ratings for tranches of CDOs consisting of the lowest-quality subprime mortgages, there is no formula to yield an exact correct price at any given time. (Of course, the efficient market hypothesis believers would contend that this price is the market price.) Therefore, while these examples provide compelling illustrations of apparent drastic mispricings, they fall short of the solidity of a mathematical proof of mispricing due to investor irrationality. The Palm/3Com episode provides such incontrovertible evidence of investor irrationality and prices that can be shown to be mathematically incorrect.

On March 2, 2000, 3Com sold approximately 5 percent of its holdings in Palm, most of it in an IPO. The Palm shares were issued at $38. Palm, the leading manufacturer of handheld computers at the time, was a much sought-after offering, and the shares were sharply bid up on the first day. At one point, prices more than quadrupled the IPO price, reaching a daily (and all-time) high of $165. Palm finished the first day at a closing price of $95.06.

Since 3Com retained 95 percent ownership of Palm, 3Com shareholders indirectly owned 1.5 Palm shares for each 3Com share, based on the respective number of outstanding shares in each company. Ironically, despite the buying frenzy in Palm, 3Com shares fell 21 percent on the day of the IPO, closing at 81.181. Based on the implicit embedded holding of Palm shares, 3Com shares should have closed at a price of at least $142.59 based solely on the value of the Palm shares at

[5]Source for this section: see chapter, "The Curious Case of Palm and 3Com," in *Mastering Investment* by James Pickford (Upper Saddle River, NJ: Financial Times Prentice Hall, 2002).

their closing price ($1.5 × $95.06 = $142.59). In effect, the market was valuing the stub portion of 3Com (that is, the rest of the company excluding Palm) at –$60.78! The market was therefore assigning a large negative price to all of the company's remaining assets excluding Palm, which made absolutely no sense. At the high of the day for Palm shares, the market was implicitly assigning a negative value well in excess of $100 to the stub portion of 3Com. Adding to the illogic of this pricing, 3Com had already indicated its intention to spin off the remainder of Palm shares later that year, pending an Internal Revenue Service (IRS) ruling on the tax status, which was expected to be resolved favorably. Thus 3Com holders were likely to have their implicit ownership of Palm converted to actual shares within the same year.

The extreme disconnect between 3Com and Palm prices, despite their strong structural link, seems to be not merely wildly incongruous; it appears to border on the impossible. Why wouldn't arbitrageurs simply buy 3Com and sell Palm short in a ratio of 1.5 Palm shares to one 3Com share? Indeed, many did, but the arbitrage activity was insufficient to close the wide value gap, because Palm shares were either impossible or very expensive to borrow (a prerequisite to shorting the shares). Although the inability to adequately borrow Palm shares can explain why arbitrage didn't immediately close the price gap, it doesn't eliminate the paradox. The question remains as to why any rational investors would pay $95 for one share of Palm when they could have paid $82 for 3Com, which represented 1.5 shares of Palm plus additional assets. The paradox is even more extreme when one considers the much higher prices paid by some investors earlier in the day as Palm shares traded as high as $165. There is no escaping the fact that these investors were acting irrationally.

Given the facts, it is clear that either the market was pricing Palm too high or it was pricing 3Com too low, or some combination of the two. It is a logical impossibility to argue that both Palm and 3Com were priced perfectly, or for that matter even remotely close to correctly. At least one of the two equities was hugely mispriced.

What ultimately happened? Exactly what would have reasonably been expected: Palm shares steadily lost ground relative to 3Com, and the implied value of the 3Com stub rose steadily from deeply negative to over $10 per share at the time of the distribution of Palm shares to 3Com shareholders less than four months later. Arbitrageurs who were able to short Palm and buy 3Com profited handsomely, while Palm investors who bought shares indirectly by buying 3Com fared tremendously better than investors who purchased Palm shares directly. Gaining advantage through obvious mispricings for a high-profile IPO that was prominently discussed in the financial press is something that should have been impossible if the efficient market hypothesis were correct.

So what is the explanation for the paradoxical price relationships that occurred in the Palm spin-off? Quite simply that, contrary to the efficient market hypothesis contention that prices are always correct, sometimes emotions will cause investors to behave irrationally, resulting in prices that are far removed from fundamentally justifiable levels. In the case of Palm, this was another example of investors getting caught up in the frenzy of the tech buying bubble, which peaked only about a week after the Palm IPO. Figure 2.2 shows what happened to Palm shares after the initial IPO. (Note that this chart is depicted in terms of current share prices—that is, past prices have been adjusted for stock splits and reverse splits, which equates to a 10:1 upward adjustment in the March 2000 prices.) As can be seen, in less than two years, Palm shares lost over 99 percent of what their value had been on the close of the IPO day.

The fact that some mispricings, such as Palm/3Com, can be demonstrated with mathematical certainty lends credence to the view that numerous other cases of apparent mispricings are indeed price aberrations, even when such an absolute proof is not possible. There is an

Figure 2.2 Palm (Split-Adjusted), 2000–2002
SOURCE: moneycentral.msn.com.

important difference between this point of view and the efficient market hypothesis framework. Whereas the efficient market hypothesis view of the world argues that it is futile to search for opportunities because the market price is always right, a view that investor emotions can cause prices to deviate widely from reasonable valuations implies that there are opportunities to profit from market prices being wrong (that is, routinely trading at premiums or discounts to fair value).

The Market Is Collapsing; Where Is the News?

In the world described by the efficient market hypothesis, price moves occur because the fundamentals change and prices adjust. Large price moves therefore imply some very major event.

On October 19, 1987, a day that became known as Black Monday, equity indexes witnessed an incredible plunge. The Standard & Poor's (S&P) 500 index lost 20.5 percent, by far the largest single-day loss ever. Moreover, the actual decline was far worse. The cash S&P index, which normally is kept tightly in line with S&P futures by arbitrageurs, dramatically lagged the decline in futures on October 19, 1987, because the New York Stock Exchange (NYSE) order processing system couldn't keep up with the avalanche of orders. These mechanical delays resulted in stale limit orders (that is, orders placed earlier in the day when index prices were higher) being executed. Thus the cash market index close on October 19, 1987, was itself stale and significantly understated the actual decline. The more liquid futures market, which did not embed such stale pricing and therefore was a far more accurate indicator of the actual decline, fell by an even more astounding 29 percent! Even Black Tuesday, the October 28, 1929, crash, failed to come close, losing a mere 12.94 percent.[6] Although the 1929 Black Tuesday decline was followed the next day by an additional 10.2 percent decline, even the loss on these two days combined was still one-third smaller than the S&P futures decline on October 19, 1987. All other historic daily declines in

---

[6]The data on historical S&P daily percentage declines comes from *Stock Market Volatility: Ten Years after the Crash*, a 1997 study by G. William Schwert (Brookings-Wharton Papers on Financial Services, 1998: 65–99).

stocks were less than one-third as large (using S&P futures as the comparison). In short, the October 19, 1987, crash towers above all other historic declines, including the infamous October 1929 crash.

So what extraordinary, earth-shattering event sparked this largest one-day loss in history—and by a wide margin? Well, market commentators had to scramble to find a reason. The best they could do in identifying a catalyst was to attribute the trigger to a statement by Treasury Secretary James Baker that he favored a further weakening of the dollar versus the German mark. Statements by administration officials suggesting a weaker dollar policy are hardly momentous events for the stock market, and one can even find instances where such news was viewed as bullish. Another explanation that has been trotted out to explain the October 19, 1987, crash is that legislation coming out of a House of Representatives committee proposed eliminating tax benefits related to financing mergers. Although this development did indeed prompt selling, it occurred three full trading days earlier, so it is quite a stretch to attribute the October 19 crash to it, not to mention that such a delayed full response would still contradict the efficient market hypothesis model of prices instantaneously adjusting to new information.

What, then, caused the enormous price collapse on October 19, 1987? There are two plausible answers, which in combination are probably more helpful in explaining the price move than any contemporaneous fundamental developments:

1. **Portfolio insurance.** This market hedging technique refers to the preprogrammed sale of stock index futures, as the value of a stock portfolio declines, in order to reduce risk exposure. Once reduced, the net long exposure is increased back toward a full position as the stock index price increases. The use of portfolio insurance had grown dramatically in the years prior to the October 1987 crash, and by that time, large sums of money were being managed with this hedging technique that effectively dictated the need for automatic selling when market prices declined. The theory underlying portfolio insurance presumes that market prices move smoothly. When prices witness an abrupt, huge move, the results of the strategy may differ substantially from the theory. Such a move occurred on October 19, 1987, when prices gapped below threshold portfolio insurance sell levels at the opening, triggering an

avalanche of sell orders that were executed far below the theoretical levels. This selling, in turn, pushed prices lower, triggering portfolio insurance sell orders at lower levels, a process that repeated in a domino-effect pattern. Moreover, professional traders who recognized the potential for underlying portfolio insurance sell orders being triggered went short in anticipation of this selling, further amplifying the market's downward move. There is no denying that portfolio insurance played a major role in magnifying the price loss on October 19, 1987. Indeed, this is the basic conclusion reached by the Brady commission that was formed to study the causes of the market's collapse that day.

2. **The market was overvalued.** A simple explanation for the October 1987 market decline was that it was a continuation of the market's adjustment from overvalued price levels. At the market's peak in mid-1987, the dividend yield (dividend divided by price) had fallen to 2.7 percent, a level near the low end of the prior historical range. In this context, the collapse on October 19, 1987, can be seen as an accelerated adjustment toward fair market valuation.

Both of these explanations, however, are inconsistent with the efficient market hypothesis. In the first instance, according to the efficient market hypothesis, price declines are responses to negative changes in fundamentals rather than selling begetting more selling, as was the case in portfolio insurance. In the second, the efficient market hypothesis asserts that the overall market price is always correct—a contention that makes an adjustment from a price overvaluation a self-contradiction.

The efficient market hypothesis is inextricably linked to an underlying assumption that market price changes follow a random walk process (that is, price changes are normally distributed[7]). The assumption

[7]To be precise, the assumption is that price changes are *lognormally distributed*—that is, the logarithms of price changes are normally distributed. A lognormal distribution assumption is necessary because prices can increase by more than 100 percent, but a decrease of more than 100 percent would result in negative prices, which is an impossibility. In a lognormal distribution, the probability of an increase by a factor (k) would be equal to the probability of a price decline by the inverse of that factor ($1/k$). For example, if $k = 2$, a lognormal distribution would imply that the probability of a doubling of price is equal to the probability of a halving of price.

of a normal distribution allows one to calculate the probability of different-size price moves. Mark Rubinstein, an economist, colorfully described the improbability of the October 1987 stock market crash:

> Adherents of geometric Brownian motion or lognormally distributed stock returns (one of the foundation blocks of modern finance) must ever after face a disturbing fact: assuming the hypothesis that stock index returns are lognormally distributed with about a 20% annualized volatility (the historical average since 1928), the probability that the stock market could fall 29% in a single day is 10^{-160}. So improbable is such an event that it would not be anticipated to occur even if the stock market were to last for 20 billion years, the upper end of the currently estimated duration of the universe. Indeed, such an event should not occur even if the stock market were to enjoy a rebirth for 20 billion years in each of 20 billion big bangs.

Actually, Rubinstein drastically understated the improbability in order to create his striking description. The calculated probability of 10^{-160} is infinitesimally smaller than the 20 billion squared implied by his example. How small? 10^{-160} is roughly equivalent to randomly picking a specific atom in the universe and then randomly picking the same atom in a second trial. (This calculation is based on the estimate of 10^{80} atoms in the universe. *Source:* www.wolframalpha.com.)

There are two ways of looking at the 1987 crash in the context of the efficient market hypothesis.

1. Wow, that was really unlucky!
2. If the efficient market hypothesis were correct, the probability of the 1987 crash is clearly in the realm of impossibility. Therefore, if the model implies the impossible, the model must be wrong.

The Disconnect between Fundamental Developments and Price Moves

The efficient market hypothesis assumes that fundamental developments are instantaneously reflected in market prices. This is a theory that could be held only by someone who has never traded markets or is impervious to contradictory empirical evidence. There are continually situations in which market prices move well after the news has been known for some time. The following are a few examples.

Copper: Delayed Response to Shrinking Inventories

In 2002, copper inventories reached enormous levels. Not surprisingly, the copper market languished at low prices. Inventories then began a long decline, but prices failed to respond for over a year (see Figure 2.3). Beginning in late 2003, prices finally adjusted upward to a higher plateau, as inventories continued to slide. Prices then continued to move sideways at this higher level for about one year (early 2004 to early 2005), even though inventories fell still further. This sideways drift was followed by an explosive rally, which saw prices nearly triple in just over one year's time. Ironically, this enormous price advance occurred at a time when inventories had actually begun to increase moderately.

The long delay between the start of the decline in inventories in 2002 and the beginning of the bull market more than a year later is not difficult to explain within the confines of a rational market. Inventory levels at their peak in 2002 were simply so enormous that even a substantial decline still left a surplus and little concern regarding supply availability. The second delay, however, seems far more puzzling. Why did prices move sideways during the period from early 2004 to early 2005 while inventories continued to move even lower, and then witness a delayed soaring bull market?

An important clue is provided by the price spreads between near and distant contract months on the London Metal Exchange (LME) (copper is traded in standardized contracts deliverable on different forward dates). Normally, price spreads in copper (as well as other storable commodities) trade in a *contango* structure, a technical term that simply means that contract months further in the future trade at higher prices than more nearby contracts. This premium for more distant contracts makes sense because there is a cost in holding inventories (e.g., interest on financing, storage charges). If supplies are ample, holders of the stored commodity must be compensated, and therefore forward contracts will trade at a premium. In contrast, in times of shortage, everything changes. Here, concerns over running out of supplies will trump storage costs as buyers

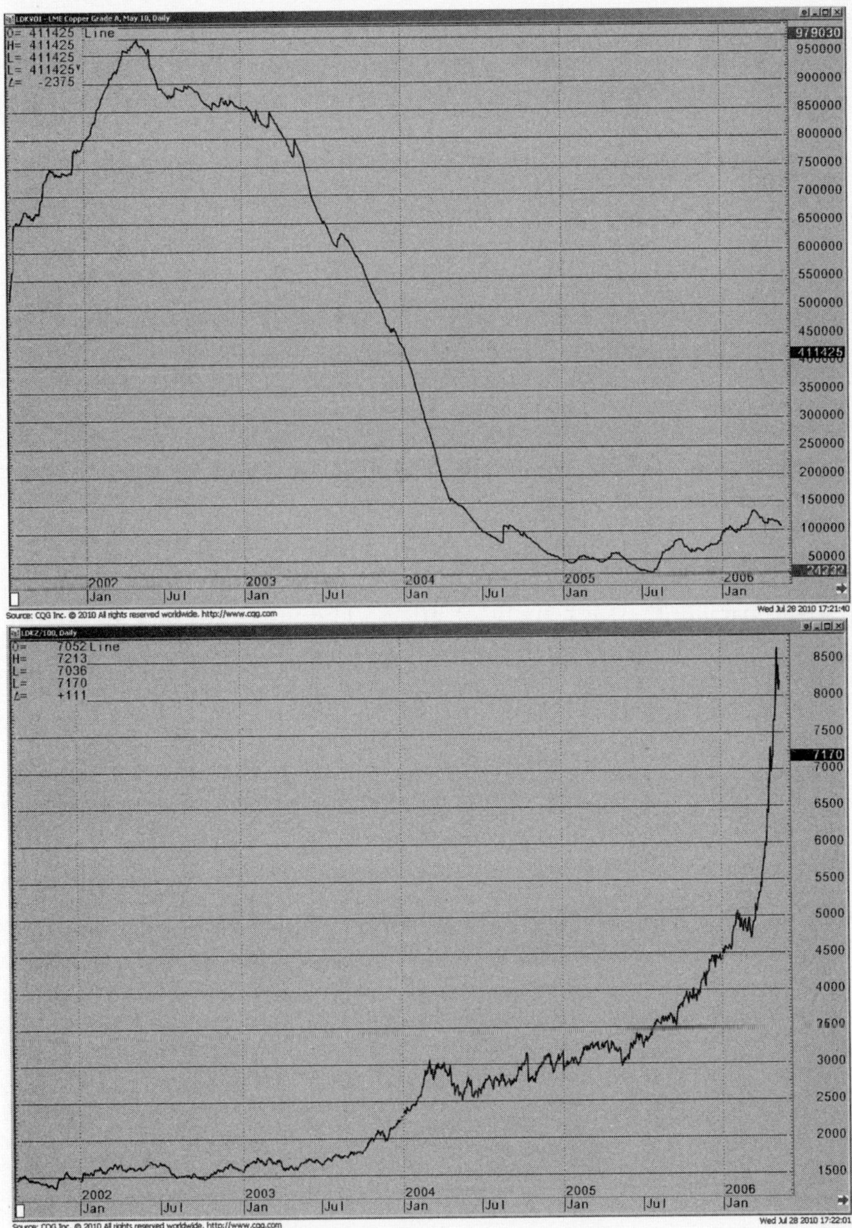

Figure 2.3 LME Copper Inventories (Top) versus LME Prices
SOURCE: CQG, Inc. © 2012 All rights reserved worldwide.

are willing to pay a premium for immediate supplies, and nearby months will trade at higher levels than more forward-dated months—a market structure termed *backwardation*.

When the market is in backwardation, producers will be less inclined to hedge their anticipated forward output, because they would be locking in a price below the current price. Even more critical, if cash price levels remain unchanged or go higher, forward short hedge positions will generate large margin calls as their prices rise to meet the cash level with the approach of the contract expiration date. The combination of reduced hedge selling and especially producer short covering, as it becomes too expensive to meet margin calls, can cause a price advance to become near vertical. In this sense, besides merely acting as a barometer of supply tightness, widening spreads between nearby and forward prices can exert a direct bullish market impact.

Figure 2.4 shows the price spread between three-month forward and 27-month forward copper. The movement of this spread seems to closely parallel the movement of prices. The initial advance of copper prices in late 2003 to a higher plateau in early 2004 coincided with the shift of the spread structure from contango to backwardation (compare

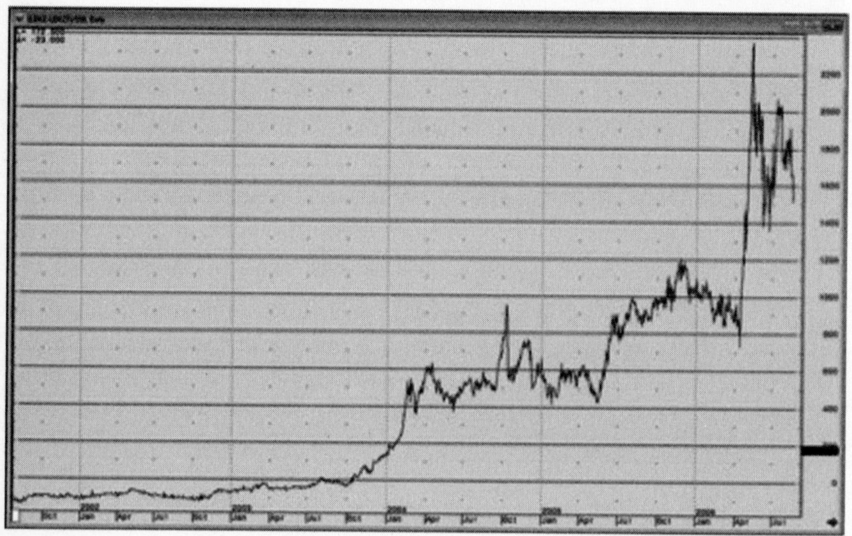

Figure 2.4 Spread Three-Month Forward/27-Month Forward LME Copper

Figure 2.3 to Figure 2.4). The subsequent yearlong sideways movement of prices followed by a huge rally approximately paralleled similar movements in the spread structure. The fact that the delayed response of copper price moves to changes in inventory is explained by the timing of changes in the price spread structure does not get efficient market hypothesis proponents off the hook. After all, the spread structure is itself determined by price levels. So if we use the spread structure to explain prices, the question then becomes: Why did the spread structure—a price-based measure—respond with long delays to the changing fundamentals?

Price responses (both price levels and spreads) followed major changes in the fundamentals (inventory levels) with long lags. The market in 2006 traded at dramatically higher price levels (and spreads at much wider backwardation) on the same fundamentals as it did in early 2005. These long lags between changes in fundamentals and price adjustments contradict the immediate price adjustments implied by the efficient market hypothesis. The more plausible explanation is that the shift in market psychology from complacency regarding ample supply availability to heightened sensitivity over supply shortages occurred gradually over time rather than as an immediate response to changing fundamentals.

Countrywide Flies High as Housing Engine Sputters

There were many reasons for the 2008 financial meltdown and the subsequent Great Recession, but certainly chief among them was the housing bubble, which saw housing prices far exceed historical norms. For over a century since the starting year of the Case-Shiller Home Price Index, the inflation-adjusted index level fluctuated in a range of approximately 70 to 130. At the peak of the 2003–2006 housing bubble, the index more than doubled its long-term median level (see Figure 2.5).

The extremes of the housing bubble were fueled by excesses in subprime mortgage lending in which loans were made to borrowers with poor credit, requiring little or no money down and in its later phases no verification of income or assets. The competition among mortgage lenders to find new borrowers seemed like a race to issue the poorest-quality mortgages possible, and in terms of both market share and excesses, Countrywide seemed to be the clear winner in this dubious contest.

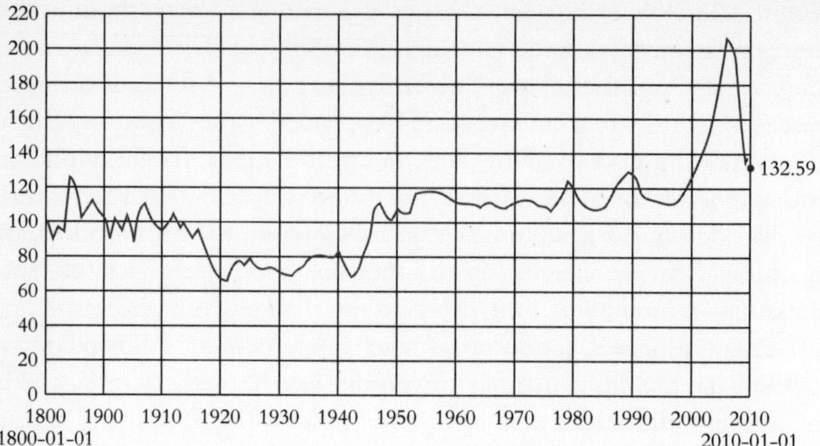

Figure 2.5 Case-Shiller National Home Price Index, Inflation-Adjusted
Source: www.multpl.com/case-shiller-home-price-index-inflation-adjusted/; underlying data: Robert Shiller and Standard & Poor's.

During the early bubble years, Countrywide was issuing loans to subprime borrowers at effectively zero cash down (by offering piggyback loans for the down payment portion of the mortgage).[8] Adding to the excess, approximately half of its loans were adjustable-rate mortgages (ARMs) with low teaser rates in the first year, which drastically increased thereafter. If you thought it was not possible to go any lower in quality than a no-money-down, adjustable-rate subprime mortgage, you would be underestimating Countrywide's creativity in finding new ways to further cheapen the quality of its loans. Countrywide came up with a mortgage called an option ARM, a mortgage in which the borrower had the option of paying less than the stipulated monthly payment, effectively increasing the principal. Countrywide was also a leader in minimizing verification. Borrowers would only need to state their income rather than provide any documentation. Countrywide's own employees aptly called these loans "liar loans." If by any chance the initial mortgage application was rejected, Countrywide loan officers

[8]The details regarding Countrywide's lending policies and practices are taken from Roger Lowenstein, *The End of Wall Street* (New York: Penguin Press, 2010).

would assist the client (read: help the applicant lie) in filling out a new application, which would invariably be approved.

Effectively, Countrywide was issuing subprime mortgages for no money down, with no required verification of income or assets, and in the case of the option ARMs, the potential for negative amortization. Given the structure and extremely poor quality of the loans, it is clear that any downturn in housing prices would mean that borrowers with inadequate financial means would immediately be underwater on their loans (owe more on the mortgage than the value of the house)—a recipe for disaster. In short, Countrywide seemed inordinately dependent on a housing market with ever-increasing prices and was particularly vulnerable to any signs of weakness in residential real estate.

The S&P/Case-Shiller Home Price Index peaked in the spring of 2006 (see Figure 2.6). At the same time, the rate of delinquencies and foreclosures on subprime ARMs rose steadily throughout 2006 and accelerated in 2007 (see Figures 2.7 and 2.8). Despite these ominous developments, Countrywide's stock price continued to trade at lofty levels, even moving to new highs in January 2007 and remaining strong

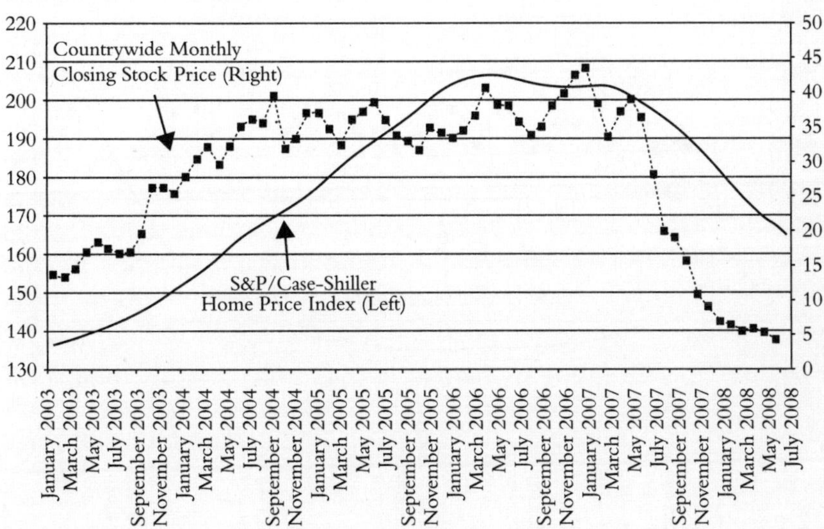

Figure 2.6 The S&P/Case-Shiller Home Price Index (20-City Composite, Seasonally Adjusted) versus Countrywide Monthly Closing Price
SOURCE: S&P Dow Jones Indices and Fiserv.

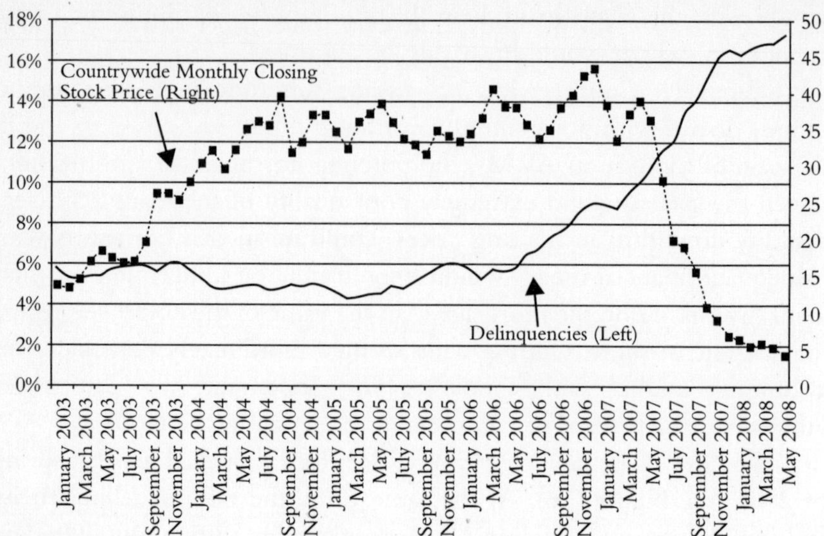

Figure 2.7 Subprime ARM Total Delinquencies versus Countrywide Monthly Closing Price
SOURCE: OTS (delinquency data).

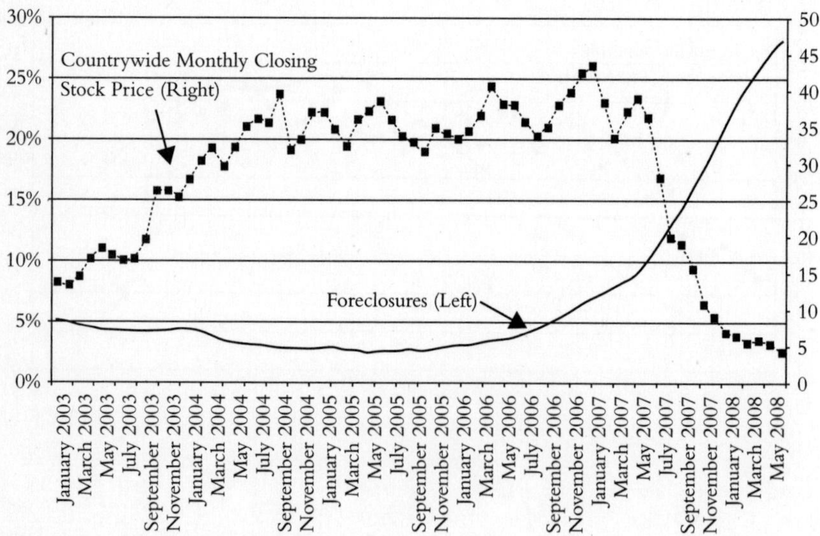

Figure 2.8 Subprime ARM Foreclosures and Real Estate Owned (REO) versus Countrywide Monthly Closing Price
SOURCE: OTS (delinquency data).

through the first half of 2007. It was not until more than a year after housing prices had peaked and a similar period of sharply rising delinquencies and foreclosures that Countrywide's stock began its collapse in July 2007. The long lag in Countrywide's response to the seriously deteriorating fundamentals, which is clearly evident in Figures 2.6, 2.7, and 2.8, seems in direct contradiction to the efficient market hypothesis assumption that prices instantaneously adjust to changing fundamentals.

Subprime Bonds Ignore Rising Foreclosures

We have already described the absurd pricing of subprime bonds. Here, however, we are concerned with another issue—the delayed response of these securities to sharply deteriorating fundamentals. Given the extremely poor quality of the subprime mortgages that were the building blocks of these bonds (adjustable rates, no verification, etc.), these securities were extraordinarily vulnerable to any downturn in the housing market. So surely at the first sign of trouble in the housing market subprime bond prices should have fallen sharply below par. Figure 2.9 shows the prices of the ABX-HE-AAA index, an index of credit default swaps tied to

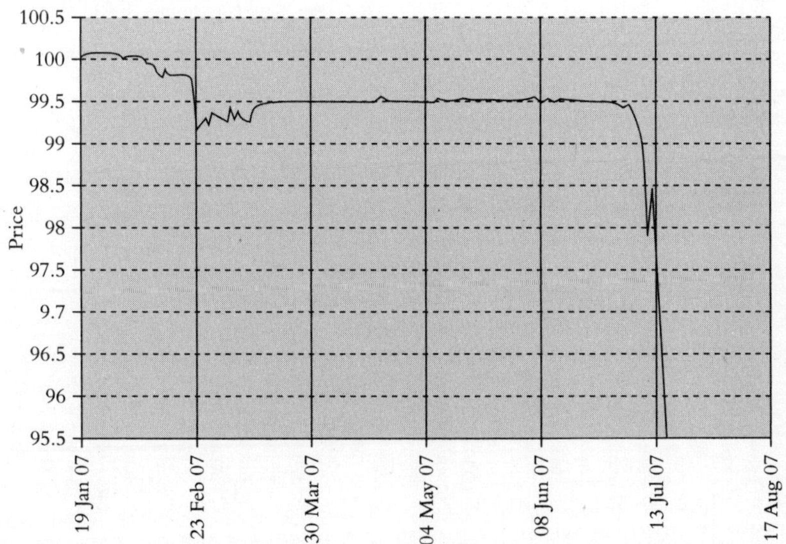

Figure 2.9 ABX-HE-AAA 07-1 Index, January to August 2007
SOURCE: Markit.com.

20 subprime-loan bonds rated AAA. (Credit default swaps are derivatives that mirror the risk premiums of the reference bonds.) Note that prices remained near par until early July 2007 when they went over a cliff.

Did the real estate market suddenly worsen in early summer 2007, as one might infer from this price chart? Figure 2.10 shows that subprime delinquencies actually reached multiyear highs a year earlier and continued to climb steadily higher. By the time the subprime mortgage bond market finally broke in July 2007, delinquencies had more than doubled from their sideways drift of earlier years. Foreclosures (also shown in Figure 2.10) started to accelerate a few months later, but by mid-2007, they had more than tripled from earlier levels.

Given the susceptibility of subprime mortgage bonds to a weakening residential real estate market, the market's yearlong complacency in the face of sharply rising delinquency and foreclosure rates is remarkable, but perhaps not as remarkable as the efficient market contention that markets immediately discount all new information. Here is new information that is critical to the market's pricing structure, and the market ignores it

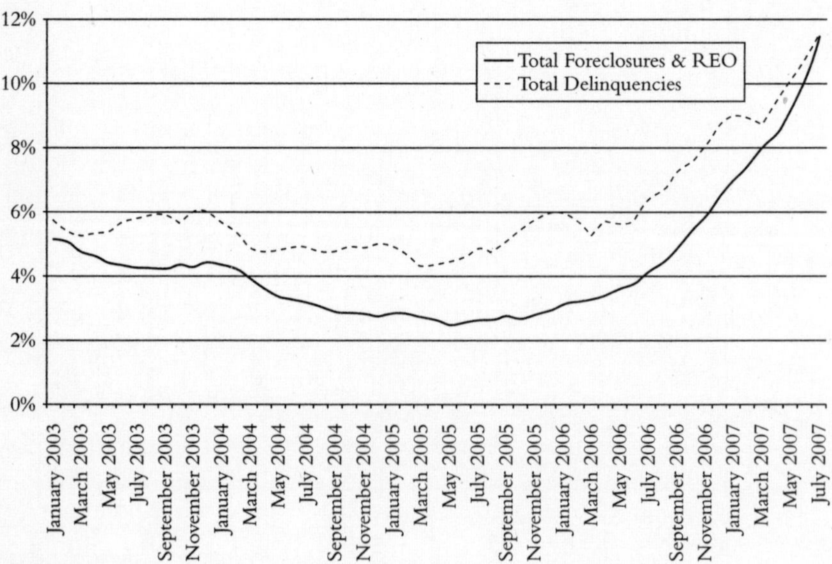

Figure 2.10 Subprime ARM Total Delinquencies and Foreclosures (including REO)
SOURCE: OTS.

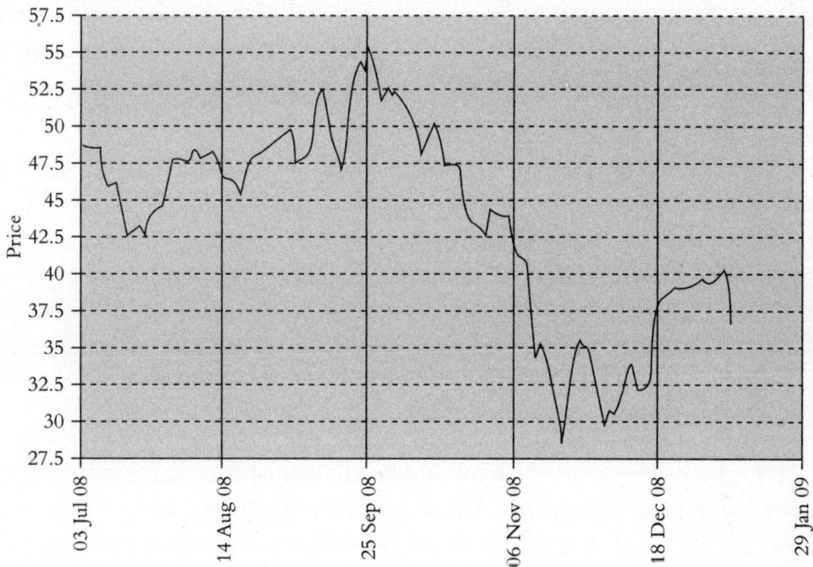

Figure 2.11 ABX-HE-AAA 07-1 Index, July 2008 to January 2009
SOURCE: Markit.com.

for a year—hardly an immediate response. To underline how susceptible subprime bonds were to the housing downturn, Figure 2.11 is the counterpart of Figure 2.9 approximately one year later, by which time the same index had fallen to the area of 30 cents on the dollar. Investors who, in some cases, bought bonds that paid as little as ¼ of 1 percent interest over Treasuries lost as much as 70 percent in one year.

Price Moves Determine Financial News

Of course, major *unexpected* developments will have an immediate market impact when they become known, but for the most part the efficient market hypothesis assumption that prices instantaneously adjust to fundamental news has it exactly backwards. It is far more accurate to say that the financial news will instantaneously adjust to price changes. Whether the market is up or down on a given day, financial reporters have to find an explanation for the price move. Therefore, an explanation will be drawn from the coincident news developments on that day, regardless of whether they are pertinent. This routine process can lead to the comical situation of the same development being used as both a bullish and a bearish explanation on days when the market traverses widely between up and down.

August 26, 2011, offered a perfect example. On that day, the market sold off in the morning, and then rallied sharply into the afternoon. The key focus of market attention was a speech by Federal Reserve Chairman Ben Bernanke. The following two headlines led stock market news stories issued by the *same* newswire service on the same day:

Wall Street Slides after Bernanke Comments
Wall Street Bounces as Bernanke Keeps Hopes Alive

The first story read, "Major indexes fell more than 1 percent after Federal Reserve Chairman Ben Bernanke said the U.S. economic recovery was much less robust than hoped but stopped short of signaling further action to boost growth." The second story saw things a bit differently and explained, "Bernanke raised hope the Fed could consider further stimulus measures for the economy at an extended policy meeting in September."

Now, you could believe that the same event was bearish before it was bullish. It seems considerably more plausible, though, to believe that the interpretation of the event was altered to fit the market price action. I can assure you that if the market had failed to rebound, there would not have been any stories about how the market ignored Bernanke's constructive comments. The market action determines the interpretation of the news, not the other way around.

Quite frequently prices move up on the same longer-term fundamentals that have been known for some time or in reaction to a prior decline that took prices too low based on the underlying fundamentals. But while these types of longer-term underlying factors are what really move prices, rather than the often minor or irrelevant developments that are coincident on the same day, they apparently do not make acceptable news copy. When was the last time you saw a financial page headline that read "Market Rallies Sharply Because Bullish Fundamentals Unchanged" or "Market Surges as Prices Correct Recent Excessive Decline"?

Is It Luck or Skill? Exhibit A: The Renaissance Medallion Track Record

Efficient market hypothesis proponents have a ready explanation for why some investors are able to repeatedly outperform the market: luck. They would argue that given a large number of investors, probability dictates that there will be a few lucky ones who will outperform a surprisingly large percentage of the time. For example, if we assume the odds of beating a specific market benchmark in a given year are 50 percent, in a group of 100,000 investors, the odds that at least one of them will outperform 15 years in a row are better than 95 percent. Thus, in a group this size, it would be far more surprising if no one beat the market in all 15 years, even though the odds for any specific investor achieving this feat are extremely small: 3/1,000 of 1 percent. Efficient market hypothesis supporters would contend that given the large number of market participants, it is inevitable that there will be some investors who outperform a large majority of the time and there is no reason to assume they are skilled rather than lucky. This argument as presented is entirely correct. It, however, overlooks a critical point: the degree of outperformance. It is not simply a matter of some managers having reached above-benchmark returns a large percentage of the time, but rather that they have achieved outperformance by wide margins. In assessing the probability of attaining certain track records if the efficient market hypothesis were true, it is essential to consider the degree of outperformance, not simply the frequency.

There are too many examples of extraordinary performance in the markets to be consistent with a theoretical framework that asserts that the only way to beat the market is by chance. We need consider only one such track record to make the point: the Renaissance Medallion fund, which was headed by the mathematician Jim Simons and supported by a brilliant team of mathematicians and scientists. Over a 19-year period (1990 to early 2009) for which we have results, the fund realized an average monthly gross return of 4.77 percent with 90 percent of the months being positive. (We used gross returns in our analysis instead of net returns because we are interested in calculating the probability of attaining the track record, not the implied return to investors after fees.)

A $1,000 investment at the start without deducting performance fees would have grown to $35 million.

When confronted with evidence of starkly superior track records, efficient market hypothesis supporters are fond of resorting to the "Shakespearian monkey" argument—namely, if you have enough monkeys banging at typewriters, one monkey will eventually type *Hamlet*. The implied analogy is that if you have enough traders, you will get some great track records simply by chance. Both these contentions are true. The relevant question, however, is: How many monkeys do you need to get one that types *Hamlet*? Or, in the more pertinent market performance case: How many traders do you need to get a Renaissance Medallion track record by chance? It turns out that the odds of getting Medallion-like performance results if markets were truly efficient would be infinitesimally small (10^{-48}). In fact, you would need the number of traders to be far closer to the number of estimated atoms in the earth than to the number of people on the planet (let alone the much smaller number of market participants) to get a track record as good as Renaissance Medallion simply by chance.[9]

The Flawed Premise of the Efficient Market Hypothesis: A Chess Analogy

The efficient market hypothesis assumes the markets can't be beat because everyone has the same information. This reasoning is conceptually flawed. Even if everyone had all the same information, there's no reason to assume they would reach the same decision as to the appropriate price of a market or security. For example, in a chess tournament, all the players know the same rules and have access to the same chess books and records of past games by world champions, yet only a small minority excel. There is no reason to assume that all the players will use the same information with equal effectiveness. Why should the markets, which in a sense represent an even more complex game than chess (there are more variables, and the rules are always changing) be any different?

[9]This statement is based on estimate of 10^{50} atoms in the earth. *Source:* www.wolframalpha.com.

In a chess tournament, a few highly skilled players will win most of the games by exploiting the mistakes of weaker players. Much like chess, it seems only reasonable to expect a few highly skilled market participants to interpret the same information—the current position of the market chessboard, so to speak—differently from the majority, and reach variant conclusions about the probable market direction. In this conceptual framework, mistakes by a majority of less skilled market participants can drive prices to incorrect levels (that is, prices out of line with the unknown equilibrium level), creating opportunities for more skilled traders. Quite simply, equal dissemination of knowledge does not imply equal use of knowledge.

Since all market participants pay commissions and are subject to slippage, the majority of participants are doomed to below-average results. This statement is true by definition for zero-sum markets, such as futures, where the total dollars long are always exactly equal to the total dollars short.[10] In fact, if hypothetically it were possible to restrict the trading in futures markets to the 100 best traders in the world, you could safely make the prediction that a large majority of them would be losers. The situation for markets in which the vast majority of participants are long, such as the stock market, is more subtle. Here the relevant question is not whether market participants have made money, but whether they have done better than the representative stock index, which is a proxy for the systematic return of the entire market. In this regard, there is overwhelming evidence that a substantial majority of stock market participants do worse than the market. Over time, academic studies have repeatedly shown that a large majority of *long-only* funds underperform the stock indexes.[11] For that matter, so do individual investors, market analysts, and market letter writers who provide

---

[10]Of course, some market participants in the futures markets, particularly hedgers and arbitrageurs, will have offsetting positions in other markets. But to avoid unnecessarily complicating the argument, we focus on futures as a self-contained market.

[11]The qualification of "long-only" is critical to the statement's veracity. Equity hedge funds, which carry a significant short position (albeit they are still net long on average), do outperform equity indexes in return/risk terms. Insofar as hedge funds are both long and short, however, a stock index is no longer the appropriate benchmark.

testable recommendations. I know of no study that demonstrates that any of these groups have done better than the market over any extended length of time (although there will certainly be individuals in all these groups who do).

The fact that the majority of participants in all markets are consistently unable to beat the market gives the efficient market hypothesis the illusion of truth. But the fact that the markets are very difficult to beat does not imply they *can't* be beat. It is entirely consistent to believe that a very large majority of market participants will underperform and, at the same time, to believe that a few highly skilled traders will outperform the markets (in numbers and by margins that exceed those explainable by probability arguments). Just as some chess masters can consistently win at tournaments, a small minority of skilled traders can significantly outperform the markets. Indeed, in both arenas, it can be argued that the mistakes of the majority create the winning opportunities for the few who are more skilled.

Some Players Are Not Even Trying to Win

Not only are some market participants more skilled than others, but some key market players have motivations other than profit. The efficient market hypothesis assumes that market participants acting on available information will drive prices to economically correct levels. Some market participants, however, are not seeking to maximize profits, but are operating on different agendas. We consider two such classes of market participants:

1. **Hedgers.** This group uses markets as a form of insurance to reduce risk. For example, a corn farmer may sell corn futures not because he thinks the price is too high, but rather to lock in a price. The farmer may even believe corn prices are too low and still be a seller in order to avoid the business risk of corn prices moving still lower before the crop is harvested. Analogously, a cereal manufacturer would be a buyer of corn futures to lock in its input costs, rather than to express any bullish assessment of the market. Decisions based on a desire to reduce risk may cause both buy and sell hedgers to act in a way that drives prices away from rather than toward equilibrium.

2. **Governments.** Intervention in the markets to meet economic goals or comply with international agreements can also act as a catalyst to drive prices away from natural equilibrium levels. Perhaps the classic example was the Bank of England's support of the British pound in 1992. At the time, the United Kingdom was part of the exchange rate mechanism (ERM)—a European currency agreement among participant nations to keep the relative valuations of their currencies within defined boundaries. At the time, Germany's prime motivation was to control inflation during the postunification period, a goal that led the Bundesbank to keep interest rates high. In order to prevent currency outflows from the pound to the mark, which would push the pound below its lower boundary versus the mark, the Bank of England was forced to raise interest rates as well. The problem was that the UK economy was in recession, an economic state that dictated a need for the Bank of England to lower rates, not raise them.

    At even the lower boundary of the range specified by the exchange rate mechanism, the pound was well above the equilibrium level vis-à-vis the mark implied by the divergent economic conditions in the two countries. In order to prevent the pound from sinking to a naturally lower level versus the mark, the Bank of England had to intervene to support the pound. This was a striking example, but hardly an unusual one, in which government intervention in the market pushed prices away from natural equilibrium levels, creating a profit opportunity for speculators. The Bank of England's attempts to support the pound were eventually overwhelmed by speculative selling, including the famous massive $10 billion short position by George Soros and his colleague, Stanley Druckenmiller. Once the Bank of England gave up its intervention efforts, the pound plummeted to a much lower equilibrium level. Soros and Druckenmiller earned an estimated $1 billion in profits on the trade.[12]

[12]For a detailed narrative on this episode, see Sebastian Mallaby, *More Money Than God* (New York: Penguin Press, 2010), which provides a superb history of the hedge fund industry and its key players.

> Some observers draw the wrongheaded conclusion from this episode that the pound crashed because of selling by Soros, Druckenmiller, and other speculators. The correct interpretation is that the pound didn't fall earlier because of the supportive intervention by the Bank of England. Once this intervention was withdrawn, the pound immediately sank to the natural lower equilibrium dictated by economic forces. In effect, the speculators caused an earlier end to an artificially maintained high price rather than causing any unwarranted price decline. The cannon shot may trigger the avalanche, but it is the unstable structure that is the true cause.

In short, market actions by hedgers and governments can cause price disequilibriums and implied profit opportunities, which are not supposed to exist according to the efficient market hypothesis.

The Missing Ingredient

If an efficient market hypothesis proponent wrote a cookbook, the list of ingredients for a chicken soup recipe might look like the following:

- 1 tablespoon olive oil
- 2 onions
- 2 quarts boiling water
- Salt
- 2 bay leaves
- 1 large carrot
- 1 celery stalk
- ½ teaspoon dried thyme
- ¼ cup fresh parsley leaves
- Ground pepper

Not a bad recipe, except that there is a missing ingredient that real-world cooks might consider important: the chicken.

For those who have actually traded markets, a market pricing theory that left out the role and influence of human emotions would be as complete and helpful as a chicken soup recipe without the chicken. The efficient market hypothesis implicitly assumes that markets always respond rationally—a representation that ignores the fact that markets are traded by people, not robots, and people often react more on emotion than on information.

As has been well demonstrated by behavioral economists, people inherently make irrational investment decisions. For example, in one classic experiment conducted by Kahneman and Tversky, pioneers in the field of prospect theory, subjects were given a hypothetical choice between a sure $3,000 gain versus an 80 percent chance of a $4,000 gain and a 20 percent chance of not getting anything.[13] The vast majority of people preferred the sure $3,000 gain, even though the other alternative had a higher expected gain (0.80 × $4,000 = $3,200). Then they flipped the question around and gave people a choice between a certain loss of $3,000 versus an 80 percent chance of losing $4,000 and a 20 percent chance of not losing anything. In this case, the vast majority chose to gamble and take the 80 percent chance of a $4,000 loss, even though the expected loss would be $3,200. In both cases, people made irrational choices because they selected the alternative with the worse expected gain or greater expected loss. Why? Because the experiment reflects a quirk in human behavior in regards to risk and gain: People are risk averse when it comes to gains, but are risk takers when it comes to avoiding a loss. This behavioral quirk relates very much to trading, as it explains why people tend to let their losses run and cut their profits short. So the old cliché, but not any less valid advice, to "let your profits run and cut your losses short" is actually the exact opposite of what most people tend to do.

Bankrupt companies provide a perfect example of how human nature leads to letting losses run. In the event of a bankruptcy, common stock shareholders are the last to be paid off—that is, after all classes of bondholders, creditors, employees, government if taxes are due, and

[13]Daniel Kahneman and Amos Tversky, "Prospect Theory: An Analysis of Decision under Risk," *Econometrica* 47, no. 2 (March 1979): 263–291. Prospect theory is a branch of decision theory that attempts to explain why individuals make decisions that deviate from rational decision making by examining how the expected outcomes of alternative choices are perceived (definition source: www.qfinance.com).

preferred equity holders. If there were enough money to pay off all these parties after the sale of assets, the company would probably not be in bankruptcy in the first place. So, with rare exceptions, once it is certain that a company will file for bankruptcy, the stock should be worthless. Yet bankrupt stocks continue to trade at some level meaningfully above zero for quite some time before finally fading into oblivion. Why? Because even though the likelihood of the stock eventually going to zero is virtually 100 percent, people will rationalize, "I bought this stock at $30 and it is down to $1. I have already lost $29, and the worst case is only a $30 loss. I might as well take a chance." People are risk takers when it comes to trying to avoid a total loss, a fact that explains a lot of market behavior.

Rational behavior and basic economic theory would suggest that people would be decreasingly likely to purchase an item as its price increases. Security prices, however, often reflect the perverse opposite pattern, wherein steadily rising prices may attract more buyers, as they become increasingly concerned about missing a bull market. If carried to extremes, the result is a price bubble. Similar fundamentals can be associated with wildly different prices due to the chaotic and unpredictable nature of human psychology. The Internet bubble discussed earlier provides a perfect example. The Internet index increased sevenfold and then surrendered the entire gain, all in the space of three years. It is far easier to explain the parabolic price ride of these stocks as a reflection of changing emotions—euphoria to panic—rather than as a response to a contemporaneous dramatic improvement in fundamentals followed by drastic deterioration in fundamentals.

The essential point is that the efficient market hypothesis leaves out any role for human emotions to impact prices and in so doing is by necessity an incomplete theory of price behavior. Indeed, virtually all the contradictions to the efficient market hypothesis we have cited can be traced back to the potential for human emotions and irrational behavior to distort prices. Markets do not accurately discount all known fundamentals, but rather they overdiscount or underdiscount this information, depending on the market's emotional environment, and indeed this is one of the sources of investing or trading opportunities.

A much more realistic model of how markets actually work is that prices are determined by a combination of fundamentals and emotions.

The same exact set of fundamentals can lead to different prices given different emotional environments. The long history of market bubbles and crashes provides overwhelming empirical evidence that the "madness of crowds"[14] can take market prices far beyond any rational level based on value and fundamentals and that market panics can result in precipitous price declines completely removed from any contemporaneous changes in fundamentals. There is a clear line from the Tulipmania of seventeenth-century Holland when "houses and lands were . . . assigned in payment of bargains made at the tulip-mart"[15] to the huge demand for mortgage-based securitizations in the early 2000s when investors eagerly bought AAA-rated tranches of securitizations backed entirely by no-verification ARM subprime mortgages for the tiny yield premium they offered. It is impossible to explain these episodes and the multitude of similar financial events based on fundamentals and the timing of changes in fundamental information. These and similar events can be explained only by acknowledging the obvious and sometimes overpowering impact of human emotions, which can and often do lead to completely irrational behavior.

Right for the Wrong Reason: Why Markets Are Difficult to Beat

Advocates of the efficient market hypothesis are absolutely correct in contending that markets are very difficult to beat, but they are right for the wrong reason. The difficulty in gaining an edge in the markets is not because prices instantaneously discount all known information (although they *sometimes* do), but rather because the impact of emotion on prices varies greatly and is nearly impossible to gauge. Sometimes emotions will cause prices to wildly overshoot any reasonable definition of fair value—we call these periods market bubbles. At other times, emotions will cause prices to plunge far below any reasonable definition of fair value—we call these periods market panics. Finally, in perhaps the majority of the time, emotions will exert a limited

[14]Part of the title of Charles Mackay's classic 1841 book, *Extraordinary Popular Delusions and the Madness of Crowds* (New York: Broadway Books, 1995).
[15]Ibid.

distortive impact on prices—market environments in which the efficient market hypothesis provides a reasonable approximation. So either market prices are not significantly out of line with fair valuations (muted influence of emotions on price) or we are faced with the difficult task of determining how far the price deviation may extend.

Although it is often possible to identify *when* the market is in a euphoric or panic state, it is the difficulty in assessing *how far* bubbles and panics will carry that makes it so hard to beat the market. One can be absolutely correct in assessing a fair value for a market, but lose heavily by taking a position too early. For example, consider a trader who in late 1999 decided the upward acceleration in technology stocks was overdone and went short the NASDAQ index as it hit the 3,000 mark. Although this assessment would have been absolutely correct in terms of where the market traded in the decade beginning the year after the bubble burst (the 1,100 to 2,900 range), our astute trader would likely have gone broke as the market soared an additional 68 percent before peaking at 5,048 in March 2000 (see Figure 2.12). The trader's market call would have been fundamentally correct and only four months off in picking the top of a 10-year-plus bull market, yet the trade would still have been a disaster. There is certainly no need to resort to the assumption of market prices being perfect to explain why winning in the markets is difficult.

The acknowledgment that emotions can exert a strong, and even dominant, price influence has critical implications. According to this view of market behavior, markets will still be difficult to beat (because of the variability and unpredictability of emotions as a market factor), but

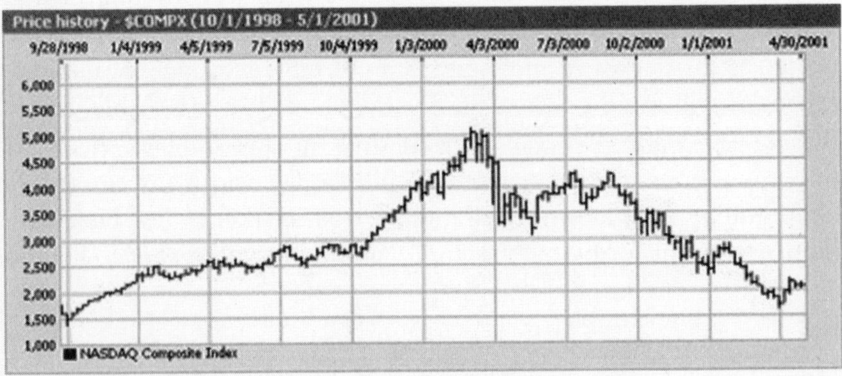

Figure 2.12 NASDAQ Index, October 1998 to May 2001
SOURCE: moneycentral.msn.com.

importantly, not impossible to beat. In fact, the impact of emotions causing prices to move far out of line with true valuations will itself create investing and trading opportunities.[16]

Diagnosing the Flaws of the Efficient Market Hypothesis

We are now in a position to identify the exact points at which the line of reasoning of the efficient market hypothesis is flawed. The efficient market hypothesis can be summarized as follows:

1. The markets incorporate all known information.
2. Therefore prices are always correct.
3. The arrival of new information is random.
4. Changes in prices depend on new information.
5. Therefore you can't beat the market.

Now let's consider the validity of each of these five arguments.

1. The markets incorporate all known information.
   - ASSUME TRUE.
2. Therefore prices are always correct.
   - FALSE!
   - Markets are traded by people, not robots, and people often react on emotion more than on information.[17] The influence of

[16]There is no intended duality between emotions and reason, but rather a complex interaction between the two. For example, it may be entirely rational to participate in an emotion-driven bubble. The key point is simply that the influence of emotions can lead to price behavior that is inconsistent with the efficient market hypothesis model.

[17]Although a segment of trading is run by computerized programs, this consideration does not alter the fact that a large portion of trading activity will reflect human decision making. Moreover, computerized programs are still subject to revisions and override, and thus even computerized trading can reflect human emotions. A classic example of this phenomenon was the meltdown of statistical arbitrage funds in August 2007. Statistical arbitrage is a market neutral, mean reversion strategy that uses mathematical models to identify short-term anomalies in stock movements, balancing sales of stocks witnessing upside deviations (as defined by its models) with purchases of stocks witnessing downside deviations.

emotion can cause irrational behavior and result in prices being much too high or low vis-à-vis an objective assessment of the fundamentals.

3. The arrival of new information is random.
   - ASSUME TRUE
4. Changes in prices depend on new information.
   - FALSE!
   - Price moves often lag the information.
   - Price moves often occur in the absence of new information (e.g., market bubbles and crashes where momentum feeds on itself).
5. Therefore you can't beat the market.
   - FALSE!
   - Prices can be significantly out of line with reasonable valuations.
   - Prices don't move in tandem with information.
   - Some people are more skilled in interpreting information.

Why the Efficient Market Hypothesis Is Destined for the Dustbin of Economic Theory

Supporters of the efficient market hypothesis are reluctant to give up the theory, despite mounting contradictory evidence, because it provides the foundation for a broad range of critical financial applications, including risk assessment, optimal portfolio allocation, and option pricing. The unfortunate fact, however, is that these applications can lead to erroneous conclusions because the underlying assumptions are

---

Since the strategy will normally embed multidimensional neutrality (e.g., market, sector, capitalization, region, etc.), significant leverage is typically employed to achieve desired return levels. As a group, statistical arbitrage funds will often have significant overlap in the stocks they are long and short. In August 2007, large liquidations by some statistical arbitrage funds caused other funds in this strategy to suddenly see their portfolios behaving perversely, with longs falling and shorts simultaneously rallying. The resulting losses were magnified by the leverage that is an inherent part of the strategy. The sudden breakdown of the models and abrupt losses encouraged liquidation by other statistical arbitrage funds, setting off a chain reaction. In this highly chaotic and stressful environment, human decision making, and with it emotions, played an essential role in a strategy that is normally considered to be in the domain of automated trading.

incorrect. Moreover, the errors will be most extreme in those periods when the cost of errors will be most severe (i.e., market bubbles and panics). In some sense, efficient market hypothesis proponents are like the proverbial man looking for dropped car keys in the parking lot under the lamppost because that is where the light is. The flaws of the efficient market hypothesis are both serious and numerous:

- If true, the impossible has happened—and many times! The magnitude of some price moves would be a statistical impossibility if the efficient market hypothesis were true.
- Some market participants have achieved track records that would be a statistical impossibility if the efficient market hypothesis were true.
- The assumed mechanism for prices adjusting to correct levels is based on a flawed premise, since the price impact of informed traders can be outweighed temporarily by the actions of less knowledgeable traders or by the activity of hedgers and governments, which are motivated by factors other than profit.
- Market prices completely out of line with any plausible valuation are a common occurrence.
- Price moves often occur well after the fundamental news is widely known.
- Everyone having the same information does not imply that everyone will use information with equal efficiency.
- The efficient market hypothesis fails to incorporate the impact of human emotions on prices, thereby leaving out a key market price influence that throughout history has at times (e.g., market bubbles and crashes) dominated the influence of fundamental factors.

Investment Misconceptions

Investment Misconception 2: Market prices are perfect and discount all known information.

Reality: Market prices are frequently far removed from any reasonable measure of fair valuation. Sometimes market prices are too high given the prevailing fundamentals; sometimes they are too low.

Investment Misconception 3: Markets can't be beat.

Reality: Markets are difficult, but not impossible, to beat—a critical distinction that implies that some winners are winners because they are skilled, not because they are lucky (although some winners will merely be lucky). The difficulty in beating the market deceives many people into believing the task is impossible except by luck.

Investment Misconception 4: Price moves are immediate responses to changes in fundamentals.

Reality: Price moves commonly lag changes in fundamentals. Also, sometimes prices are driven by emotional factors rather than fundamentals.

Investment Misconception 5: The assumption of an efficient market model allows historical price changes to be used to derive probability estimates for various size price moves.

Reality: Efficient market–based models implicitly assume price changes are normally distributed—an assumption that will yield reasonably accurate estimates of the probabilities associated with moderate price changes, but will drastically understate the probability of large price changes. The consequences of this deficiency are critical: The risk of a large loss is much greater than implied by conventional risk models based on an efficient market assumption.

Investment Insights

Most of key assumptions related to the efficient market hypothesis, which underlies much of investment theory, are simply inconsistent with the way markets actually behave. Although markets are often efficiently priced (or approximately so), there are many exceptions, and it is the exceptions that provide skilled market participants the opportunity for outperformance. Markets are indeed difficult to beat, and recognition of this fact means that for many investors, the best choice might well be traditional academic advice: Invest in index funds so that you can at least match the market. But there is a big difference between hard to beat and impossible to beat. Investors with an interest in markets who are willing to put in the hard work to develop an investment or trading methodology and who have the discipline to follow a plan should not be dissuaded from that endeavor by the efficient market hypothesis.

The model of market prices being determined strictly by fundamentals is overly simplistic. Prices are determined by both fundamentals and human emotions. Sometimes, the impact of human emotions can completely swamp the fundamentals. For example, I find it far more plausible to view the sevenfold price increase in Internet stocks and subsequent complete retracement, all in the span of three years, in the context of a market bubble and its aftermath, as opposed to reflecting a back-to-back enormous improvement and deterioration in fundamentals. Not only can human emotions exert an important price impact, but the distortive impact of emotions often creates the best investment opportunities.

Chapter 3

The Tyranny of Past Returns

How do people decide when to invest? How do investors select among different alternatives? In virtually all investment decisions, the key driver is past returns. The investor calculus is simple: High returns are good; low returns or losses are bad. When the stock market has been rising, investor buying interest will increase. Conversely, after a period of market decline, investors will be more prone to liquidate than to invest.

The strong relationship between market returns and investor net flows into equity mutual funds is clearly evident in Figure 3.1. When Standard & Poor's (S&P) 500 index returns turn significantly negative, the normal inflows into equity mutual funds are reversed. Net outflows from equity mutual funds occurred in 2002 and 2008 following large declines in equity prices. In each case, equity prices surged in the following year (2003 and 2009, respectively).

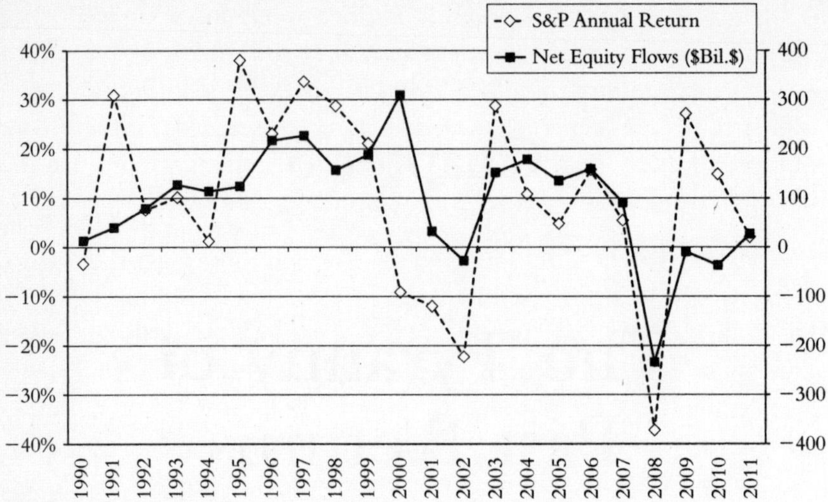

Figure 3.1 Net Flows into Equity Mutual Funds (Right) versus S&P Annual Returns (Left)

DATA SOURCE: S&P returns: Standard & Poor's; mutual fund flows: *2011 Investment Company Fact Book* (Washington, DC: Investment Company Institute).

Returns determine not only when people invest but also what they invest in. Investments that have registered strong two-, three-, and five-year average returns will draw buying interest, while those with low, let alone negative, returns will be shunned. This investor behavior is quite understandable and influenced by numerous factors. To begin, it seems entirely logical to select investments that have demonstrated an ability to provide good returns. In addition, those investments that have done the best in recent years will also be the ones scored most highly by rating services. Not surprisingly, return-based advertising will feature funds that have done well, providing another spur to investor activity. Financial articles in newspapers and magazines will also focus on funds that have performed well. Investors who use software to select funds from a database will invariably select investment criteria that will generate a list of funds with strong recent returns, automatically filtering out lower-return funds. Portfolio optimization software, which is heavily dependent on returns, will also tend to select investments that have generated high past returns, albeit subject to volatility and correlation constraints. All of these factors will reinforce the natural investor tendency to select funds with high recent returns and to exclude laggards.

Clearly, people tend to invest in markets following periods of good performance and also tend to select investments that have demonstrated the best recent returns. The key question is: How well does this near-automatic reliance on past returns in making investment decisions serve investors? In quest of an answer, in subsequent sections we provide the analysis to answer the following four specific questions:

1. How does the U.S. equity market perform in those years that follow high returns in recent-year periods?
2. Do long-term investments in U.S. equities (i.e., 5 to 20 years) perform better if initiated after extended periods of high or low returns?
3. Does an investment strategy of annually rotating to the strongest-performing S&P sector of recent years yield any improvement over the average performance of all sectors?
4. Does the strongest-performing hedge fund strategy of recent years outperform the average of all strategies in the current year?

Clarifying Note: The following studies draw inferences from past market, sector, and strategy style performance following periods of high and low returns. There is, of course, no certainty that future results would show similar patterns. In all cases, however, the underlying assumption is that past performance patterns are indicative of the more likely patterns for the future. Readers should bear in mind that since the conclusions are based on empirical studies, they should be viewed as indications rather than absolute truths. Still, it seems more reasonable to invest in accordance with the empirical evidence than in opposition to it.

S&P Performance in Years Following High- and Low-Return Periods

We segmented annual S&P returns for the 1871 to 2011 period into four quartiles and then compared the average returns in years following highest-quartile and lowest-quartile years.[1] Returns following

[1]S&P data based on series compiled by Robert Shiller, which uses Cowles stock index data prior to 1926.

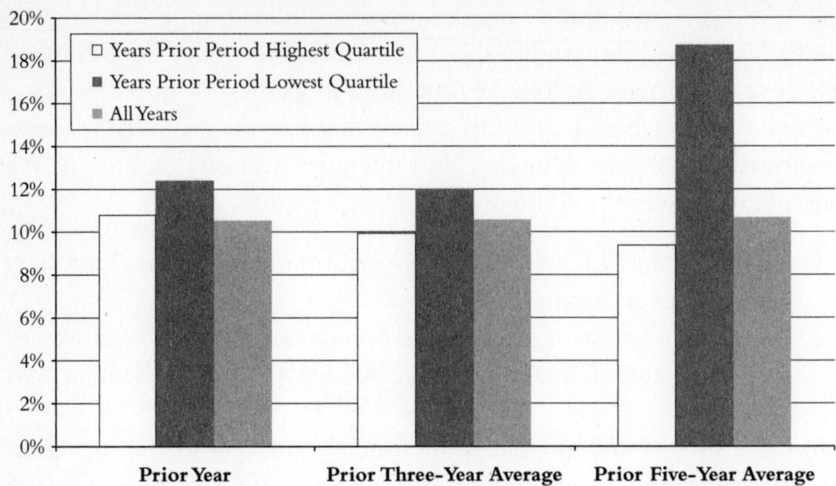

Figure 3.2 S&P Returns, Including Dividends: Comparison of Years Following Highest- and Lowest-Quartile Performance, 1872–2011

DATA SOURCE: Moneychimp.com, which is based on Robert Shiller's data and Yahoo!. Prior to 1926 (first year of S&P index), data is based on Cowles stock index data.

lowest-quartile years averaged 12.4 percent versus 10.8 percent following highest-quartile years and 10.5 percent in all years. We repeated an analogous process using three-year returns. The results were similar, but more pronounced, with average returns in years following lowest-quartile three-year returns outpacing returns following highest-quartile periods: 12.0 percent versus 9.9 percent. Finally, we repeated the test using past five-year periods. Here the difference was truly striking. The average return in years following lowest-quartile five-year returns was almost exactly double that of years following highest-quartile five-year returns (18.7 percent versus 9.4 percent). These results are summarized in Figure 3.2. The consistent superior performance of years following low-quartile return periods versus years following high-quartile return periods is clearly evident.

There is always a trade-off between more data and more relevant data. It can reasonably be argued that by going back as far as the 1870s, we included a period of history that is not representative of the current market. We therefore repeated the exact same analysis for the years 1950 forward. The results are summarized in Figure 3.3. Once again, years following low-quartile return periods significantly outperformed

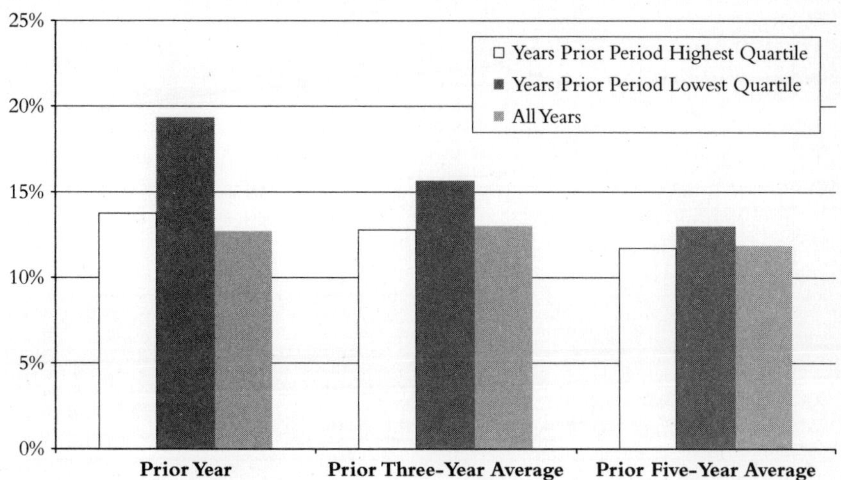

Figure 3.3 S&P Returns, Including Dividends: Comparison of Years Following Highest- and Lowest-Quartile Performance, 1950–2011
DATA SOURCE: Moneychimp.com, which is based on Robert Shiller's data and Yahoo!.

years following high-quartile periods, with the difference being 6 percent for the one-year period and nearly 4 percent for the three-year period.

The lesson is that the best prospective years for realizing above-average equity returns are those that follow low-return periods. Years following high-return periods, which are the times most people are inclined to invest, tend to do slightly worse than average on balance.

Implications of High- and Low-Return Periods on Longer-Term Investment Horizons

In the prior section, we examined the performance of the S&P in the single years following highest-return periods. Although the historical evidence suggests that these years performed significantly worse than years following low-return periods, an even more important question is: How do longer-term investments launched after high-return periods fare versus those started after low-return periods?

We segmented annual S&P 10-year returns for the period beginning in 1880 and ending between 1991 and 2011 into four quartiles. (The exact ending year depends on the length of the forward holding period tested.) Figure 3.4 shows the average annual return in the 5, 10,

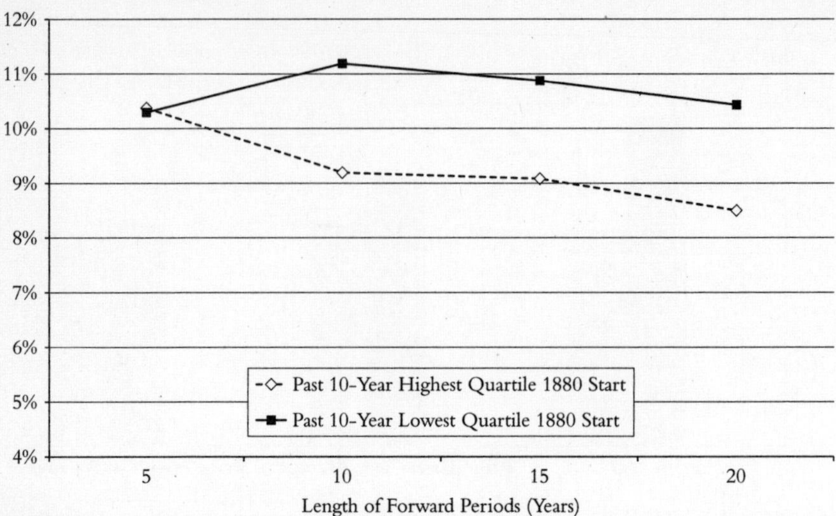

Figure 3.4 S&P Forward Period Average Annual Compounded Returns, Including Dividends, 1880–2011: Comparison of Years When Past 10-Year Returns Were in Lowest and Highest Quartiles
DATA SOURCE: Moneychimp.com, which is based on Robert Shiller's data and Yahoo!. Prior to 1926 (first year of S&P index), data is based on Cowles stock index data.

15, and 20 years following both high- and low-quartile 10-year returns. There was little difference between the two for the 5-year forward period, but for the 10-, 15-, and 20-year forward periods, returns were about 2 percent per year higher following low-quartile 10-year returns than following high-quartile 10-year returns.

We then repeated an analogous experiment segmenting the data based on past 20-year returns. These results are shown in Figures 3.5. Returns were consistently higher in the forward periods follow low-quartile past returns by amounts ranging between 1.4 percent and 5.4 percent per year. On average across the four forward periods, returns were a substantive 3.5 percent per year higher following low-quartile periods than following high-quartile periods.

Although, generally speaking, there is a benefit in using more data, perhaps going back as far as the late 1800s introduces data that is unrepresentative of the modern era and serves to distort the results. To address this possibility, we also repeated the same analysis for years 1950 forward. Restricting the analysis to this more recent data, the

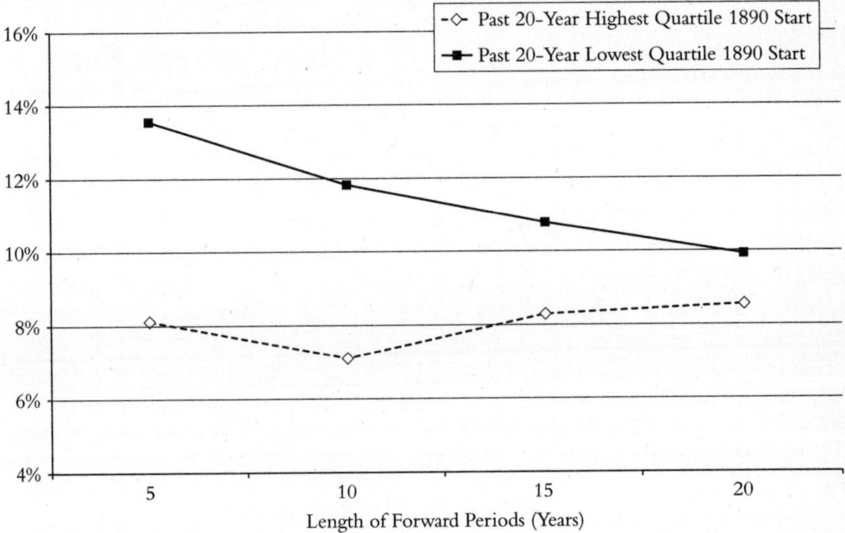

Figure 3.5 S&P Forward-Period Average Annual Compounded Returns, Including Dividends, 1890–2011: Comparison of Years When Past 20-Year Returns Were in Lowest and Highest Quartiles

DATA SOURCE: Moneychimp.com, which is based on Robert Shiller's data and Yahoo!. Prior to 1926 (first year of S&P index), data is based on Cowles stock index data.

outperformance of post-lowest-quartile periods vis-à-vis post-highest-quartile periods was even more imposing. As shown in Figure 3.6, returns were higher following lowest-quartile 10-year returns in each of the four forward periods by amounts ranging from 1.1 percent to 6.4 percent.

Based on past 20-year returns, the results were particularly striking. Returns in the periods following lowest-quartile 20-year returns exceeded returns following highest-quartile 20-year returns by amounts ranging between 6.6 percent and 11.0 percent!

The message is clear. The best time to start a long-term investment in equities is after an extended period of low returns—not surprisingly, the periods when investors are most likely to be disenchanted with stocks as an investment—and the worst time is after extended high-return periods (e.g., the late 1990s) when investors tend to most enthusiastic about stocks.

Readers might well wonder what the implications of past returns are for the current long-term investment horizon. As of the end of 2011 (the most recent year-end as of this writing), the past 10-year return was

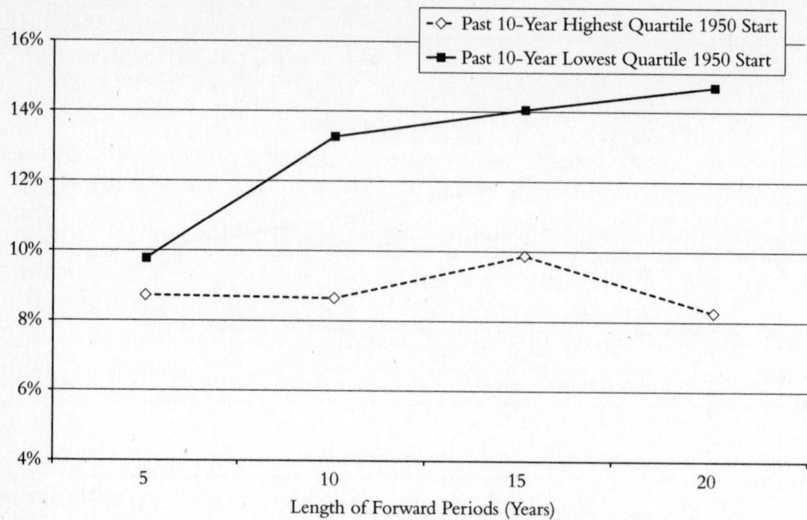

Figure 3.6 S&P Forward-Period Average Annual Compounded Returns, Including Dividends, 1950–2011: Comparison of Years When Past 10-Year Returns Were in Lowest and Highest Quartiles
DATA SOURCE: Moneychimp.com, which is based on Robert Shiller's data and Yahoo!.

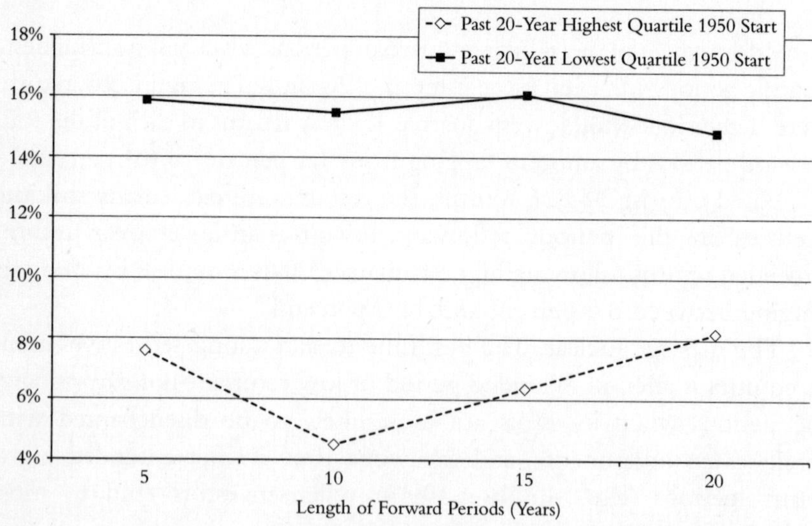

Figure 3.7 S&P Forward-Period Average Annual Compounded Returns, Including Dividends, 1950–2011: Comparison of Years When Past 20-Year Returns Were in Lowest and Highest Quartiles
DATA SOURCE: Moneychimp.com, which is based on Robert Shiller's data and Yahoo!.

2.9 percent per annum and the past 20-year return was 7.8 percent per annum (see Figure 3.7). These are relatively low return levels that correspond to the 14th and 11th percentiles, respectively, for the 10-year and 20-year average per annum returns for all year-ends since 1950. The only other year-ends when both these percentiles were below the 25th percentile were 1974, 1975, 1976, 1977, 1978, 1979, 1981, 1982, 2008, 2009, and 2010. Excluding the last three of these years, for which 10-year forward returns are not yet available, the forward average 10-year and 20-year returns for these years were both just under 16 percent per annum. Both the 10-year and 20-year return percentiles will remain below the 25th percentile as long as the 2012 return is 28 percent or less. In short, at this juncture (2012), barring a plus 28 percent return in 2012, the relatively poor performance of the stock market during the past 10-year and 20-year periods has constructive implications for stocks as a long-term investment.

Is There a Benefit in Selecting the Best Sector?

Searches for the highest-return mutual funds will invariably generate lists that are replete with sector focus funds because some sectors will always outperform broad market funds. Investors who select mutual funds based on highest past returns—a common approach—will end up indirectly investing in the sector or sectors that have realized the highest past returns in recent years. The obvious question is: Does the best-performing sector in recent years (and by implication most funds with the same sector focus) continue to perform better in the current year? To provide an answer, we utilize the 10 S&P sector indexes (see Table 3.1).

To evaluate the relative performance of the past best sector, we compare the outcome of three investment strategies:

1. **Select the best.** Each year invest in the S&P sector with the highest return during the recent past period.
2. **Select the worst.** Each year invest in the S&P sector with the lowest return during the recent past period.
3. **Select the average.** Diversify by allocating 10 percent to each of the 10 sectors. This approach will yield an annual return equal to the average of all the sectors.

Table 3.1 S&P Sector Indexes

Number	Index
1	Consumer Discretionary
2	Consumer Staples
3	Energy
4	Financials
5	Health Care
6	Industrials
7	Information Technology
8	Materials
9	Telecommunication Services
10	Utilities

In the first test, we use past one-year returns to define the best and worst sectors. Since 1990 is the first full year for which S&P sector index data is available, 1991 is the first year in the comparison analysis. Figure 3.8 illustrates the net asset value[2] (NAV) graphs that result from each of the three investment strategies. Selecting the best past year sector at the start of each year results in a dramatically lower ending NAV than the equal allocation annual rebalancing implied by the average and does only modestly better than picking the prior year's worst-performing strategy.

Next, we conduct an analogous test using past three-year returns to define the best and worst sectors. Here, the first test year is 1993 because three prior years of data are needed to define the best and worst sectors. The NAV graphs for each of the three strategies are shown in Figure 3.9. In this instance, selecting the past best sector not only underperforms the average, but also lags picking the worst past sector.

We repeat the process a third time using the past five-year period to define the best and worst sectors. Since five years of data are needed

[2]The net asset value (NAV) indicates the equity at each point of time (typically month-end) based on an assumed beginning value of 1,000 (sometimes 100). For example, an NAV of 2,000 implies that the original investment has doubled as of the indicated time. The NAV at any point is equal to the chain of compounded returns. For example, if the first three monthly returns were +10 percent, +5 percent, and −8 percent, the NAV would be equal to 1,062.6 ($1{,}000 \times 1.10 \times 1.05 \times 0.92 = 1{,}062.6$).

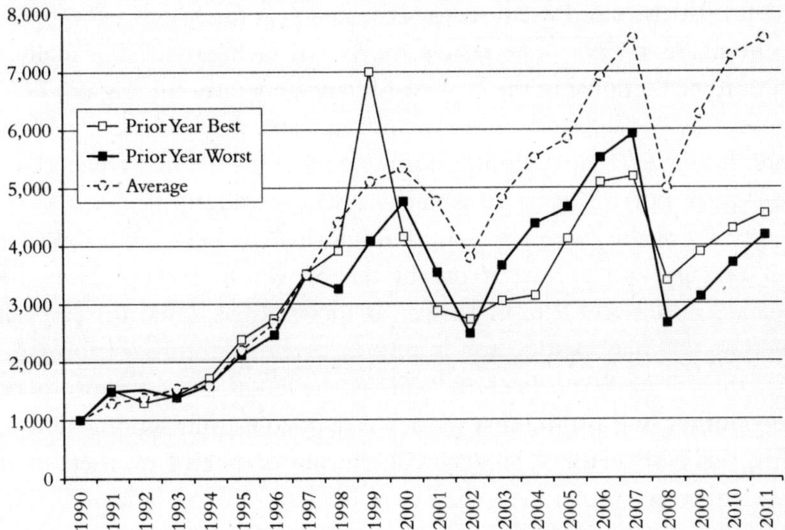

Figure 3.8 NAV Comparison: Prior One-Year Best S&P Sector versus Prior Worst and Average
DATA SOURCE: S&P Dow Jones Indices.

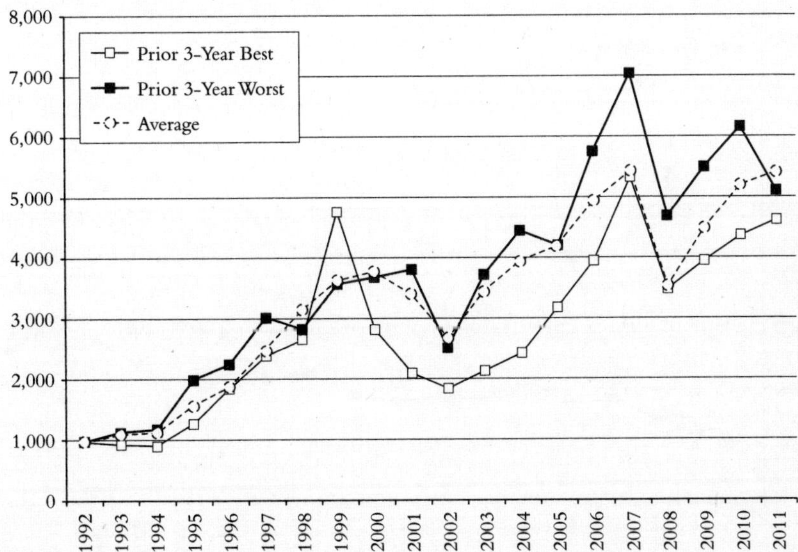

Figure 3.9 NAV Comparison: Prior Three-Year Best S&P Sector versus Prior Worst and Average
DATA SOURCE: S&P Dow Jones Indices.

to define the best and worst sectors, the first year for which a comparison can be made is 1995. The results are shown in Figure 3.10. Finally, in this third test, choosing the best past sector generates the highest NAV, significantly outdistancing both the average and the worst sector NAVs. Note, however, that the outperformance is achieved in a roller coaster ride—an important point to which we will soon return.

In two of the three test periods, choosing the best sector did worse than average and in one it did better. How can we combine these disparate results to yield an answer as to whether, based on past data, selecting the best past sector improves or hurts future performance? Since there is no a priori reason to favor one length of past return period over another, we assume that money is divided equally among all three. Thus, the best sector approach will allocate one-third of assets to the best-performing sector in the past year, one-third to the best-performing sector during the past three years, and the final third to the best-performing sector of the past five years. (Sometimes two or all three of

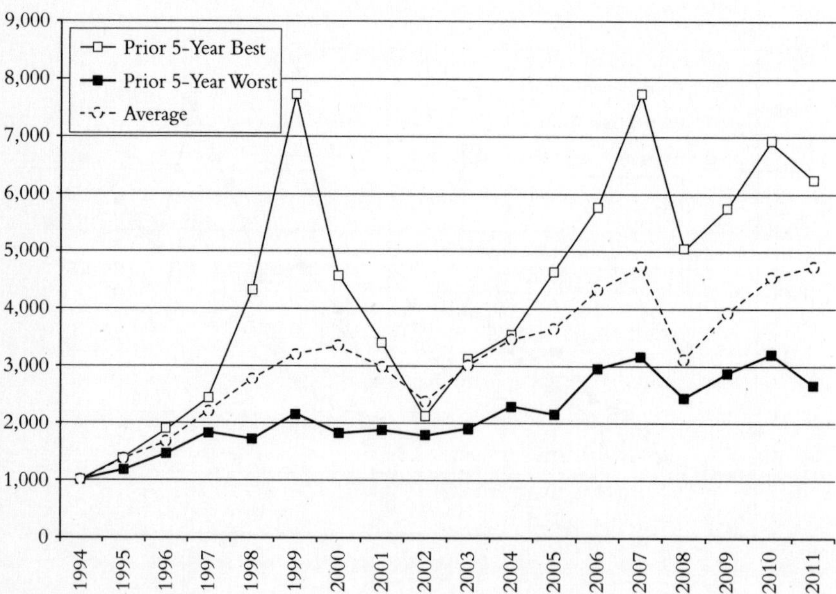

Figure 3.10 NAV Comparison: Prior Five-Year Best S&P Sector versus Prior Worst and Average
DATA SOURCE: S&P Dow Jones Indices.

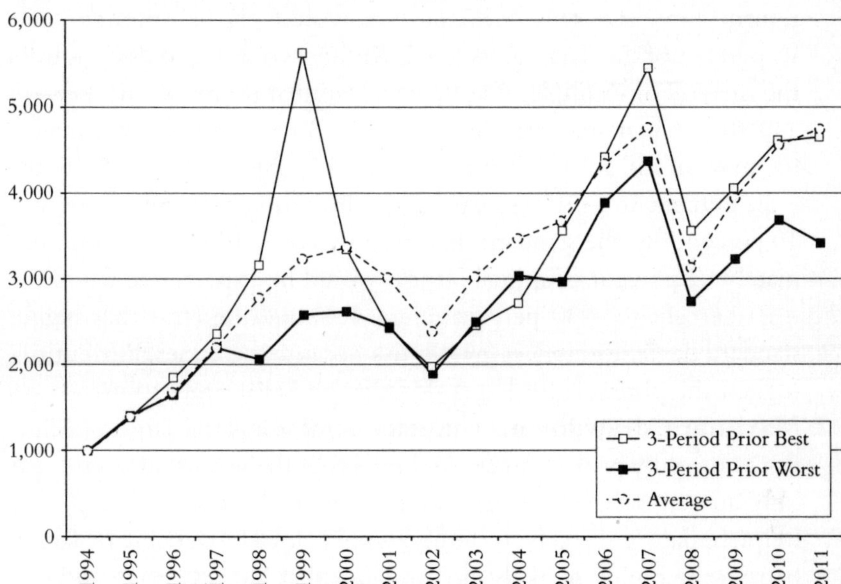

Figure 3.11 NAV Comparison: Three-Period Prior Best S&P Sector versus Prior Worst and Average
DATA SOURCE: S&P Dow Jones Indices.

these may be the same sector.) The worst sector approach will use an analogous allocation methodology. The average allocation will be the same as before. The results for the three-period combined analysis are shown in Figure 3.11. Selecting the best sector does slightly worse than the average but at least it does better than selecting the past worst sector. Based on these results, it might seem that although choosing the past best-performing sector doesn't help, at least it doesn't seem to hurt much, either. But the story does not end there.

So far, the analysis has only considered returns and has shown that choosing the best past sector would have yielded slightly lower returns than an equal-allocation approach (that is, the average). Return, however, is an incomplete performance metric. Any meaningful performance comparison must also consider risk (a concept we will elaborate on in Chapter 4). We use two measures of risk here:

1. **Standard deviation.** The standard deviation is a volatility measure that indicates how spread out the data is—in this case, how broadly the

returns vary. Roughly speaking, we would expect approximately 95 percent of the data points to fall within two standard deviations of the mean. For example, if the average annual return was 10 percent and the annual standard deviation was 30 percent, approximately 95 percent of annual returns would be expected to fall in the −50 percent to +70 percent range. In contrast, if the return was 10 percent but the standard deviation was only 10 percent, approximately 95 percent of annual returns would be expected to fall in the −10 percent to +30 percent range. It should be clear that higher standard deviations reflect greater risk because the wider distributions suggest the potential for larger declines (and also larger gains).

2. **Maximum drawdown.** This statistic measures the largest decline from an equity peak to an equity low. Note that our analysis employs only annual data. Therefore, the maximum drawdown using more frequent data (e.g., daily, monthly) would almost invariably be larger, barring the highly unlikely circumstance that both the high and low equity points of the drawdown occur on the last trading day of the year.

Figure 3.12 compares the best sector, worst sector, and average results in terms of these two risk measures. The worst sector and average have similar risk levels in terms of both statistics. The best sector, however, has a significantly higher standard deviation and a far larger maximum drawdown. Calculating risk is not merely an academic exercise. Higher risk can dramatically alter the outcome of an investment. Although the best sector approach delivered only a slightly lower cumulative return than the average (Figure 3.11), any investors who followed this strategy would have been much more likely to abandon the investment in midstream because of its proclivity to huge drawdowns. These investors might likely never have realized an outcome near equal to the average. After all, in real time, investors don't know that an investment will recover. In other words, the greater the risk, the more likely the investment would be liquidated at a loss.

Figure 3.13 combines return and risk into two return/risk ratios. Both ratios show similar results: In return/risk terms, the best sector not only does much worse than the average, but it even underperforms the worst sector. The implications are that investors would be better off diversifying to achieve average returns than to concentrate their

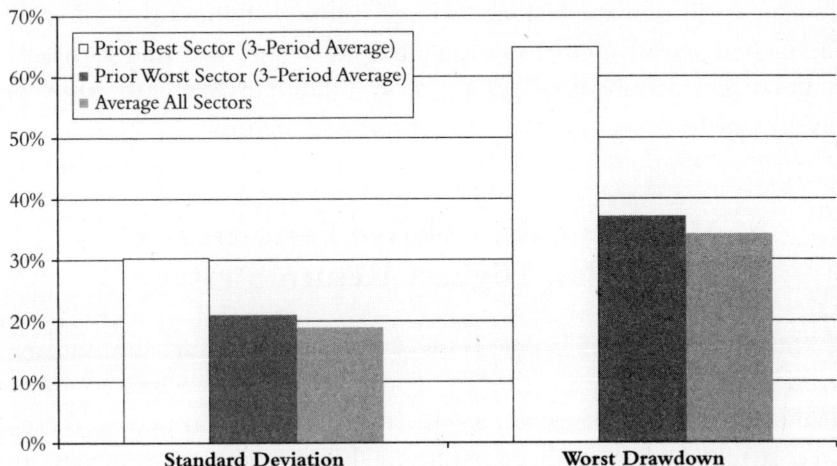

Figure 3.12 Standard Deviation and Maximum Drawdown: Prior Best Sector (Three-Period Average) versus Prior Worst Sector and Average of All Sectors, 1995–2011
DATA SOURCE: S&P Dow Jones Indices.

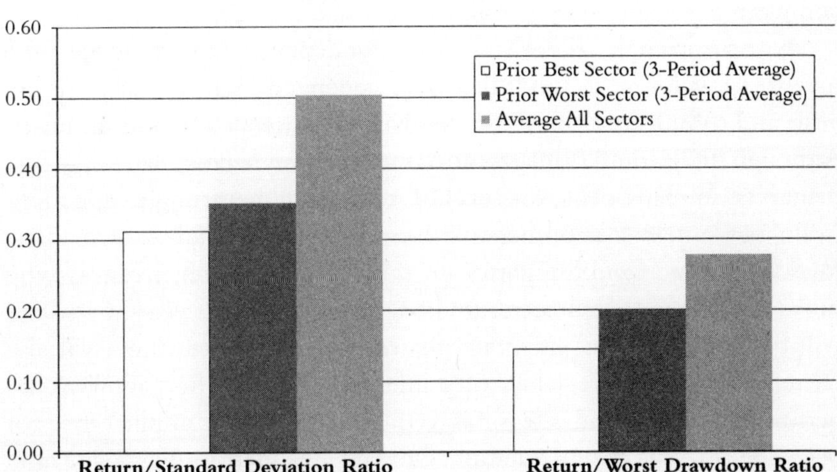

Figure 3.13 Return/Standard Deviation and Return/Maximum Drawdown Ratios: Prior Best Sector (Three-Period Average) versus Prior Worst and Average of All Sectors, 1995–2011
DATA SOURCE: S&P Dow Jones Indices.

investment in the past best-performing sector. It follows that selecting the highest-return mutual funds of the past would also lead to subpar return/risk performance because these funds are likely to have an investment focus on the past best-performing sectors.

Hedge Funds: Relative Performance of the Past Highest-Return Strategy

If your knowledge of hedge funds doesn't extend much beyond the latest episode of your favorite TV drama series—if it's a mystery, hint: The hedge fund manager did it—the only key fact you need to know here is that hedge funds encompass a broad range of strategies. In contrast to mutual funds, which primarily consist of long equity or long bond investments (or a combination of the two), hedge funds include a wide range of strategies, which differ in markets traded (equities, fixed income, foreign exchange [FX], credit, commodities); geographic focus (developed countries, emerging markets, single country, specific region); net exposure (net long, market neutral, net short, dynamically ranging); and directional versus relative value market orientation. A complete overview of hedge funds is provided in Chapter 11.

Not surprisingly, there is a strong tendency for many hedge fund investors to allocate to funds that have generated high returns in recent years and to redeem from those that have experienced significant losses. Although hedge fund managers are far more idiosyncratic than long-only managers, in many cases, the level of returns will be strongly influenced by the investment environment for the specific strategy style—particularly for some hedge fund categories. In this sense, although investors who move assets from the worst-return hedge funds in recent years to the best will be responding to individual manager performance, they will also be reflecting an indirect bias of shifting funds from the past weakest-performing hedge fund categories to the strongest. This implicit investor behavior raises the critical question: Does the best-performing hedge fund strategy category in recent years (and by implication most funds within that category) continue to perform better in the current year? To provide an answer, we utilize the 23 hedge fund sector indexes calculated by Hedge Fund Research, Inc. (HFRI), which are listed in Table 3.2.

Table 3.2 HFRI Hedge Fund Strategy Indexes*

	Index
1	HFRI Equity Hedge (Total) Index
2	HFRI Equity Hedge: Equity Market Neutral Index
3	HFRI Equity Hedge: Quantitative Directional
4	HFRI Equity Hedge: Sector—Energy/Basic Materials Index
5	HFRI Equity Hedge: Sector—Technology/Health Care Index
6	HFRI Equity Hedge: Short Bias Index
7	HFRI Event-Driven (Total) Index
8	HFRI Event-Driven: Distressed/Restructuring Index
9	HFRI Event-Driven: Merger Arbitrage Index
10	HFRI Event-Driven: Private Issue/Regulation D Index
11	HFRI Macro (Total) Index
12	HFRI Macro: Systematic Diversified Index
13	HFRI Relative Value (Total) Index
14	HFRI Relative Value: Fixed Income—Asset Backed
15	HFRI Relative Value: Fixed Income—Convertible Arbitrage
16	HFRI Relative Value: Fixed Income—Corporate Index
17	HFRI Relative Value: Multi-Strategy Index
18	HFRI Relative Value: Yield Alternatives Index
19	HFRI Emerging Markets (Total) Index
20	HFRI Emerging Markets: Asia ex-Japan Index
21	HFRI Emerging Markets: Global Index
22	HFRI Emerging Markets: Latin America Index
23	HFRI Emerging Markets: Russia/Eastern Europe Index

*Excludes fund of fund indexes, which combine multiple strategies.

The hedge fund strategy category indexes are not investable. So, it is not possible to replicate the returns of the indexes. The assumption for our test is that by randomly selecting a subset portfolio of one or more funds in the hedge fund category, the category index would serve as a proxy estimate for the expected return of the portfolio. Although the returns of any selected subset within a strategy could vary significantly from the index, there would be no bias to the direction of variation, and the strategy index return would serve as the best estimate of the single-strategy portfolio return. We compare the outcomes of three investment strategies.

1. **Select the best.** Each year invest in hedge funds in the category with the highest return during the recent past period. For testing

purposes, the simplifying assumption is that the return of this single-strategy portfolio will approximate the return of the hedge fund category index.

2. **Select the worst.** Each year invest in hedge funds in the category with the lowest return during the recent past period. For testing purposes, the simplifying assumption is that the return of this single-strategy portfolio will approximate the return of the hedge fund category index.
3. **Select the average.** Diversify by allocating equally to each of the 23 hedge fund categories defined by HFRI, and rebalance annually. For testing purposes, the simplifying assumption is that this approach will yield an annual return equal to the average of the 23 strategy categories.

In the first test, we use past one-year returns to define the best and worst hedge fund strategy categories. Figure 3.14 illustrates the net asset value (NAV) graphs that result for each of the three investment strategies. Selecting the hedge fund strategy with the highest return

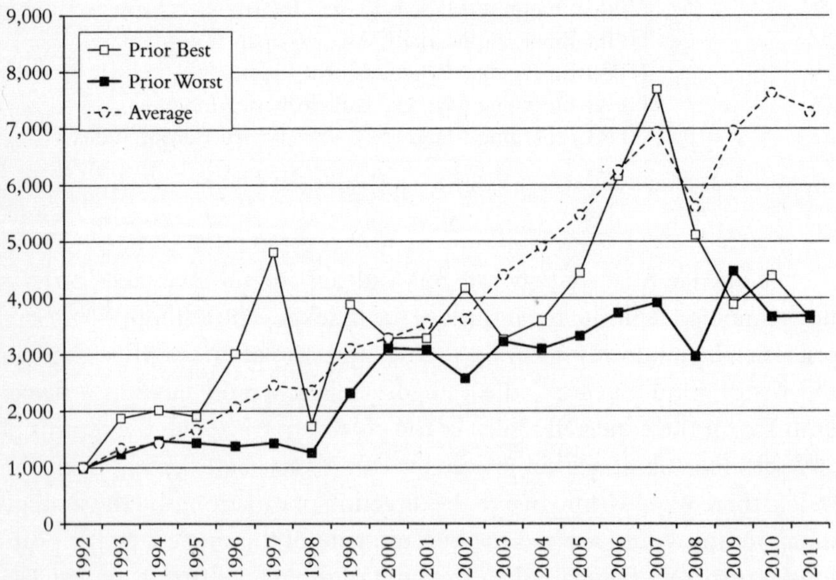

Figure 3.14 NAV Comparison: Prior One-Year Best HFRI Strategy Style versus Prior Worst and Average

SOURCE: Data from HFR (www.hedgefundresearch.com).

in the prior year ends up with a much lower final NAV than an investment that replicates the average of all strategies, and it even results in a slightly lower cumulative return than selecting the past year's lowest-return strategy.

Next, we conduct an analogous test using past three-year returns to define the best and worst hedge fund strategy categories. The NAV graphs for each of the three strategies are shown in Figure 3.15. In this instance, the underperformance of the past best sector is particularly striking. The final NAV based on an annual return equal to the average of all sectors is more than double the best sector's ending NAV, while the worst sector's ending NAV is nearly four times as high as the best.

We repeat the process a third time using the past five-year period to define the best and worst hedge fund strategies. The results are shown in Figure 3.16. Here again, the best sector substantially underperforms both

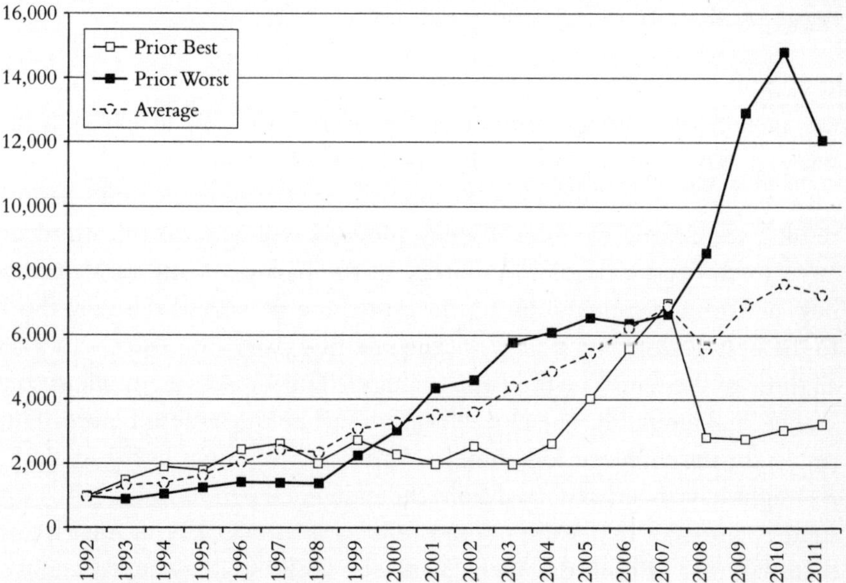

Figure 3.15 NAV Comparison: Prior Three-Year Best HFRI Strategy Style versus Prior Worst and Average

SOURCE: Data from HFR (www.hedgefundresearch.com).

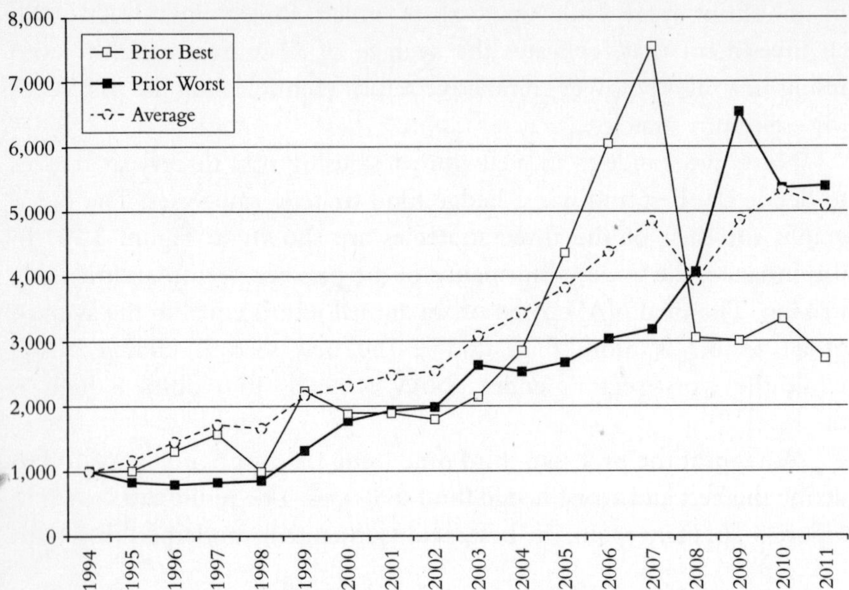

Figure 3.16 NAV Comparison: Prior Five-Year Best HFRI Strategy Style versus Prior Worst and Average
SOURCE: Data from HFR (www.hedgefundresearch.com).

the average and the worst strategy approaches, each of which ends up with an NAV nearly double the final NAV of the best sector.

To derive a single composite result that combines all three period results, we assume the best strategy method will allocate one-third of assets to the best-performing strategy in the past year, one-third to the best-performing strategy during the past three years, and the final third to the best-performing strategy of the past five years. (Sometimes two or all three of these may be the same strategy.) The worst strategy allocation will be analogous. The average allocation will be the same as before. The results for the three-period combined analysis are shown in Figure 3.17. As might have been expected from the individual period results, the best strategy provides by far the poorest return, with a final NAV that is less than half that of both the average and the worst strategy approaches.

As poorly as the best strategy performed in relative return terms, this is not the full story. Investing in the best strategy not only resulted in delivering much lower returns, but it did so with much greater risk. Figure 3.18

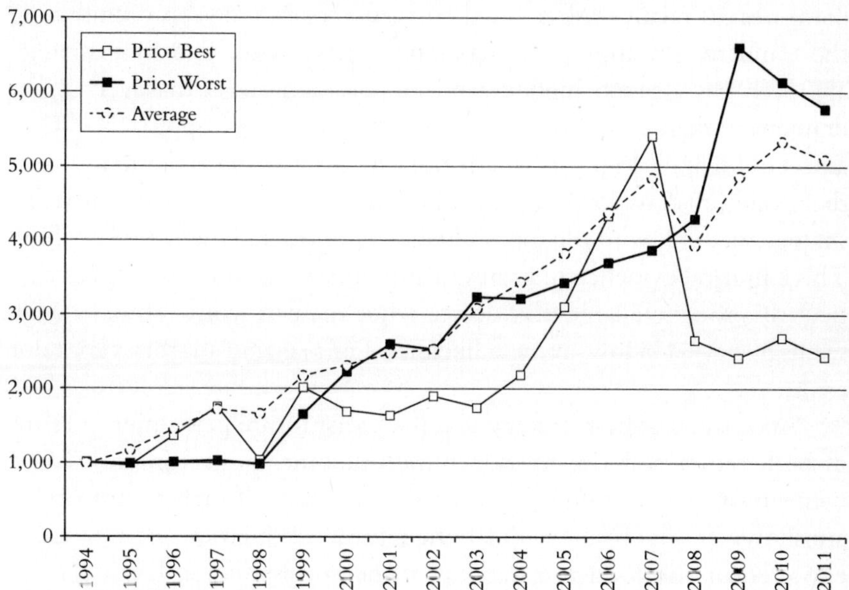

Figure 3.17 NAV Comparison: Three-Period Prior Best HFRI Strategy Style versus Prior Worst and Average

SOURCE: Data from HFR (www.hedgefundresearch.com).

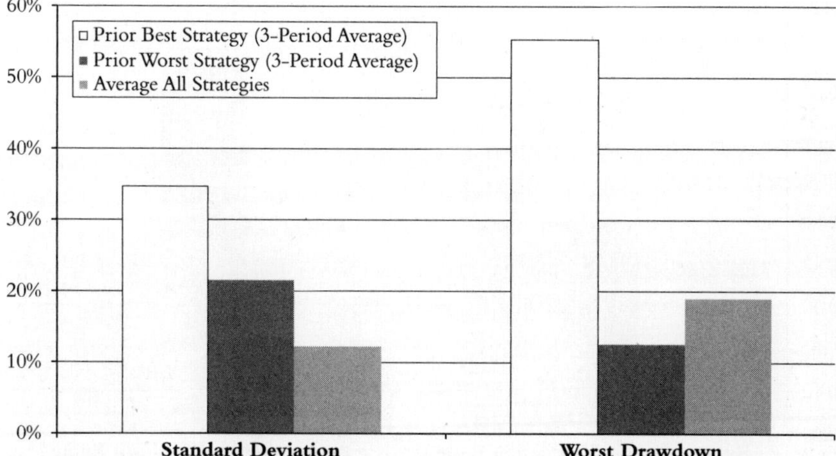

Figure 3.18 Standard Deviation and Maximum Drawdown: Prior Best Strategy (Three-Period Average) versus Prior Worst Strategy and Average of All Sectors, 1995–2011

DATA SOURCE: S&P Dow Jones Indices.

compares the relative risk of the three-period composite approaches using the standard deviation and maximum drawdown. The best strategy approach has a much higher standard deviation and a massively larger drawdown than both the average and worst strategy approaches. One aspect of Figure 3.18 is particularly notable: the enormous chasm between the maximum drawdown using the best strategy approach versus the worst strategy method, with the former being very high and the latter very low. This empirical evidence indicates that the past best-return strategy is particularly prone to a large drawdown, while the past worst-return strategy seems to have a below-average likelihood of realizing another very poor return year.

Since the past best strategy was the worst future performer in terms of both return and risk measures, the outcome of a return/risk-based comparison is a foregone conclusion. The results of such a comparison are shown in Figure 3.19. For both return/risk metrics, the best strategy's return/risk level is a fraction of the corresponding levels for the worst strategy and average of all strategies.

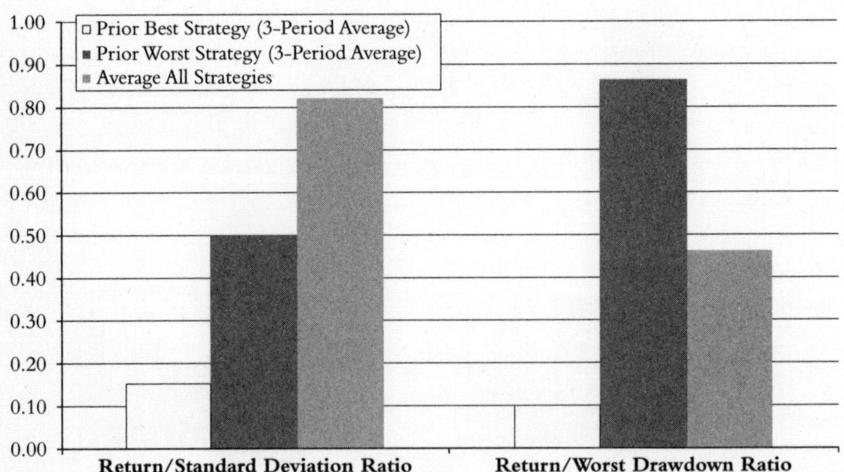

Figure 3.19 Return/Standard Deviation and Return/Maximum Drawdown Ratios: Prior Best Strategy (Three-Period Average) versus Prior Worst and Average of All Strategies, 1995–2011

DATA SOURCE: Standard & Poor's.

The lesson seems quite clear: In regard to hedge fund investing, favoring the best-return strategies of the past represents a highly misguided approach. As a general principle, an investor would be much better off doing the exact opposite—investing in the worst-return strategies of the past. To the extent that the performance of many hedge funds will be heavily influenced by the strategy category, the foregoing analysis implies that shifting assets from low-return to high-return managers may well degrade rather than improve future performance. This general conclusion, however, would not apply to hedge funds whose performance is relatively uncorrelated to their hedge fund category. Also, to avoid any confusion, our analysis showed only that past high-return strategies tend to underperform in the future. We did not at all address the question of whether the past best-performing funds in a given hedge fund category do better than the worst-performing funds *in the same category*.

Why Do Past High-Return Sectors and Strategy Styles Perform So Poorly?

We have seen that for equities, selecting the best sector provides only average returns, but with much greater risk. And for hedge funds, where the dispersion of returns across alternative investment strategies is far greater, choosing the prior best strategy drastically underperformed both the average and prior worst strategy. These observations raise the question of why the best-return investments of the past perform so poorly going forward. There are four plausible explanations:

1. **Change in fundamentals.** Typically, a sector or strategy will do particularly well because of a prevailing highly favorable fundamental environment. There is no reason, however, to assume that the conditions that provided strength in the past will remain prevalent in the future. An analogous statement would apply to the low-return sectors and strategies of the past. For example, consumer-discretionary stocks will fare very poorly during recessions. Unless recession conditions are expected to be extended into the future, this past performance history is not only irrelevant but also

misleading in regard to future potential returns. Shifting fundamentals can explain why the past lowest-return investment sectors could outperform the past highest-return sectors in the future.

2. **Lagged shifts in supply.** If the companies in a sector are very profitable, this situation will spur expansion by existing firms as well as draw increased competition into the sector. The resulting lagged increases in supply will negatively impact profit margins in future years.
3. **Strategy overcrowding.** If a given hedge fund strategy is very profitable, it will draw more managers into the strategy, as well as attract increased investor allocations. The increases in managers and assets in a strategy will reduce profit margins, as there is more competition for the same trades, and will increase losses during liquidation phases.
4. **Emotional price distortions.** Strong bull markets attract speculative buying that can cause prices to move well beyond equilibrium levels. (Although this statement contradicts the efficient market hypothesis, for reasons we fully detailed in Chapter 2, we believe this view is far closer to reality.) In this context, the sectors and strategies with the highest past returns are exactly the ones most likely to be excessively priced and hence most vulnerable to retracement.

Wait a Minute. Do We Mean to Imply . . . ?

Some readers may be uncomfortable about where this chapter seems to be heading. In the preceding sections, we showed that investing after high-return periods yielded poorer results than investing after low-return periods and that selecting the past best-performing equity sector or hedge fund strategy resulted in subpar future performance. Do these results imply that using past returns to select funds is a waste of time and possibly even counterproductive? Do we mean to imply that investors might be better off choosing funds with poor past performance than those with superior returns? The answer is yes and no—it depends on the degree to which a fund's performance is determined by the market or sector.

Long-Only Funds (Mutual Funds)

If a fund is highly correlated to the market (or a sector)—as is true for virtually all long-only funds—its performance will be far more a reflective of the market than the fund's investment process and skill. For example, a so-called closet index fund—a fund that is managed so that its performance does not deviate much from the selected index—would by design be highly correlated to the market. For a closet index fund, high returns would simply mean that the market had witnessed similar high returns and would provide no additional information about the fund's relative merits. Although closet index funds may represent an extreme case, most long-only mutual funds are still highly correlated to whichever index most closely resembles the types of stocks in their portfolios (an index representing similar capitalization companies, sector, and country or region) and could be described as quasi-closet index funds. In contrast, a market neutral fund—a fund in which long and short positions are equally balanced—would likely have a low correlation to the market. In this case, performance results would reflect the fund manager's stock-picking skill rather than the market direction.

Imagine you are watching cable news and see an ad for an energy sector fund with striking two-, three-, and five-year returns. Does this performance record imply that the fund manager is particularly skilled or that the fund is a good investment prospect? If this same fund is very highly correlated to the energy sector index, as is typically the case, then the fund's performance would be nothing more than a reflection of the sector's performance. And, as we have seen, superior sector performance is a poor, if not inverse, indicator of future performance.

Most long-only funds are far more influenced by a specific benchmark index than by any idiosyncratic management skill. In the world of long-only funds, even when skill plays a contributing role in achieving past performance, it is typically dwarfed by the market or sector influence. The lesson is that when you are looking at the past performance of long-only funds, you are primarily seeing the past performance of the market or sector—and that information, as the research studies in this chapter have shown, will be unhelpful, if not detrimental, in selecting investments for future performance.

Hedge Funds and CTA Funds

The relevance of past returns in selecting hedge funds and CTA funds[3] is a far more complex issue. Although for these types of managers past performance may reflect manager skill, there are still a number of major limitations to drawing conclusions about potential future performance based on past performance.

1. **Strategy Style Impact on Performance.** For many hedge funds, returns will be more dependent on the investment environment for their strategy style than on their particular execution of the strategy. This dependency is particularly dominant in some hedge fund strategy styles. We now look at two hedge fund strategies to illustrate the impact of strategy category on performance:
   - *Merger arbitrage.* When a merger deal is announced, the target company's stock price will jump to some level below the announced acquisition price. The discount exists because there is some uncertainty whether the deal will be completed. This discount will diminish over time as the likelihood of a successful transaction increases, and will approach zero if the merger is successfully completed. Merger arbitrage funds seek to profit by buying shares in the target company (and hedging with sales of the acquiring company if the merger deal is a stock exchange at a specified ratio rather than cash acquisition). Merger arbitrage funds will profit from the closing of the discount if the deal is completed and will minimize losses to the extent they are able to avoid deals that break.

     Merger arbitrage funds are highly dependent on the level of merger activity and the level of discounts. When there is a sharp expansion in

[3]The term CTA stands for commodity trading adviser, the official designation for managers registered with the Commodity Futures Trading Commission (CFTC) and members of the National Futures Association (NFA), and is a misnomer on at least two counts: (1) A CTA is a fund or account manager with direct investment responsibility, and not an adviser as the name appears to suggest. (2) CTAs do not necessarily trade only commodities as the name implies. The vast majority of CTAs also trade futures contracts in one or more financial sectors, including stock indexes, fixed income, and FX. And, ironically, many CTAs do not trade any commodities at all, but trade only financial futures.

merger activity, such as occurred in 1999–2000 and 2006, merger arbitrage funds will do well. However, periods of depressed merger activity, such as 2001 to 2005, will be accompanied by low or negative returns. The level of returns of any merger arbitrage fund is more likely to be a reflection of the level of past merger activity than of manager skill, and there is no reason to assume that past merger conditions will have any predictive value for the level of future merger activity. On the contrary, the cyclical tendency in mergers may even suggest that the conditions in recent years—and by implication the level of merger arbitrage returns in recent years—are an inverse indicator.

- *Convertible arbitrage.* A convertible bond is a corporate bond that holders can convert into a fixed number of shares at a specified price. In effect, a convertible bond is a combination of a corporate bond and a call option. Because the embedded option has monetary value, convertible bonds will pay lower interest rates than corporate bonds. Convertible arbitrage funds will typically buy convertible bonds and hedge by shorting sufficient stock to neutralize the long exposure implied by the embedded call option (an activity called "delta hedging").

  Convertible arbitrage funds will do well when the implied optionality in convertible bonds is priced low and normal liquidity conditions prevail. Conversely, if the strategy becomes overcrowded, pushing up prices, effectively making the embedded optionality expensive, and there is a liquidity crunch because too many hedge funds are liquidating at the same time, the strategy will perform very poorly. A classic example occurred in 2008 when large investor redemptions forced heavy liquidation by hedge funds. Since the vast majority of hedge funds are on the same side (long), this selling led to a supply/demand imbalance, depressing convertible bond prices. Managers who initially had been unaffected by investor redemptions experienced losses as other hedge fund managers liquidated the same positions they held. These losses prompted some of their investors to redeem. The vicious circle of hedge funds liquidating in an illiquid market led to more losses and, in turn, more investor redemptions, causing convertible prices to spiral downward. Virtually all convertible arbitrage funds witnessed losses in 2008, often by record amounts. The HFRI convertible arbitrage index was down a staggering 33.7 percent in 2008—nine times its prior worst annual loss!

A mirror image prevailed in 2009. The forced liquidation selling in 2008 pushed convertible bond prices to extremely undervalued levels. In some cases, prices fell so low that the bond's optionality was being valued at less than zero—providing the proverbial "free option." The extremely oversold conditions of 2008 sowed the seeds for a massive bull market in 2009, as bonds rebounded to fair valuation once liquidation selling had run its course, and the rally was amplified by an upside reversal in the equity market, which dramatically increased the implied option values of the bonds. The HFRI convertible arbitrage index was up 60.2 percent in 2009—more than triple its prior largest annual return. The 2009 return primarily recovered the 2008 loss, and at the end of 2009 the index was approximately 6 percent higher than it had been at the start of 2008.

In both cases—the bear market of 2008 and the bull market of 2009—the results of the individual convertible arbitrage funds were far more influenced by the prevailing conditions in the convertible bond market than by the investment strategies of the managers. Even the best convertible arbitrage managers lost money in 2008, and even the worst managers did well in 2009. Looking at the extreme losses of convertible arbitrage managers in 2008 would have told you nothing about the skill level of the managers and would have served as an extraordinarily poor indication of future performance.

Similar to the situation for merger arbitrage and convertible arbitrage, the investment environment for the specific strategy plays a critical role in determining returns for managers in many other hedge fund categories as well. Therefore, for many hedge funds, past returns may be more an indication of the prior environment for a given strategy than a refection of the manager's relative merits. And, insofar as the best-performing strategies in recent past years tend to dramatically underperform the worst-performing strategies going forward (as was demonstrated earlier in this chapter), it follows that for strategy-dependent managers, high return levels in recent years may be a negative rather than positive indicator.

2. **Market Dependency.** For some hedge funds and CTAs, past performance results are still dominated by the market direction rather than by the fund's investment process (albeit not to the degree as long-only funds). For example, many equity hedge funds routinely maintain significant net long positions, and hence their returns will be highly dependent on the direction of the equity market. Many credit hedge funds will typically assume credit risk, and for these managers, the direction of credit spreads—that is, whether the premium of high yield bonds (or other credit instruments) to U.S. Treasuries is widening or narrowing—may be the dominant determinant of performance results.

   In regard to CTAs, a majority of managers pursue trend-following strategies. These managers will tend to do well when markets exhibit extended trends and will do especially poorly when markets are gyrating back and forth—price action that will lead to many false trend signals and what are called whipsaw losses. For trend-following CTAs, the degree of trendiness in the markets will normally be a more critical determinant of performance than the specific trading systems employed. When many futures markets are trending, even inferior trend-following managers will achieve good returns, while in choppy market conditions, even the best trend-following managers will have difficulty avoiding some losses. For trend-following CTAs, the true measure of performance is not their absolute return or return/risk levels, but rather their return/risk measured relative to other trend-following CTAs.
3. **Hidden Risk.** Many hedge funds pursue strategies that appear low-risk most of the time, but are vulnerable to sporadic large risks that may not have appeared in the track record. For these funds, past performance may be very misleading, as it masks inherent risks in the strategy that have not yet been manifested. Hidden risk is a critical concept in hedge fund investing and will be discussed in much greater detail in Chapter 4.
4. **Weak Correlation between Past and Future Performance.** Although some of the best-performing managers of the past continue to exhibit superior performance in the future, there are more instances in which past leading performers degrade sharply in the future. Overall, the link between past and future performance is weak.

For all these reasons, past returns may also be a useless, or even misleading, indicator in selecting hedge fund investments. Still, there is no intention to draw a broad-based conclusion that past returns are always irrelevant in selecting hedge funds and CTAs. Clearly, there are fund managers that achieve superior performance through skill. The Renaissance Medallion fund, which we detailed in Chapter 2, provides a prime example. So it would be at least theoretically possible to select potential future superior hedge fund managers on the basis of past returns. The bottom line for hedge funds is that past returns are often a poor indicator, but sometimes they may be useful; discerning between the two, however, is difficult. One guideline is that the more dependent a manager's returns are on the market or strategy category, the less relevant past returns are.

Investment Misconceptions

Investment Misconception 6: Invest in equities when the market is performing well.

Reality: Empirical evidence strongly indicates that the stock market performs significantly better across a broad range of investment horizons following low-return periods. The best time to invest in equities is after periods of poor performance.

Investment Misconception 7: Focus hedge fund investments in the hedge fund strategy categories that are performing best.

Reality: Investing in the past highest-return strategy categories has historically yielded especially poor performance—a combination of both subpar returns and high risk. Indeed, the empirical evidence suggests that the exact opposite investment approach—that is, picking the past worst-performing strategies—is a far better tactic.

Investment Misconception 8: Invest in funds with strong return records.

Reality: The return levels of long-only funds are far more dependent on the contemporaneous performance of a market or sector than the investment skill of the individual fund manager. Since, as demonstrated, high returns for a market or sector are more likely to be followed by subpar, rather than superior, performance, especially in return/risk terms, selecting high-return long-only funds would also be expected to result in below-average performance. A similar conclusion would apply to hedge funds whose return levels are closely linked to their strategy category or to a broad market direction. Since the past highest-return hedge fund category tends to perform poorly in the future, investing in funds in the same category (because of their high returns) would also be likely to result in inferior performance, especially in return/risk terms. Although there are some exceptions in the hedge fund sphere, on balance, the empirical evidence indicates that selecting funds with the highest returns in recent years (and absent other criteria) is not merely unhelpful, but doing so may even have a detrimental impact on future performance.

Investment Insights

Investor decisions are often driven by past returns. But there are good reasons, both theoretical and empirical, to question the relevance of past performance in timing or selecting investments. In fact, insofar as past returns have any relevance as an investment decision input, their significance is more often the exact reverse of what most investors believe it to be—that is, past high returns are more likely to be a negative rather than positive indicator.

Past superior performance is relevant only if the same conditions are expected to prevail—an expectation that is often unfounded and sometimes starkly contradicted by evolving events. As essayist George J. Church once wrote, "Every generation has its characteristic folly, but the basic cause is the same: People persist in believing what happened in the recent past will go on happening into the indefinite future, even when the ground is shifting under their feet."

Chapter 4

The Mismeasurement of Risk

Worse Than Nothing

More money has been lost through the mismeasurement of risk than by the failure to measure risk. It would be safer to drive a car without a speedometer than a speedometer that understated true speeds by 25 percent. If you had no mechanical gauge of speed, you would be conscious of that absence of information and take extra caution as a result. If, instead, you are relying on a speedometer you believe is providing correct readings but, in fact, is significantly understating actual speed, you will be more prone to an accident. Similarly, in trading and investment, relying on risk measurements that significantly understate true risk may be far more dangerous than not using any risk measurement at all. Indeed, many of the catastrophic losses suffered by investors have been a direct consequence of inaccurate risk measurement rather than the absence of risk measurement.

Perhaps the most spectacular example of how faulty risk measurement can lead to a drastically worse outcome than no risk measurement at all is the trillion-dollar-plus losses suffered by investors in 2007 and 2008 in debt securitizations linked to subprime mortgages, an episode detailed in Chapter 2. Investors bought these securities because the rating agencies assigned them AAA ratings—a risk evaluation that was based on assumptions that had no bearing to the underlying data (holdings that consisted entirely of unprecedentedly low-quality subprime mortgages). Imagine that investors were offered *unrated* debt securities whose collateral consisted of subprime mortgages with no down payment and no income, job, or asset verification, paying as little as a fraction of a percentage point above U.S. Treasury bonds. How much of these securities would they have bought? It is difficult to imagine any consequential amount being invested. Yet investors bought huge quantities of these securities because of the implicit assurance provided by credit ratings. The highly flawed risk assessment conducted by the credit rating agencies enabled enormous investor losses and widespread bank and financial institution failures that otherwise would not have occurred. Erroneous risk evaluations may give investors comfort where none is warranted, and in this sense are much worse than a complete absence of risk assessment, where the lack of such information would itself engender a far more cautious approach.

Volatility as a Risk Measure

Volatility, as measured by the standard deviation, is the ubiquitous measure of risk. The standard deviation is a measure of dispersion. The more widespread returns are around the expected return (commonly assumed to be the average of historical returns), the higher the standard deviation. To provide a sense of what standard deviation values mean, assuming returns are normally distributed,[1] returns would be expected to

[1]*Normally distributed* means that returns will fall within the typical bell-shaped pattern—more returns near the mean (i.e., average) and fewer and fewer returns

Table 4.1 Comparison of Two Managers' Performances

	Average Annual Return	Annualized Standard Deviation	95% Probability Range for Expected Returns
Manager A	15%	5%	5% to 25%
Manager B	15%	20%	–25% to 55%

fall within one standard deviation of the expected return 68 percent of the time and within two standard deviations 95 percent of the time. For example, consider two managers, both with the same 15 percent average annual return (assumed to be the future expected return), but with widely different standard deviations of 5 percent and 20 percent. These two managers are compared in Table 4.1.

Although both managers have the same average return (and assumed future expected return), the uncertainty of the expected return is much greater for Manager B. There is a 95 percent probability that Manager A's annual return will fall within the 5 percent to 25 percent range. Thus, for Manager A, there is a high probability that returns will exceed +5 percent, even in the worst case (at the 95 percent probability level). In contrast, the same 95 percent probability range allows for Manager B's annual return to be anywhere between a very high 55 percent to a

---

for values more distant from the mean. A normal distribution is commonly assumed in a wide range of calculations in finance because it usually provides a reasonable approximation and because it greatly simplifies the calculation of many statistics. (Any normally distributed data series can be fully represented by just two numbers: the mean and the standard deviation.) In reality, however, many markets and return streams deviate from normal distributions by having more instances of returns widely removed from the mean—a characteristic that causes the assumption of a normal distribution to lead to a serious underestimation of the probabilities associated with extreme events. A classic example of this failing was the October 19, 1987, stock market crash, discussed in Chapter 2, an event that the assumption of a normal distribution would have implied was impossible. Here we are concerned with illustrating the concept of standard deviation, which implicitly assumes returns are normally distributed to make probability statements about future returns, rather than evaluating the validity of the normal distribution assumption.

significant loss of −25 percent. It is in this sense of greater uncertainty of return that higher volatility is associated with greater risk. Typically, when investors refer to low-risk funds, they are talking about low-volatility funds (that is, funds with low annualized standard deviations).

In essence, the standard deviation measures the ambiguity of the expected return. It should be intuitively clear that if the standard deviation is low, it implies the return will be relatively close to the expected return, which is typically assumed to equal the average past return (assuming, of course, that the past return is considered the best estimate for the expected return). In contrast, if the standard deviation is high, it suggests that the actual return may vary substantially from the expected return. The standard deviation is a type of average deviation of returns from the mean—one in which bigger differences are weighted more heavily—and this description provides another intuitive interpretation of what the standard deviation represents.[2]

It is important to understand that the standard deviation measures the variability in returns and does not necessarily reflect the risk of losing

---

[2]The standard deviation calculation is readily available in any spreadsheet program, but for those readers who want to know how it is calculated, there are five simple steps:

1. Take the difference between each past return (e.g., each monthly return) and the average of all returns.
2. Square each of these deviations and then sum.
3. Divide by $N - 1$, where N equals the number of returns.
4. Take the square root.
5. Assuming monthly returns are used in the calculation, multiply the standard deviation derived in step 4 by the square root of 12 to get the annualized standard deviation.

The squaring of the differences between individual returns and the mean (step 2) assures that negative deviations have same impact on the standard deviation as positive deviations (rather than offsetting them) and also acts to give greater weight to wider deviations. Step 4 counterbalances the squaring of deviations in step 2. The formula for the standard deviation is:

$$\mathrm{SD} = \sqrt{\left[\sum (R_i - M)^2 / N - 1\right]},$$

where R_i is the individual return for month "i", M is the mean, and N is the number of returns.

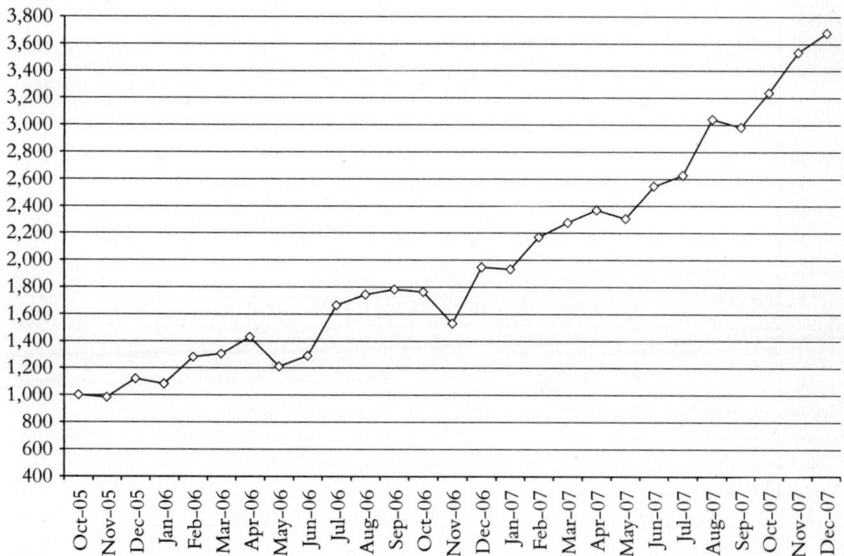

Figure 4.1 Fund X: Steady Performer

money. Consider a fund, for example, that lost 1.0 percent every month. Such a fund would have a standard deviation of 0.0 (because there is no variability in returns), but an absolute certainty of losing money.[3]

Let's consider an example where the standard deviation is used to gauge a 95 percent probability range for future 12-month returns. Figure 4.1 shows the net asset value (NAV) of an actual fund, which we label "Fund X." Although Fund X has relatively high volatility—10 percent monthly standard deviation, which annualizes to 35 percent—the high volatility appears to be more than counterbalanced by a lofty 79 percent average 12-month return. Fund X also appears to be a consistently strong performer with over 70 percent winning months, only two months with losses greater than 4 percent, and a maximum drawdown (equity peak to trough decline) limited to 15 percent, which lasted only one month. Fund X's return and standard deviation numbers imply that there is a 95 percent probability that any 12-month return would fall in a 9 percent to 149 percent range [79% +/− (2 × 35%)].

[3]This quirky example was provided by Milt Baehr, the cofounder of Pertrac, in a conversation we had years ago.

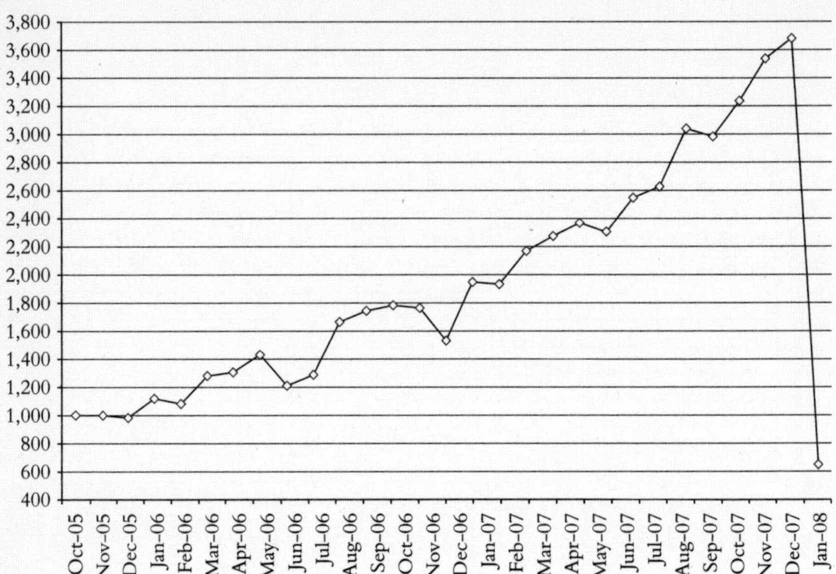

Figure 4.2 Fund X: Oops!

This extremely wide range of possibilities is a consequence of the high volatility, but note that even the low end of the range implies that there is a 95 percent probability that any 12-month return will equal or exceed positive 9 percent.

In Figure 4.2, we add one additional month of data. Based on this single additional month return, the most recent 12-month return drops from +89 percent to −66 percent! This negative 66 percent return is drastically below the positive 9 percent low end of the 95 percent probability range implied by the standard deviation. What happened? Why did the standard deviation provide such a highly misleading gauge of the low end of the probable return range?

The Source of the Problem

The answers to these questions lead to an absolutely critical point regarding risk measurement: Volatility is useful in defining approximate downside risk *only if historical returns are representative of the returns that can be expected in the future.* While we can never be sure this assumption is true (at least not in the case of trading returns), there are definitely cases where we can be sure that it is false—and Fund X provides a prime example. To understand why this is the case, we have to examine the strategy employed by Fund X.

Note: Readers unfamiliar with options might find the primer on options in Appendix A helpful in better understanding the remainder of this section.

Fund X's trading strategy involved selling out-of-the-money options. For example, if a stock index was trading at 1,000, this type of fund might sell calls with an 1,100 strike price (giving the buyer the right to buy the index at 1,100) and puts with a 900 strike price (giving the buyer the right to sell the index at 900). In the vast majority of cases, the market would not move sufficiently to reach either of these levels during the life span of the options, and the options would expire worthless. In this case, the fund would profit by the full premiums collected for the options sold. As long as the market did not witness any abrupt, very large price moves—that is, large enough to reach the strike prices of either the calls or the puts sold—the strategy would be profitable. Since markets only infrequently witness sudden, huge price moves, this type of strategy tends to register steady gains in a large majority of months.

The vulnerability in the strategy is that if the market witnesses a sharp price move in either direction, the strategy is prone to severe and accelerated losses. The losses occur for two reasons. First, there is a loss directly related to the price move. For example, if the market moves to 800, a seller of the 900 put would lose 100 points on the trade, less the small premium collected for selling the option (small because the option was far out-of-the-money when it was sold and would have been perceived as having a small probability of expiring in a profitable range). Second, volatility might increase sharply in the event of a steep market sell-off, further increasing the value of the options sold.

The real crux of the problem for the option seller, however, is that losses will increase exponentially as a price move continues. The reason for this behavior is related to the relationship between changes in the underlying market price and changes in the option price. The percentage that an option price will change for a given small change in the underlying market price is called the option's delta. A delta of 50 (representative of options with strike prices near the market level) implies that the option will move by one-half point for every point move in the market. Out-of-the-money options, because they have a low probability of expiring with any value, will have low deltas. For example, the types of options sold by Fund X might have deltas as low as 0.1, meaning that initially, for every point the market moved toward its strike level, these options would have lost only 1/10 of a point. As a market move progressed, however, the delta would steadily increase, crossing the 0.5 level once the market reached the option strike price and approaching 1.0 as the option became more in-the-money. Thus, the exposure would steadily increase as the market moved adversely to the position, leading to accelerated losses. In short, the strategy pursued by Fund X is one that would win the majority of times, but occasionally could be vulnerable to a mammoth loss.

The period depicted in Figure 4.1 was generally one of low volatility and moderate price moves, a market environment very beneficial to an option selling strategy. Thus, it is hardly surprising that Fund X did very well. As for the large magnitude of its gains, these results simply imply that the fund was taking on a great deal of exposure (i.e., selling a lot of options). The types of episodes that could result in large losses for an option selling strategy did not occur during the period coincident with the fund's prior track record. If an investor understood the strategy the fund was pursuing, it would have been clear that the historical record was not representative of the reasonable range of possibilities and hence could not be used to infer future risk, either through the standard deviation or by any other risk measure for that matter.

The core of the problem highlighted by the Fund X example is not so much a matter of volatility providing a misleading risk gauge, but rather the broader consideration that any track-record-based risk calculation would yield erroneous implications if the track record period is unrepresentative (e.g., it coincided with an overly favorable environment for the strategy). Volatility-based estimates underlie most erroneous risk evaluations simply because volatility is the track-record-based statistic most commonly used to measure risk.

The critical point is that risk assessments based on the past track record (the standard deviation or any other statistics) are prone to be highly misleading if the prior market environment for the strategy was more favorable than what could generally be anticipated over a broader time frame. The reason why investment risk estimates so often prove to be fatally flawed is that they are based only on visible risk—that is, losses and volatility evident in the track record—and do not account for hidden risks—that is, sporadic event-based risks that failed to be manifested during the track record period.

Hidden Risk

Hidden risk is risk that is not evident in the track record because the associated risk event did not occur during that time period. Hidden risks occur only sporadically, but when they occur, they can have a major negative impact. The key types of hidden risk include:

- **Short volatility risk.** This is the type of risk faced by strategies, such as that of Fund X, that seek to profit from stable and declining volatility periods, but in exchange are prone to accelerated risk during volatility spikes in the market—periods that tend to be associated with financial crises and sharply falling prices, both of which often occur simultaneously.
- **Market risk.** Although hedge funds typically employ both long and short positions, a number of hedge fund strategy styles will exhibit a strong net long bias (e.g., equity hedge, emerging markets). Therefore, the performance of many hedge funds in these strategy categories will be heavily dependent on the market direction. For example, Figure 4.3 illustrates the strong correlation between the S&P 500 and an index of equity hedge funds. Funds with a significant net long bias in the market sector they trade will be prone to significant losses in the event of sliding market prices. If the track record for such a fund does not contain any significant bear market phases, market risk—that is, the risk of a declining market—would be a hidden risk in the track record.
- **Liquidity risk.** Funds that hold illiquid positions may sometimes face large losses if they need to promptly liquidate these positions either to exit trades they no longer like or to meet investor

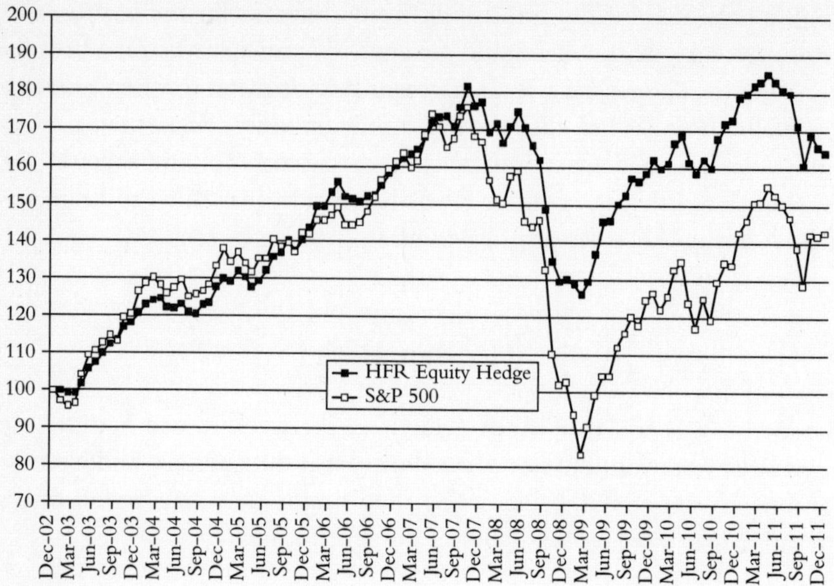

Figure 4.3 HFR Equity Hedge Fund Index versus S&P 500 (January 1, 2003 = 100)

redemptions. Getting out of illiquid positions may require selling at a very large discount, especially if the order size is large. Liquidity is prone to large variation. When markets are rising and volatility is low, even less liquid holdings may be able to be liquidated without creating a major negative impact. In a bear market, however, the value at which an illiquid portfolio can be closed out is likely to be far lower than implied by the most recent price prints. Investors should realize that for illiquid portfolios, market prices may not reflect portfolio value and may greatly exaggerate the dollar amount that would be realized if the portfolio were liquidated. Some examples of strategies that embed significant illiquidity risk are equity microcap long/short and credit strategies that hold low-liquidity credit instruments.

Ironically, liquidity risk is most problematic at the most inopportune times. Liquidity conditions will be worst during crisis periods when a flight-to-safety market psychology prevails and heavy investor redemptions force funds to liquidate their holdings.

The fact that many funds hold similar positions amplifies the gap between supply and demand during risk-aversion periods, resulting in especially wide bid/asked spreads, and extracting a large penalty from those forced to liquidate. The financial panic of September and October 2008 provided a classic example of the dangers of liquidity risk.

- **Leverage risk.** Certain hedge fund strategies require substantial leverage to be executed. For example, convergence strategies are a category of hedge funds that buy and sell very closely related securities, looking for their price differences to narrow when they move beyond a statistically defined normal band. But since the price movements sought in these types of trades tend to be relatively small, a consequence of matching long and short positions across multidimensional characteristics, the positions have to be put on in relatively large size to provide a meaningful return. Thus these types of strategies will typically use large leverage. These funds can exhibit extended periods of low volatility and moderate equity drawdowns. During market liquidation events, however, price deviations between related instruments can widen well beyond normal boundaries and stay at abnormal levels for protracted periods. Such events could lead to large losses directly related to the leverage of the positions.

  Some hedge funds, across a variety of strategies, will use leverage to boost returns. Such a use of leverage will also amplify losses during adverse market periods. If conditions for the strategy are favorable, the risk of such leverage may not be readily evident in the track record other than through high returns.

  Another problem with leverage relates to the kind of leverage instrument used. A mismatch occurs when funds use short-duration leverage instruments to enhance the returns of a longer-duration asset, such as using short-term commercial paper to fund mortgage-backed collateralized debt obligations (CDOs). Here there is risk of not being able to roll over funding.

  Although excessive or unwarranted use of leverage is one of the main factors responsible for episodes of large losses by hedge funds, including those severe enough to result in the fund's demise (blowups), it is important to note that leverage can also be used as a tool to reduce risk through hedging, as in the case of the classic Jones model hedge fund detailed in Chapter 10. Also, the confusion between leverage and risk is one of the major misconceptions among hedge fund investors—a point fully discussed in Chapter 15.

- **Credit risk.** Many hedge funds in the credit space pursue a strategy of borrowing money at a relatively low interest rate and investing the proceeds in higher-yielding instruments (e.g., junk bonds). If money is borrowed at, say, 4 percent, and the junk bonds bought yield an average of 8 percent, then the hedge fund will earn a profit of 4 percent on borrowed amounts (and a full 8 percent on the assets under management, which do not have a borrow cost), assuming bond prices are unchanged. If the amount borrowed is equal to assets under management (leverage factor of two), the total gross return will be 12 percent (again assuming no change in bond prices). The larger the borrowings are (that is, the greater the leverage), the greater the potential return. If credit spreads (that is, the difference between high yield instruments, such as junk bonds, and U.S. Treasuries) are narrowing, profits will be even greater, as hedge funds will not only return a multiple of the yield difference between securities they buy and borrowing costs, but will also earn capital gains from appreciating bond prices (narrower credit spreads imply higher bond prices[4]).

  When credit spreads are stable or narrowing, most credit funds will exhibit steadily rising NAV levels with infrequent and modest losses. The event risk in this strategy, however, is that credit spreads do not follow a one-way street. Although credit spreads will fluctuate in moderate trading ranges most of the time, occasionally, during periods of financial crisis or elevated bankruptcies, credit spreads will widen sharply. During these events, steeply declining values in high-yielding debt securities (e.g., junk bonds, emerging market bonds) can lead to capital losses far greater than the yield differential earned. Note, for example, in Figure 4.4 the sustained negative returns in the HFR Fixed Income Corporate Index (an

[4]Assuming interest rate levels do not increase by enough to offset yield reduction due to credit narrowing.

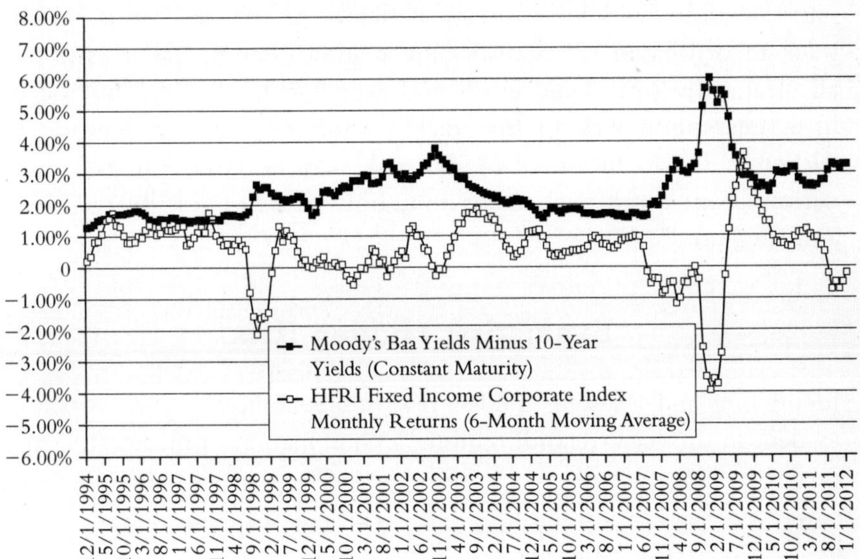

Figure 4.4 HFR Fixed Income Corporate Index Monthly Returns (Six-Month Average) versus Credit Spread (Moody's Baa Yield Minus 10-Year Treasury Note Yield)

index of credit hedge funds) from mid-2007 through early 2009, coincident with the sharp widening of credit spreads. In these instances, credit risk and leverage risk will exhibit a negative synergistic effect, as the larger the leverage, the greater the credit investment losses.

In all these instances (except perhaps for market risk, where adverse periods may be more frequent), strategies prone to the foregoing event risks will exhibit relatively smooth performance and limited equity drawdowns during most periods, interspersed with occasional episodes of large drawdowns. In effect, these strategies exhibit two different phase states with sharply contrasting characteristics. Drawing general conclusions based on a period that contains only the benign phase can prove harmful to investor health.

An adequate risk assessment requires not only an examination of the track-record-based risk statistics (e.g., standard deviation, maximum drawdown), but also an evaluation of hidden risks. If hidden risks are pertinent to the strategy, then track-record-based risk statistics alone will be seriously deficient as risk indicators. While track-record-based risk statistics are readily quantifiable, it is not at all clear how one could assess and weigh risks that did not occur in a meaningful way in the track record. So the key question is: Although the inclusion of hidden risk may be critical to risk evaluation, from a practical standpoint, how can this risk be identified and measured?

Evaluating Hidden Risk

Identifying and assessing hidden risk (susceptibility to event risk not evident in the track record) requires a combination of quantitative and qualitative approaches.

Quantitative Measures

Even when the track record does not contain loss episodes remotely reflective of the risk inherent in a fund or strategy, it still can be used to identify these risks. Some examples of track-record-based measures that can be used to identify hidden risks include:

- **Correlation.** This statistic measures how closely two variables move with each other. Correlation values can range between –1.0 and 1.0. The closer the correlation is to 1.0, the more synchronized the value changes in the two variables are (in the same direction). Correlation doesn't prove cause and effect, but it can signal its potential presence. (Correlation is explained in detail in Chapter 9.) For example, assume a hypothetical hedge fund had a track record similar to the equity hedge fund index shown in Figure 4.3. Through October 2007, the track record would have reflected a steady uptrend with minimal equity drawdowns, the worst being only a slight 3 percent. The risk implied by this track record would appear to be very low.

  However, an examination of the correlation between this set of returns and the S&P 500 returns through October 2007 (the NAV peak for both sets of returns) would have revealed a correlation value of 0.72—a relatively high level that implies a potential strong relationship between the two series. Since through October 2007 the

S&P 500 had also witnessed a steady uptrend with very contained pullbacks, a high correlation would imply that the fund's limited downside movements might reflect the prior highly favorable environment for equities rather than low risk. High correlation would also imply that if the stock market experienced a reversal, the fund would likely also move sharply lower—as indeed occurred. In effect, the fund's vulnerability to losses if the stock market reversed its uptrend could have been ascertained, even though the track record did not contain any significant losses. Correlation can also be used to gauge a fund's susceptibility to other market-based risk factors, such as widening credit spreads.

- **Beta.** The beta of a fund versus a benchmark index is the factor by which a fund's return is expected to change for a given change in the index. For example, a beta of 0.7 would imply the fund could be expected to gain 0.7 percent for each 1 percent gain in the index and lose 0.7 percent for each 1 percent decline in the index. Once again assuming a hypothetical fund with a return series equivalent to the equity hedge fund index shown in Figure 4.3, its beta versus the S&P 500 through October 2007 would have been 0.47, implying it could be expected to lose about half as much as the S&P 500 index in a market decline. Although considerably less risky than the index, the fund's beta would still have implied significant exposure to equities. Interestingly, the subsequent drawdown to the end-of-month low in February 2009 was 30 percent, or slightly more than half the corresponding 53 percent decline in the S&P 500.

  Beta and correlation are mathematically related and provide two different ways of examining similar information. Correlation indicates the degree of the relationship between a return series and a benchmark, while beta indicates the estimated changes in the series for each 1 percent change in the benchmark.[5]
- **Average return in negative months.** Funds prone to risk often perform poorly in negative market environments. In assessing risk, it

[5]Mathematically, beta is equal to correlation times the ratio of the series standard deviation to the benchmark standard deviation. So, for example, if the correlation equals 0.8 and the series has a standard deviation half as large as the benchmark, the beta would be equal to 0.4.

is often more instructive to examine a fund's return during negative market months only than across all months—the proverbial less is more. For example, a fund may exhibit small losses because its track record coincides with a period of rising equity prices rather than because of any inherent risk management. If, however, the fund has a significant negative average return in those months in which the market was down, it would suggest a vulnerability to risk if the market environment turned unfavorable.

- **Percentage of profitable months in negative market months.** The percentage of times a fund is up when the market is down is another useful statistic in gauging vulnerability to a bear market.

Qualitative Assessment

The track record is only a starting point in risk assessment. While evidence of high risk in the track record indicates the potential for high risk in the future, the reverse is not true: Low risk in the track record does not necessarily imply low risk. Investors need to ask themselves the question: What was the source of past returns? Specifically, investors need to determine to what extent past returns were due to taking on market exposure or credit risk, selling volatility, holding illiquid positions, or using leverage—all approaches that can lead to smooth or high returns in most times, but also abrupt losses in risk-averse environments.

The qualitative assessment can be quantified by assigning a rating score to each risk considered. For example, each risk factor can be assigned a value between 1 and 10, with 1 representing very low risk and 10 extremely high risk. Using such an approach, a foreign exchange (FX) fund trading only G-7 currencies might be assigned a liquidity risk of 1, while a fund with $1 billion under management trading microcap stocks might have a liquidity risk of 8 to 10. As another example, a market neutral equity fund would have a market risk rating of 1 or 2, while a long-only fund would have a risk rating closer to 10. In this way, each risk can be assessed and codified. Although the approach is unavoidably subjective, it can be very helpful in highlighting potentially risky funds, regardless of whether any significant risk is evident in the track record. Consider two funds, both of which have equivalent low volatility and moderate equity drawdowns, but differ in their qualitative

Table 4.2 Exposure to Selected Risk Factors

	Market	Credit	Volatility	Liquidity	Leverage
Fund A	3	1	1	1	3
Fund B	8	8	7	8	7

risk ratings as shown in Table 4.2. Whereas the track records might suggest they have equivalent risk, the qualitative risk assessment score approach clearly indicates that Fund B is far riskier.

The Confusion between Volatility and Risk

Volatility is often viewed as being synonymous with risk—a confusion that lies at the heart of the mismeasurement of risk. Volatility is only part of the risk picture—the part that can be easily quantified, which is no doubt why it is commonly used as a proxy for risk. A comprehensive risk assessment, however, must also consider and weigh hidden (or event) risks, especially since these risks may often be far more important.

The confusion between volatility and risk often leads investors to equate low-risk funds with low-volatility funds. The irony is that many low-volatility funds may actually be far riskier than high-volatility funds. The same strategies that are most exposed to event risk (e.g., short volatility, long credit) also tend to be profitable a large majority of the time. As long as an adverse event does not occur, these strategies can roll along with steadily rising NAVs and limited downside moves. They will exhibit low volatility (relative to return) and look like they are low-risk. But the fact that an adverse event has not occurred during the track record does not imply that the risk is not there. An option selling strategy, such as Fund X, will appear to be low-risk (relative to return) as long as volatility remains muted. But as soon as volatility spikes, the risk explodes. The behavior of investments vulnerable to event risk operates in two radically different states: the predominant phase when conditions are favorable and the sporadic phase when an adverse event occurs. It is folly to estimate overall performance characteristics based on just one of these phases. Assuming that low volatility implies that a fund is low-risk is like assuming a Maine lake will never freeze based on daily temperature readings taken only during the summer.

Funds can be both low-volatility and high-risk. Funds that fall into both categories would have the following characteristics:

- They employ a strategy that has a high probability of moderate return and a small probability of large loss.
- Their track record overlaps a favorable market environment for the strategy.
- There were no major stress events for the fund's strategy during its track record.

Our intention is to caution that low volatility does not necessarily imply low risk. There is, however, no intention to suggest that low volatility implies high risk. Of course, some low-volatility funds will also be low-risk funds. The key is determining the reason for the low volatility. If low volatility can be attributed to a strategy that assumes a trade-off of frequent moderate wins in exchange for the risk of occasional large losses (e.g., selling out-of-the-money options, leveraged long credit positions), then the risk evaluation must incorporate the implications of an adverse event, even if one did not occur during the fund's track record. If, however, low volatility can be attributed to a strategy that employs rigorous risk control—for example, a risk management discipline that limits losses to a maximum of ½ percent per trade—then low volatility may indeed reflect low risk.

Not only does volatility, as typically measured by the standard deviation, often dramatically understate risk in circumstances when hidden risks apply, but in some cases, volatility can also significantly overstate risk. Some managers pursue a strategy that curtails the downside but allows for large gains. Consider the example of Fund Y, in which the manager buys out-of-the-money options at times when a large price move is anticipated. The losses on these trades would be limited to the premiums paid, but the gains would be open-ended. If, on balance, the manager was successful in timing these trades, the track record might reflect high volatility because of large gains. The risk, though, would be limited to the losses of the option premiums. In effect, the manager's track record would exhibit both high volatility and low risk.

Fund Y is not the inverse of Fund X, which consistently sold out-of the-money options. The opposite strategy of consistently buying out-of-the-money options might have limited monthly losses, but it would certainly be prone to large cumulative drawdowns over time because of the potential of many consecutive losing months. Also, since option sellers are effectively selling insurance (against price moves), it is reasonable to assume that they will earn some premium for taking on this risk. Over broad periods of time, consistent sellers of options are likely to earn some net profit (albeit at the expense of taking on large risk exposure), which implies an expected net negative return for buyers of options. In order for a long option strategy to be successful, as well as to exhibit constrained drawdowns over time, the manager needs to have some skill in selecting the times when options should be brought (as opposed to being a consistent buyer of options).

So high volatility is neither a necessary nor a sufficient indicator of high risk. It is not a necessary indicator because frequently the track record volatility may be low, but the strategy is vulnerable to substantial event risks that did not occur during the life span of the record (that is, hidden risks). It is not a sufficient indicator because in some cases, high volatility may be due to large gains while losses are well controlled.

The Problem with Value at Risk (VaR)

Value at risk (VaR) is a worst-case loss estimate that is most prone to serious error in worst-case situations. The VaR can be defined as the loss threshold that will not be exceeded within a specified time interval at some high confidence level (typically, 95 percent or 99 percent). The VaR can be stated in either dollar or percentage terms. For example, a 3.2 percent daily VaR at the 99 percent confidence level would imply that the daily loss is expected to exceed 3.2 percent on only 1 out of 100 days. To convert a VaR from daily to monthly, we multiply it by 4.69, the square root of 22 (the approximate number of trading days in a month). Therefore the 3.2 percent daily VaR would also imply that the monthly loss is expected to exceed 15.0 percent (3.2% × 4.69) only once out of every 100 months. The convenient thing about VaR is that it provides a worst-case loss estimate for a portfolio of mixed investments and adapts to the specific holdings as the portfolio composition changes.

There are several ways of calculating VaR, but they all depend on the volatility and correlations of the portfolio holdings during a past look-back period—and therein lies the rub. The VaR provides a worst-case loss estimate *assuming future volatility and correlation levels look like the past.* This assumption, however, is often wildly inappropriate. For example, in early 2007, the VaR of a portfolio of highly rated subprime mortgage bonds would have suggested minuscule risk because the prior prices of these securities had been extremely stable. There would not have been even a hint of the catastrophic risk inherent in these securities, since VaR can only reflect risk visible in prior price movements.

If the past look-back period is characterized by a benign market environment and a risk-seeking preference by investors, the VaR is likely to greatly underestimate the potential future loss if market conditions turn negative and investor sentiment shifts to risk aversion. During such liquidation phases, not only will the volatility levels of individual holdings increase sharply, but correlation between different markets will also rise steeply, a phenomenon known as "correlations going to 1." When different markets are moving in tandem, the risk at any volatility level will be magnified. In 2008, losses by funds of hedge funds greatly exceeded the extremes suggested by VaR because virtually all hedge fund strategies witnessed large losses at the same time, even those that normally had low correlations with each other. The diversification that fund of funds managers counted on disappeared. The cause was the domino effect of liquidation, as large losses in some hedge funds caused investors in need of liquidity to liquidate other unrelated fund holdings, setting off a self-reinforcing liquidation cycle. With the vast majority of hedge funds trying to liquidate the same side of trades as other hedge funds, the transitory imbalance between supply and demand resulted in extremely adverse liquidation prices and widespread losses across virtually all hedge fund styles.

VaR provides a good risk estimate for normal market conditions, which prevail most of the time. The problem is that the greatest risk lies in the sporadic episodes where markets are seized by panic liquidations and act abnormally. VaR is like an automobile speedometer that is perfectly accurate at speeds below 60, but provides inaccurately low readings for speeds above 60. It is dangerously wrong exactly at those times when accuracy is most critical! By providing a statistically based worst-case risk measure, VaR may induce unwarranted complacency in investors regarding the risk in their portfolios. In this sense, an overreliance on VaR as a risk gauge may be more dangerous than not using any risk measurement at all.

Asset Risk: Why Appearances May Be Deceiving, or Price Matters

Consider an example of two hedge funds both of which utilize long/short strategies in high yield bonds and hedge to neutralize interest rate risk. Which fund portfolio seems riskier?

1. Hedge Fund A: long high-rated corporate bonds/short low-rated corporate bonds.
2. Hedge Fund B: long low-rated corporate bonds/short high-rated corporate bonds.

Although it sounds as if portfolio B has much higher risk, the reverse *might* be true:

- A short position in a high-rated bond has very little risk because the potential for a further decline in the credit spread is very limited (that is, the upside price scope is limited), while the potential risk in a long high-rated bond can be substantial if the company is vulnerable to a credit downgrade.
- Although low-rated bonds have a higher risk of default, that risk may be fully discounted or even overdiscounted by the prevailing market price.
- Short positions in low-rated bonds generate greater losses if the bond price moves sideways because the carry is much higher (that is, the interest payments that have to be made are higher).

Moral: Credit quality alone can be a very poor indicator of risk. Risk is not a function of quality, but rather quality relative to price.

Investment Misconceptions

Investment Misconception 9: Risk measurement is always beneficial.

Reality: Faulty risk measurement is worse than no risk measurement at all, because it may give investors an unwarranted sense of security.

Investment Misconception 10: High volatility implies high risk.

Reality: Although it is usually true that high volatility will imply high risk, this assumption will be false for strategies where downside risk is contained and high volatility is due to sporadic large gains. For example, a manager with some skill in anticipating large price moves who expresses her opinions by buying out-of-the-money options might have such a profile. The use of long out-of-the-money options would limit the loss on each trade and, ironically, the better the manager's market calls, the higher the volatility (due to larger gains).

Investment Misconception 11: Low volatility implies low risk.

Reality: Low volatility implies low risk only if the past can be assumed to be a reasonable approximation of the future—an assumption that is frequently unwarranted. Low volatility may often reflect the absence of major adverse events during the track record period rather than low risk. Investors should consider the Malay proverb: Don't think there are no crocodiles because the water is calm.

Investment Misconception 12: The frequency and magnitude of past losses in a fund provide a good indication of risk.

Reality: The major risks to any strategy are often not evident in the track record because they are sporadic and may not have occurred during the life span of the fund. As a consequence of these hidden risks, past losses may greatly understate risk.

Investment Misconception 13: Market prices fairly reflect a portfolio's value.

Reality: For portfolios with significant illiquid holdings, the value that would be realized if the portfolio had to be liquidated might be considerably lower than implied by market prices because of the slippage that would occur in exiting positions.

Investment Misconception 14: Value at risk (VaR) provides a good indication of worst-case risk.

Reality: VaR may severely understate worst-case risk when the look-back period used to calculate this statistic is not representative of the *future* volatility and correlation levels of the portfolio holdings. Following transitions from benign market environments to liquidation-type markets, realized losses can far exceed the thresholds implied by previous VaR levels. By the time VaR adequately adjusts to the new high-risk environment, larger-than-anticipated losses may already have been realized.

Investment Insights

Standard risk measures are often poor indicators of actual risk. Major sources of risk frequently fail to be reflected at all by typical risk metrics. The most widely used risk measure—volatility—will fail to indicate a host of risks that are intermittent in nature. Even worse, the types of strategies that are particularly prone to sporadic large losses may often exhibit extended periods of low volatility. Thus investors seeking low-risk investments and using volatility as their guideline may perversely be drawn to higher-risk investments.

Any risk assessment that is solely based on the track record is inherently flawed. Investors also need to consider the various hidden risks discussed in this chapter—risks that are often not evident in the track record. A comprehensive risk analysis may begin with track-record-based measurements but must also include an understanding of the investment strategy and its inherent risks, as well as an evaluation of the risk management policies of the manager. Judging risk based solely on the track record is akin to an insurance company issuing a policy on a five-year-old home based strictly on its assessed value and prior claim history without considering its location—even if it is located in a floodplain! Just because there have not been any floods since the house was built doesn't mean the risk is low. Absence of evidence of high risk is not evidence of low risk.

Chapter 5

Why Volatility Is Not Just about Risk, and the Case of Leveraged ETFs

Volatility is normally considered only in the context of risk, where as we have seen, it is often an inadequate and even misleading indicator. Most investors don't realize that higher volatility also reduces return as well. An equal percentage gain and loss do not result in a breakeven outcome, but rather always imply a net loss—the larger the absolute magnitude of both the gain and loss, the greater the loss. For example, a 50 percent gain in one year and a 50 percent loss in the next (or vice versa) will result in a 25 percent net loss at the end of the two years (see Table 5.1).

The same average monthly return will result in steadily decreasing compounded returns as volatility increases. Table 5.2 compares five 12-month return streams, each of which has six months of gains and

Table 5.1 The Negative Impact of Volatility on Return

	Starting NAV	Percent Return	Ending NAV
Year 1	$1,000	+50%	$1,500
Year 2	$1,500	–50%	$ 750

Table 5.2 Five 12-Month Return Streams with Average Monthly Return = 1%

	Six Months of % Gains Equal to	Six Months of % Losses Equal to	12-Month Compounded Return
A	3%	–1%	12.4%
B	8%	–6%	9.5%
C	12%	–10%	4.9%
D	16%	–14%	–1.4%
E	20%	–18%	–9.2%

six months of losses, with the gains being 2 percent larger in magnitude. In all five cases, the average monthly return equals 1 percent. In case A, there are six months of 3 percent returns and six months of 1 percent losses (average monthly return equals 1 percent). In this instance, the annual compounded return is moderately higher than the arithmetic return (12.4 percent versus 12.0 percent).[1] Although the average monthly return remains the same, the compounded annual return steadily declines as the magnitude of the winning and losing months increases (although the magnitude difference remains at 2 percent in each case). In case E, the compounded return is significantly negative at −9.2 percent, even though the average monthly return is a positive 1 percent. Quite simply, volatility hurts returns.

Leveraged ETFs: What You Get May Not Be What You Expect

The failure of investors to understand the negative consequences of volatility on return can lead to unpleasant surprises. A good example

[1]Compounded return $= (1.03)^6 \times (0.99)^6 - 1 = 0.124$ or 12.4%. Arithmetic return $= (6 \times 3\%) + (6 \times -1\%) = 12\%$.

of this phenomenon is the experience of many investors who buy leveraged exchange-traded funds (ETFs). Typically, investors who buy a leveraged (2×) ETF expect to earn twice the amount as in the corresponding unleveraged ETF if the market advances.[2] Over any extended period of time, however, they typically find the return is less than twice the amount if the market advances and the loss more than twice the amount if the market declines. Analogous comments would apply to leveraged short ETFs[3]—that is, the gains on market declines will tend to be less than twice the market decline and the losses on price advances will tend to be more than twice the price rise.

The performance difference between seemingly similar exposures in leveraged ETFs and their underlying index counterparts can be shockingly large—a reality that is not understood by many investors in these products. To illustrate this crucial point, we will focus on ETFs for the S&P 500—the most prominent equity index. Note in Figure 5.1 that while a 2× leveraged investment in the S&P 500 index ETF (SPY) declined by 4 percent during 2007–2011, the 2× leveraged Ultra S&P 500 ETF (SSO) lost over 41 percent during the same period. In other words, an investor who bought the leveraged index ETF would have lost 37 percent more than an investor who bought the unleveraged index on 50 percent margin—a position with seemingly equivalent exposure on dollars invested.

Even more surprising is the outcome of an investment in the UltraShort S&P 500 ETF (SDS), which one might have expected to gain in a net declining market. As shown in Figure 5.2, the leveraged short ETF (SDS) lost even more than the leveraged long ETF (SSO), sliding 58 percent—a 62 percent underperformance vis-à-vis the 4 percent gain in a 2× leveraged short position in the index.

Finally, consider an investor who bought equal amounts of both the leveraged long and short ETFs (that is, equal long positions in the SSO and SDS). Although this combined investment sounds like a neutral

[2]Most leveraged ETFs are 2×, although there are some 3×-leveraged ETFs as well. All references to leveraged ETFs in this section assume 2×-leveraged ETFs. The drawbacks of leveraged ETFs discussed would apply even more strongly to the 3× versions.

[3]Short ETFs (both unleveraged and leveraged) are also called inverse ETFs.

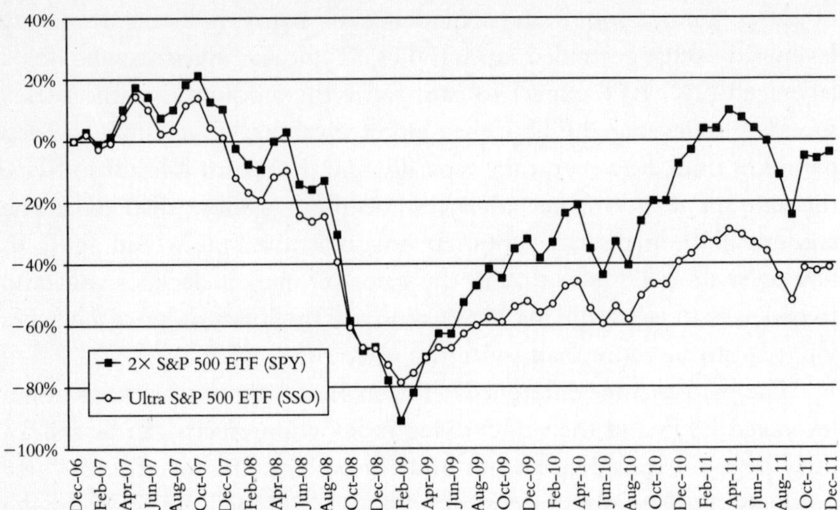

Figure 5.1 2× S&P 500 ETF (SPY) versus Ultra S&P 500 ETF (SSO): Percent Change from January 1, 2007

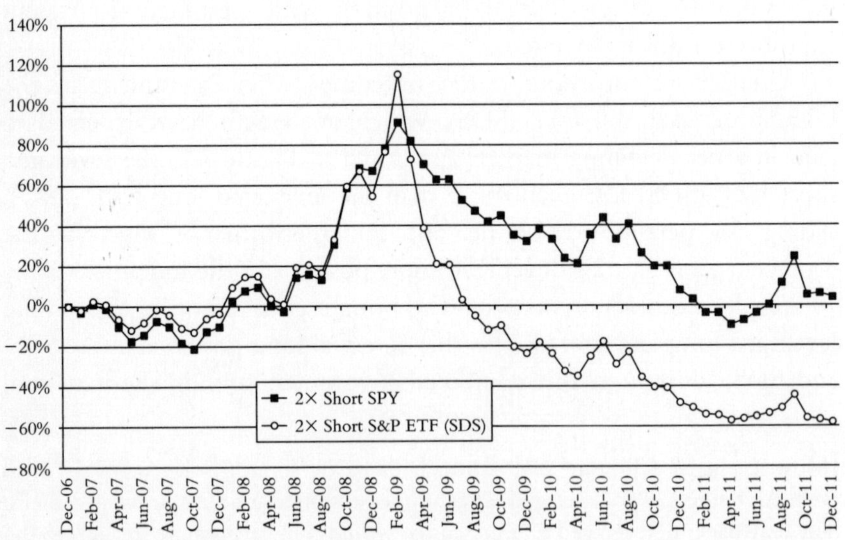

Figure 5.2 2× Short S&P 500 ETF (SPY) versus UltraShort S&P 500 ETF (SDS): Percent Change from January 1, 2007

holding in which the two positions should approximately offset each other, the reality is radically different. The combined investment would have lost the equivalent of 99 percent, measured relative to the amount invested in each ETF! (To allow for direct comparisons between this combined investment and the individual 2× long and 2× short ETFs, the percentage changes in Figure 5.3 are shown relative to the investment on *one side* of the two-position trade.)

Table 5.3 summarizes the outcomes of long and short positions in the S&P 500 index ETF (SPY) versus investments in the leveraged ETFs for the same index: Ultra S&P 500 ETF (SSO) and UltraShort S&P 500 ETF (SDS). To many leveraged ETF investors who are unfamiliar with how these contracts work, the results shown in Figures 5.1, 5.2, and 5.3 and Table 5.3 will likely be startling.

What is going on? Leveraged ETFs are rebalanced each day to maintain the target leverage factor. Therefore, on any single day, the 2× ETFs will approximately double the underlying market price change. Over time, however, the 2× ETFs can stray very far from yielding the target-level price change. In effect, by rebalancing each day, the return

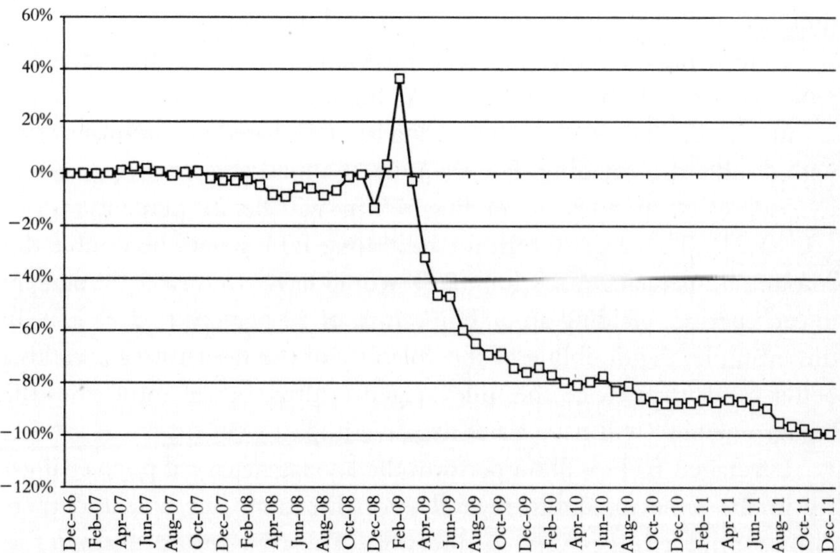

Figure 5.3 Ultra S&P 500 ETF (SSO) Plus UltraShort S&P 500 ETF (SDS): Percent Change from January 1, 2007

Table 5.3 Profit/Loss on $10,000 Alternative S&P 500 Index Investments, 2007–2011

Investment Alternative	Profit/Loss
Buy $10,000 S&P 500 ETF (SPY)	($390)
Buy $20,000 S&P 500 ETF (SPY); $10,000 leveraged 2:1	($780)
Buy $10,000 Ultra S&P ETF (SSO)	($4,140)
Sell Short $10,000 S&P 500 ETF (SPY)	$390
Sell Short $20,000 S&P 500 ETF (SPY); $10,000 leveraged 2:1	$780
Buy $10,000 UltraShort S&P 500 ETF (SDS)	($5,800)
Buy $10,000 SSO and buy $10,000 SDS	($9,940)

outcome on a 2× ETF is dependent on a return series with twice the daily volatility. It is the negative impact of volatility on return that causes the 2× ETF to underperform versus double the investment in the underlying market. Although leveraged ETFs may temporarily outperform during strongly trending markets—for example, the 2× long ETF (SSO) lost less than twice the index decline during the steep price slide in late 2008 to early 2009 (see Figure 5.1)—in most cases, over time, the leveraged ETFs will do considerably worse.

Comparing the return of a leveraged long ETF (SSO) to double the return of the underlying market (SPY) highlights the impact of volatility because, in the former case, the ending return is based on a return stream with double the volatility. For example, if a market is up 10 percent in two successive periods, its ending return will be 21 percent ($1.1 \times 1.1 = 1.21$). The target return for a 2× long ETF would be double this amount: 42 percent. A 2× long ETF would have a return of 20 percent in each period, yielding an ending return of 44 percent (1.2×1.2). In this example, the doubling of the volatility of the return stream yields a better result than twice the unleveraged returns, but in most cases the higher volatility will have a net negative impact over time.

Leveraged ETFs will outperform the leverage factor if price changes are in the same direction, regardless of direction, but will underperform if price changes vary in direction. The two-period examples in Tables 5.4 and 5.5 illustrate the general pattern for long and short leveraged ETFs.

Table 5.4 Double Market Return versus Leveraged Long ETF (2×)

	1st Period Return	2nd Period Return	End Period Return	Double Market Return (Target Return)	2× ETF versus Double Market Return
Market	+10%	+10%	+21%	+42%	
2× Long ETF	+20%	+20%	+44%	NA	+2%
Market	−10%	−10%	−19%	−38%	
2× Long ETF	−20%	−20%	−36%	NA	+2%
Market	+10%	−10%	−1%	−2%	
2× Long ETF	+20%	−20%	−4%	NA	−2%
Market	−10%	+10%	−1%	−2%	
2× Long ETF	−20%	+20%	−4%	NA	−2%

Table 5.5 Double Short Market Return versus Leveraged Short ETF (2×)

	1st Period Return	2nd Period Return	End Period Return	Double Short Market Return (Target Return)	2× ETF versus Double Short Market Return
Market	+10%	+10%	+21%	−42%	
2× Short ETF	−20%	−20%	−36%	NA	+6%
Market	−10%	−10%	−19%	+38%	
2× Short ETF	+20%	+20%	+44%	NA	+6%
Market	+10%	−10%	−1%	+2%	
2× Short ETF	−20%	+20%	−4%	NA	−6%
Market	−10%	+10%	−1%	+2%	
2× Short ETF	+20%	−20%	−4%	NA	−6%

Note the following relationships between leveraged ETFs (2×) and the target return (double the market return for leveraged long ETFs and double the return of a short market position for leveraged short ETFs):

- In same-direction price changes, the leveraged ETF will either win more or lose less.
- In opposite-direction price changes, the leveraged ETF will either win less or lose more.
- Leveraged short ETFs will vary more widely from their target return than leveraged long ETFs.
- The sequence of returns does not affect the final outcome; all that matters is whether returns are in the same direction or the opposite direction.

In very strongly trending markets (that is, markets with a preponderance of changes in one direction), leveraged ETFs will tend to either gain more or lose less than twice the return of the underlying market. In more mixed markets, however, including trending markets interspersed with price corrections, leveraged ETFs will typically gain less or lose more. Over significant lengths of time, it is possible for leveraged ETF longs to lose on balance even when the underling market is up, or for leveraged ETF shorts to lose when the market is down. The longer the holding period, the greater the intrinsic negative return bias in leveraged ETFs.

While it is possible for leveraged ETFs to equal or outperform equivalently leveraged holdings in the underlying index ETFs for temporary periods, the structure of these instruments and their susceptibility to the adverse impact of volatility will usually result in an inherent negative performance bias. Investors and longer-term traders should simply avoid buying leveraged ETFs. If larger exposure is desired, placing double the position in the unleveraged ETF will usually provide a much better outcome than buying a leveraged ETF. If leverage is a major motivation for buying leveraged ETFs, then any of the following alternative leverage tools should be considered:

- Buy double the position in an unleveraged ETF on margin. (If the intention is to buy the leveraged ETF position on margin, then use alternative funds to finance the extra exposure in the unleveraged ETF.)

- Use futures, which have low margin requirements, in markets for which a counterpart futures instrument exists.
- Buy a deep in-the-money option, which has a delta relatively close to 1.0 (that is, its price changes will be close to the market price changes).

Investment Misconceptions

Investment Misconception 15: Volatility is important only from a risk perspective.

Reality: High volatility will negatively impact return. The greater the volatility, the lower the cumulative return for any given average monthly return.

Investment Misconception 16: Leveraged ETFs are a good way to get increased exposure and will deliver approximately the indicated multiple of the target return.

Reality: Leveraged ETFs can be assumed to deliver the approximate implied return on only a day-to-day basis. Over longer periods, the compounding of the more volatile 2× returns will result in 2× ETFs diverging from their target returns. Although the divergence can be either beneficial or detrimental, in all but consistently trending markets (that is, markets with few and limited price corrections against the main trend), the leveraged ETF will tend to underperform the target return (double the underlying market return). The more back-and-forth movement a market exhibits and the longer the ETF is held, the greater the underperformance of the leveraged ETF will be. Leveraged inverse (short) ETFs are prone to even wider deviations from their target. If leveraged ETFs are held for long periods, the returns can be dramatically lower than the target return, even yielding a significant net loss when the target return is strongly positive.

Deep in-the-money options require substantially less cash outlay than outright positions.[4]

Excluding their use for short-term trades or as short-selling vehicles, leveraged ETFs are usually a bad bet for investors and, as a general rule, should be avoided.

Investment Insights

Volatility, which is typically considered only in the context of risk (where it is a flawed measure), also has important implications on the return side. Volatility reduces return. The greater the volatility, the lower the cumulative return that will result from any given average monthly return.

The negative impact of volatility on return provides a less appreciated reason in favor of diversification. An investor would be better off allocating to multiple investments, each with the same expected average return, than to just one of those investments, not only because of lower risk (the well-understood rationale) but also because the lower volatility of the diversified portfolio will yield a higher compounded return. In fact, a diversified portfolio will often yield a higher compounded return than at least some of its components with returns above the portfolio average. The implication is that unless you are confident that you can pick a significantly above-average investment, you are better off with a diversified portfolio, *even for return reasons alone*, not to mention the risk-reduction benefits. The impact of volatility on compounding is one of the reasons why in Chapter 3 the past best-performing sector or fund yielded a lower cumulative return than the average (in addition to having much higher risk). The broader message is that investors should seek to reduce volatility not only to lower risk but also to increase returns.

---

[4]Deep in-the-money options consist almost entirely of intrinsic value (that is, their price embeds very little time value); hence these options will lose relatively little to time decay. For a good article explaining this approach, see Dan Caplinger, "A Better Way to Double Your Returns," January 8, 2011, www.fool.com.

A specific implication of the impact of volatility on returns relates to leveraged ETFs. As demonstrated in this chapter, the negative impact of compounding can cause leveraged ETFs to drastically underperform an equivalently leveraged position in the underlying market. Therefore, excluding short selling and short-term trades, investors should avoid leveraged ETFs.[5]

[5]To be precise, if an investor had a high confidence level of an impending strongly trending market, a leveraged ETF would be appropriate. But, even in this case, if an investor were that confident of an imminent strong trend, a long option position would be a better way to express the trade than a leveraged ETF.

Chapter 6

Track Record Pitfalls

Track records can mislead as well as enlighten. Some of the major pitfalls in drawing inferences from track records include the following:

1. Hidden risk.
2. Irrelevant data.
3. Good performance due to high risk rather than manager skill.
4. Apples-and-oranges comparison errors.
5. Longer records that are less meaningful.

Hidden Risk

A primary way in which track records mislead is by what is not there. The track record may not reflect the types of risk inherent in a fund if it is a strategy that is exposed to sporadic risk events and no such event is contained in the track record. In this case, the track record would be unrepresentative and possibly highly misleading. This essential concept was fully discussed in Chapter 4.

The Data Relevance Pitfall

Figure 6.1 shows that the bond market has been in a general uptrend for the past 30 years. Consider the implications of this track record for the bond allocation in portfolios employing widely used portfolio optimization approaches. Portfolio optimization will provide the optimal asset mix to get the highest return for any targeted level of volatility (used as a proxy for risk). The results of portfolio optimization are based on the past return and volatility levels of the individual assets and the correlation levels between these assets. Generally speaking, the larger and more sustained an uptrend in bonds, the larger its allocation in an optimized portfolio.

The implicit assumption in portfolio optimization is that *past* track records provide a reasonable guideline for making *future* allocation decisions. How reasonable is this assumption? Specifically, in regard to bonds,

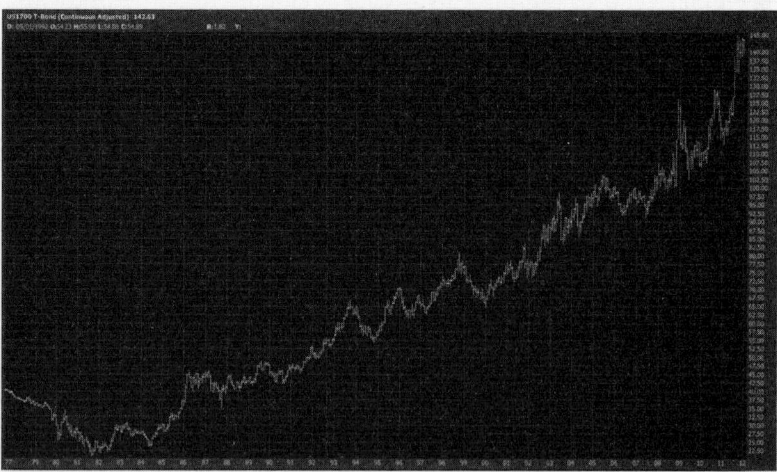

Figure 6.1 Treasury Bond Continuous Futures

Note: A continuous futures chart shows net price movement of a continuously held long position across time, adjusting for price gaps at contract rollovers.

Source: Thinkorswim for TD Ameritrade.

how relevant is the past 30-year history to the future? The driving force underlying the long-term bull market in bonds was the 22-year decline in commodity prices that began in 1980 and the simultaneous decline in inflation. Although commodity prices bottomed in 2002, inflation has remained subdued, aided by the 2008 economic collapse and its aftermath. The bull market in bonds (or equivalently, the long-term decline in interest rates) has coincided with the decline in inflation from the double-digit inflation levels of 1979 and 1980 to the sub-2 percent inflation rates in the post-2008 period.

The future outlook for bonds, however, looks very different from the past history. With 30-year bond yields having declined from near 15 percent in 1981 to 3 percent, there is much more limited scope for a further decline in interest rates under any set of assumptions. The past decline in interest rates (rise in bond prices) is not merely an unrepresentative indicator of the future, but an impossible one. We can hardly expect interest rates to move from 3 percent to −12 percent in the next 30 years. There are, however, reasons to expect a reversal in the long-term decline in interest rates. Commodity prices have already reversed to a new long-term uptrend in response to sharply increased demand from rapidly growing developing economies. Thus far, inflation has remained subdued, despite rising commodity prices, due to high unemployment. But as employment recovers, inflation is likely to begin to trend higher as well. In addition, the lagged impact of an easy monetary policy coupled with concern over billowing debt levels may also lead to higher inflation and interest rate levels (that is, lower bond prices) over the long run.

Ironically, the very factors responsible for the past bull market have bearish future implications. The extended bull market in bonds, which saw long-term interest rates decline from very high to very low levels, has left very limited room for further capital gains from rate declines, and implies an increased chance of capital losses as interest rate deviations are now more likely to be on the upside. In addition, the long-term decline in interest rates means that interest income is significantly reduced. In this context, the extremely extended climb in bond prices over the past 30 years is more an argument for lower bond prices in the future than for increasing their allocation in a portfolio.

Past track records are pertinent only if they are relevant to the future outlook. Frequently, there is no reason to make this assumption, and sometimes, as in the case of the long-term price movements in bonds, there is a stronger argument to be made for the past being an inverse indicator. *Never make investment decisions based on past track records without first asking whether there is reason to assume that past returns offer some guideline for the future.*

When Good Past Performance Is Bad

Good performance is not necessarily a positive attribute. Sometimes superior past performance may reflect the willingness to take on greater risk rather than manager skill. Consider the equity long/short managers who would have been the star performers during 1998 and 1999. Managers who were heavily net long technology and especially Internet stocks would have dramatically outperformed. During this period, the riskier the portfolio—the greater the net long exposure and the greater the concentration in Internet stocks—the better the performance. The market rewarded managers who bought extremely overvalued and even fundamentally worthless stocks, as these equities became even more overpriced. Managers who followed a prudent investment course and refrained from the speculative frenzy underperformed badly. An investor in early 2000 selecting equity hedge managers based on the criterion of best recent performance would have been more likely to pick managers with the riskiest portfolios rather than those with the greatest skill. Many of the best performers in 1998 and 1999 were among the worst performers in the ensuing years after the Internet bubble burst in March 2000 and the whole technology sector moved sharply lower through 2002.

The performance of some credit strategy hedge funds during 2003 to 2007 provides another example of superior results reflecting risk rather than skill. Long-biased hedge funds that specialize in high yield investments will profit by earning the differential between the yield on the bonds they buy and their cost of borrow. By using leverage, the profits from this differential can be multiplied. Leverage will always increase net interest income return, but may result in either greater capital gains or larger capital losses, depending on whether credit spreads are narrowing or widening. During 2003 to mid-2007, credit spreads on high yield bonds steadily narrowed, meaning that capital gains enhanced net interest income. Managers with the most leverage and credit exposure did best as leverage multiplied both interest income flow and capital gains (due to contracting spreads). The greater risk assumed by increased leverage would not have been evident because there were no episodes of a sharp expansion in credit spreads to reflect the risk of a larger net long exposure. An investor in mid-2007 selecting credit hedge funds on the basis of those with the best returns in the prior three to five years might very well have ended up choosing funds with the largest exposure to credit risk rather than superior manager skill.[1] Those funds with the largest net long exposure would have fared especially poorly in the following two years, as credit spreads widened sharply, resulting in leverage-magnified capital losses.

The investment trap is that sometimes past outperformance reflects the negative characteristic of greater risk, rather than the positive quality of manager skill. This greater risk will not be directly visible if the market environment has been very favorable—the very same condition that contributed to outperformance in the first place. Also, the types of extreme moves that most reward excessive risk taking (e.g., Internet bubble, credit market bubble) also greatly increase the chances of a major market turning point. In this sense, the past not only is unrepresentative, but may also be highly misleading. Investors always need to understand the reasons for past favorable performance and assess whether there is any reason to expect those same factors to be relevant *in the future*. A manager heavily long Internet stocks in early 2000 might have had a great track record, but an investor who understood the reason for the superior performance would have been aware of the inherent risk. As Paul Rubin observed, "Never confuse brilliance with a bull market."

[1]Of course, many credit-based managers did well during 2003–2007 without taking on excessive credit risk exposure. The point, however, is that many other managers achieved superior returns during this period primarily as function of assuming greater credit risk. Investors would need to be able to determine the source of the above-average returns in order to distinguish between the two.

The Apples-and-Oranges Pitfall

Consider the following two funds in the same strategy space, and assume we consider the maximum drawdown as the key risk metric:

1. Fund A: maximum drawdown 25 percent.
2. Fund B: maximum drawdown 10 percent.

Which fund is riskier? This may strike some readers as an inane question. Isn't Fund B obviously less risky? No, not necessarily. Actually, there is insufficient information to answer the question posed. Assume we are provided with a bit of additional information:

1. Fund A: maximum drawdown 25 percent; length of track record seven years.
2. Fund B: maximum drawdown 10 percent; length of track record three years.

It is impossible to determine which fund is riskier because the fund with the smaller drawdown also has the shorter record. What if we were told that Fund A's maximum drawdown during the past three years (the period of Fund B's track record) was only 5 percent (compared with B's 10 percent)? Then Fund A would seem less risky. The point is that we don't know how large Fund B's maximum drawdown would have been if it had traded for the same full period as Fund A. It might well have been much larger than Fund A's 25 percent.

To be meaningful, comparisons must be over the same time period. As in this example, if maximum drawdown is used as a comparison statistic, it should be measured from the later of the two start dates rather than from each fund's respective inception. The same guideline would apply to any statistic.

Assume we compare the average annual compounded return of two long-biased equity hedge funds, Fund A, which began in 1995, and Fund B, which began in 2000. If return is measured from inception, then Fund A will have a tremendous positive bias in the comparison because it traded for a number of very bullish years in which Fund B did not. In this example, the fund with the longer track record has the advantage, but in other cases, it will be the reverse. For example, an emerging market fund that launched at the start of 1999 would have a large advantage over one that started in mid-1997, as its track record would not include the major bear markets that occurred across the spectrum of emerging markets during 1997 and 1998. Here again, biased comparisons can be avoided by ignoring all data from the earlier-starting fund prior to the start date of the second fund.

The broader principle is that comparisons between funds should be across similar characteristics, including:

- **Time period.** As illustrated in the foregoing examples, if two funds started on different dates, their performance statistics should be compared for only the overlapping time period.
- **Strategy style.** It is meaningless to compare funds employing different strategies, because very often performance is highly dependent on the underlying market. A comparison between a long-biased equity hedge fund and a fixed income arbitrage fund would be biased in favor of the equity manager if the stock market was in a general uptrend during the comparison period and the reverse if stock prices were predominantly in a declining phase.
- **Markets.** Performance may often be more indicative of the market environment than the skill of the manager. Even if two managers fall into the same strategy category, if they trade different markets, then comparisons can be very misleading. For example, if two managers are both trend-following commodity trading advisors (CTAs), but one trades only commodity markets and the other trades foreign exchange (FX), a comparison when one market sector was largely trending and the other experiencing choppy price action (a highly unfavorable environment) would say more about the relative trendiness of the sectors than the skill differences between the managers.

Longer Track Records *Could* Be Less Relevant

It is commonly assumed that longer track records for a fund are more meaningful than shorter track records. This seemingly commonsense assumption is not necessarily true. Longer track records *could* be less relevant for any of the following reasons:

- **Changes in strategy and portfolio.** Large growth in assets under management over time could necessitate major changes in the strategies used and the markets traded. For example, a long/short equity manager whose biggest winners are achieved in small-cap equities may be forced to shift to increasingly larger-cap positions as assets under management grow, reducing the percentage allocation to small-cap positions or abandoning them entirely. The forced shift to larger-cap equities may diminish the manager's edge and result in a downshift in performance. Thus data from earlier years may not be representative of the current investment style and could severely overstate performance potential.
- **Declining efficacy of strategy.** The strategies responsible for a fund's success in earlier years may lose their efficacy due to either structural changes in the market or increased competition from other funds deploying similar strategies. As a result, the returns from earlier years may be much higher than more recent year returns, as they may have been achieved during a very favorable environment for the strategy that is unlikely to be repeated. A good example of this phenomenon is the performance profile of trend-following CTAs with long track records. In the 1970s, 1980s, and early 1990s, trend-following managers tended to generate high average annual returns. As more and more managers began using similar strategies, the return/risk performance of the strategy style degraded significantly. Typically, managers in this strategy space whose records stretch back to these earlier decades will have much higher return levels in the earlier years. It is not uncommon to see bifurcated track records where the earlier portion exhibits superlative performance and the latter portion mediocre results or worse. Insofar as the earlier portion of the track record was achieved under conditions no longer representative and unlikely to be repeated, its inclusion can make the strategy look much more attractive than warranted based on future performance potential.
- **Change in portfolio managers.** Funds with longer track records are more likely to see changes in portfolio managers. Over time,

the founding portfolio manager responsible for a fund's success may transition to a team leader role, delegating some, or even all, of the direct portfolio management responsibility to recruited managers. In some cases, the original manager may even partially or totally retire. In other cases, where a portfolio manager works for a larger organization, funds may continue to operate under the same name even after the original fund manager leaves and is replaced by another manager. When there are important changes in portfolio management, the earlier segment of the track record may be irrelevant and misleading.

Any or all of these factors *could* actually make a longer track record less relevant than a shorter track record.

Investment Misconceptions

Investment Misconception 17: It is reasonable to use past returns in making future investment decisions.

Reality: Past returns are misleading if there are reasons to believe that future market conditions are likely to be significantly different from those that shaped past returns, as was the case in our bond market example. Prior returns will also be misleading if there is reason to believe that a particular strategy may have lost some or all of its efficacy vis-à-vis the past.

Investment Misconception 18: High past returns, assuming they were achieved with moderate equity drawdowns, are always a positive attribute.

Reality: Sometimes high past returns reflect excessive risk taking in a favorable market environment rather than manager skill. This risk may not be evident in the track record if the risk is episodic in nature and no risk events occurred during the life span of the fund. Understanding the source of returns is critical to evaluating their implications and relevance.

Investment Misconception 19: In a quantitative assessment, a manager with a higher return/risk since track record inception is better than a manager with a lower return/risk.

Reality: When manager track records start on widely varying dates, as is often the case, the market conditions in the nonoverlapping time period may have a dominant impact on performance differences. Comparisons between managers should be made only for coincident periods (not since respective inceptions). Also, comparisons between managers are meaningful only if they are trading similar markets with similar strategy styles.

Investment Misconception 20: Longer track records are more meaningful.

Reality: Sometimes longer track records are less meaningful if there have been major changes in the strategy or portfolio management responsibility—changes that are more apt to occur in longer records.

Investment Insights

Although track records are an essential component in making investment decisions, their routine use and superficial interpretation can lead to erroneous, and even completely misleading, conclusions. The key question an investor needs to ask is whether the implications of the past track record are pertinent for the future. It some cases, they will not be. For example, the track record of an equity hedge manager that coincides with a bull market may not be at all indicative of how the manager could be expected to fare in a more two-sided market, let alone a bear market. In some cases, a good track record may reflect excessive risk taking in a benign environment rather than manager skill. In order to assess the relevance of a past track record, an investor needs to understand the source of the past gains and the risks taken to achieve them.

Chapter 7

Sense and Nonsense about Pro Forma Statistics

Pro forma is a most unfortunate and confusing term in the sense that it is used in virtually opposite contexts. Pro forma results are based on presumed representative returns as opposed to actual returns and are used when actual returns are unavailable or are considered to be in need of modification. In practice, however, pro forma returns can range from unrepresentative and misleading to more representative than so-called actual returns.

As one example of the misleading uses of pro forma numbers, consider a new fund of funds that employs a track record based on how the portfolio would have performed in the years prior to the fund's inception based on the actual track records of the funds selected for the portfolio. It's easy for investors to be fooled into believing that such pro forma results are representative because, after all, they are based on actual track records. The catch, however, is that only funds with good past performances will be selected, and the knowledge of which funds would have experienced superior performance would not have been known prior to the achievement of their outperformance. There is, in fact, no reason to assume that a largely similar portfolio, let alone the same portfolio, would have been chosen at the start of the pro forma period and subsequently maintained throughout the period without changes. Thus such pro forma results will be highly biased because, although the portfolio results are constructed from actual return data for the underlying funds, the composition of the portfolio itself is hypothetical.

Another example of misleading pro forma numbers would be a manager who after trading a diversified portfolio decides to create a new specialized program that trades only one sector in the portfolio. One can safely assume that such a carve-out portfolio will be based on a market sector subset of the whole portfolio that has done particularly well. Once again, the pro forma results are based on actual returns, a factor that seems to lend credibility. What the investor may fail to realize, however, is that the returns represent a cherry-picked subset of a broader portfolio. There will always be some portions of the portfolio that will do better than others (e.g., better-performing market sectors). There is, however, no reason to assume that the subset chosen to be a new stand-alone program will continue to do better in the future.

It is tempting to conclude that pro forma results are categorically misleading and should be dismissed, and in fact that is exactly what many investors do. This presumption, too, however, is a mistake since pro forma results can sometimes be more representative than so-called actual results. Consider, for example, a manager who launches a fund that will trade the same strategy previously utilized for a proprietary account that was not charged any fees. In this instance, the actual past returns would overstate performance potential (even assuming future returns are equivalent to those realized in the past) because they fail to reflect the fees that will be charged to investors in the fund. Clearly, the correct representation of results will be one that reduces the prior actual track record returns by amounts equivalent to the fees that investors will be charged in the new fund. Not only is there no problem with the use of pro forma results in such a situation, but the pro forma returns are unquestionably more meaningful than the actual returns.

As these contrasting examples should make clear, pro forma results can range from misleading to more representative than actual results. To lump all pro forma results together in the same derogatory context is itself misleading.

There are two key questions regarding any pro forma result:

1. Does the pro forma result embed any hindsight?
2. Is a pro forma result more representative than the actual results?

The answers to these questions determine the legitimacy or lack thereof of a pro forma return series. In the first example cited—a new fund of funds using a pro forma track record based on the prior actual track records of the underlying funds selected for the portfolio—the fund of funds manager has the benefit of hindsight in picking the funds in the portfolio. No fund of funds manager will construct a portfolio of funds that have done poorly in the past. Thus the actual results of funds in the portfolio for the period prior to their selection will be a misleading indicator of the portfolio's potential future performance. Similarly, in the example of a new fund product formed as an extraction from a broader portfolio, the choice of the subset benefits from hindsight. In contrast, where the adjustment is made to more accurately reflect the way a fund will be traded without any hindsight distortion at all—for example, a pro forma adjustment to reflect fees that new investors will be charged but that are not reflected in the track record—the pro forma returns can be more accurate and representative than the so-called actual returns.

Investment Misconceptions

Investment Misconception 21: Pro forma results provide a reasonable approximation of actual performance.

Reality: Although this assumption is true sometimes, pro forma results can be wildly misleading if they are derived with the benefit of hindsight.

Investment Misconception 22: Pro forma results are highly distorted and should never be used as a proxy for actual performance.

Reality: Although this assumption is often true, sometimes pro forma returns can provide a more appropriate performance representation for the investor than actual returns—as would be the case if the past actual returns were achieved with a lower fee structure. Generally speaking, pro forma returns are preferable to actual returns if they only adjust *past* fees to more closely represent fees paid by *current* investors and do not make any adjustments that benefit from hindsight.

Investment Insights

There is a great deal of confusion regarding pro forma results due to the term's use in nearly opposite contexts. Pro forma results are both used when they shouldn't be and dismissed when they are entirely appropriate. The key is whether pro forma results embed hindsight—a consideration that makes all the difference.

Chapter 8

How to Evaluate Past Performance

Why Return Alone Is Meaningless

You are looking for a London hotel room on the Internet. You find the same hotel room at two different sites (both including taxes) at two different prices:

- Site A: 320
- Site B: 250

Which is the better deal? The answer may seem obvious, but it's not. On one occasion, when I posed this question to a conference audience, one attendee shouted the response, "It depends whether they both include breakfast." "That would have to be a very expensive breakfast," I answered. But at least he had the right idea. The question I posed contained incomplete information. I didn't specify what currency the prices were quoted in. What if the 320 price was in dollars and the 250 price was in pounds? Changes everything, doesn't it?

"Well," you are probably thinking, "no rational person will ignore the currency denomination in comparing two prices, so what's the point?" The point is that investors make this type of error all the time when selecting investments by focusing only on returns. Comparing returns without risk is as meaningless as comparing international hotel prices without the currency denomination. Risk is the denomination of return.[1]

Consider the two managers in Table 8.1. Which is the better-performing manager? We assume that hidden risk, as discussed in Chapter 4, is not an issue and that standard deviation is therefore a reasonable proxy for risk. We also assume that the managers are considered qualitatively equivalent.

Many investors would opt for Manager B, reasoning, "I am willing to accept the higher risk to get the higher return potential." But is this reasoning rational? In Table 8.2 we add a third investment alternative—leveraging an investment with Manager A at 300 percent.[2] The leveraged investment with Manager A now has both a higher return and lower risk than Manager B. So even risk-seeking investors should prefer Manager A, using a leverage factor that raises return to the desired level.

One can picture risk as a hole—the deeper the hole, the greater the risk—and return as a pile of sand. Leverage is the shovel that, if desired, allows transferring some of the sand from the risk hole to the return pile,

---

[1]We ignore the issue here that higher returns can sometimes be a negative indicator for future performance, as was detailed in Chapter 6, and assume that performance comparisons are made over a longer period, not just recent past, and that the investor has reason to believe that manager skill is a factor in the performance difference.

[2]For strategies that use margin (e.g., futures, FX, options), managers need only a small percentage of the nominal investment to meet margin requirements. In these instances, investors can often use notional funding—that is, funding an account with a smaller amount of cash than the nominal level. For example, an investor might notionally fund an account with $300,000 cash to be traded as a $900,000 investment, implicitly leveraging the cash investment 300 percent vis-à-vis an investment that is not notionally funded. Technically speaking, although notional funding increases the exposure per dollar invested, it is not actually leveraging, since there is no borrowing involved. Our example assumes notional funding. For strategies that must be fully funded, the leveraged portion of returns would have to be reduced by borrowing costs.

Table 8.1 A Comparison of Two Managers

	Return	Risk (Standard Deviation)	Return/Risk Ratio
Manager A	10	5	2:1
Manager B	25	25	1:1

Table 8.2 A Comparison of Two Managers Revisited

	Return	Risk (Standard Deviation)	Return/Risk Ratio
Manager A	10	5	2:1
Manager B	25	25	1:1
Manager A 3×	30	15	2:1

thereby increasing return in exchange for accepting greater risk—a trade-off that may be preferred if the risk level is lower than desired. Continuing the analogy, by using negative leverage (that is, holding cash), it is also possible to transfer sand from the return pile to the risk hole, thereby reducing risk in exchange for accepting lower return. In this sense, risk and return are entirely interchangeable through leverage.

As a practical example to illustrate this concept, in Figure 8.1 we compare two actual managers. Given an assumption that we consider past performance indicative of potential future performance—at least in a relative sense—which manager provides a better investment? It would appear that the answer to this question is indeterminate: Manager C clearly achieves superior return, but Manager D displays considerably lower risk, as evidenced by much smaller equity drawdowns throughout the track record. The seeming inability to determine which manager exhibits better performance is true only in a superficial sense, however. In Figure 8.2, we again compare Managers C and D, but this time we assume that the exposure to Manager D is doubled.[3] Now it is clear that

[3]Managers C and D are CTAs who trade futures, so increased exposure could have been achieved through notional funding (i.e., without leverage through borrowing). The returns depicted in Figure 8.1 were adjusted to remove interest income, so that doubling exposure (whether through notional funding or through borrowed leverage) would multiply all the returns by a near-exact factor of 2.0. (If returns included interest income, then doubling the exposure would not fully double the returns because there would be no interest income on the additional exposure.)

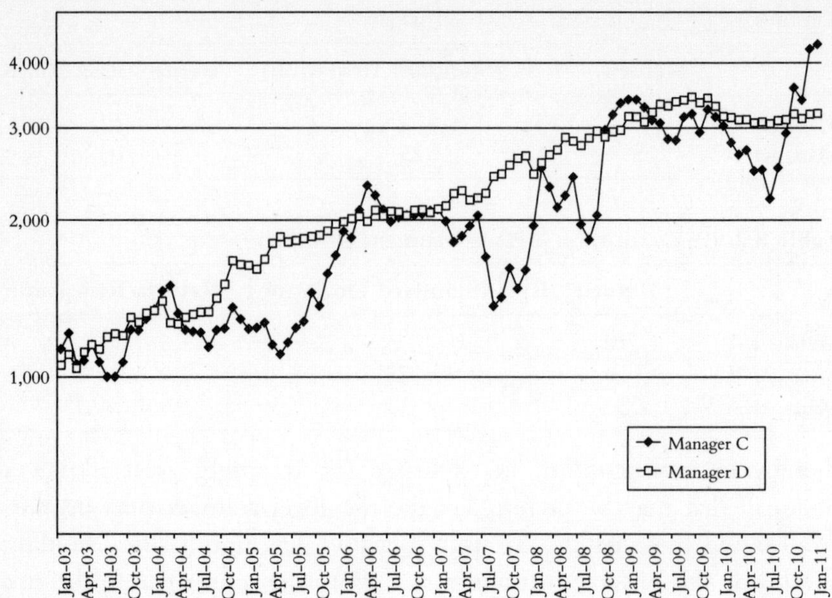

Figure 8.1 Two Paths to Return

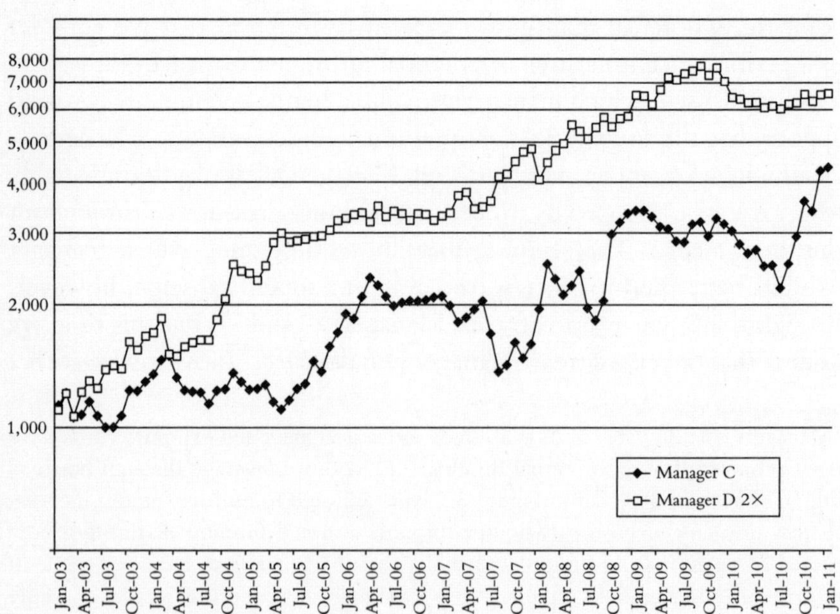

Figure 8.2 Doubling the Exposure of the Lower-Risk Manager

Manager D is superior in terms of both return and risk, achieving a significantly higher ending net asset value (NAV) and still doing so with visibly lower equity drawdowns (despite the doubling of exposure). Even though Manager C ended up with a higher return in Figure 8.1, investors could have achieved an even higher return with a 2× investment in Manager D while still maintaining less risk. The lesson is that return is a faulty gauge; it is the return/risk ratio that matters.

What if leverage is not available as a tool? For example, what if investors have a choice between Managers C and D in Figure 8.1, but there are practical impediments to increasing the exposure of Manager D? Now return and risk are inextricably bundled, and investors must choose between the higher-return/higher-risk profile of Manager C and the lower-return/lower-risk profile of Manager D. It might seem that risk-tolerant investors would always be better off with Manager C. Such investors might say, "I don't care if Manager C is riskier, as long as the end return is higher." The flaw in this premise is that investors who start with Manager C at the wrong time—and that is easy to do—may actually experience significant losses rather than gains, even if they maintain the investment, and especially if they don't. The more volatile the path of returns, the more likely investors will abandon the investment during one of the equity plunges and, as a result, never realize the higher return. After all, investors in real time do not know that the investment will eventually recover. Thus even though Manager C ends up ahead of Manager D, many investors will never survive the ride to see the eventual successful outcome (and even those who do may have initiated their investment on an upside excursion, reducing or even eliminating their net return). The greater the volatility, the larger the percentage of investors who will close out their investments at a loss.

Clearly, there is a need to use risk-adjusted returns rather than returns alone to make valid performance comparisons. In the next section we consider some alternative risk-adjusted return measures.

Risk-Adjusted Return Measures

The formulas for the performance measures in this section can be found in Appendix B.

Sharpe Ratio

The Sharpe ratio is the most widely used risk-adjusted return measure. The Sharpe ratio is defined as the average *excess return* divided by the standard deviation. Excess return is the return above the risk-free return (e.g., Treasury bill rate). For example, if the average return is 8 percent per year and the T-bill rate is 3 percent, the excess return would be 5 percent. The standard deviation is a measure of the variability of return (see the section in Chapter 4 titled "Volatility as a Risk Measure" for a detailed description). In essence, the Sharpe ratio is the average excess return normalized by the volatility of returns.

There are two basic problems with the Sharpe ratio:

1. **The return measure is based on average rather than compounded return.** The return an investor realizes is the compounded return, not the average return. The more volatile the return series, the more the average return will deviate from the actual (i.e., compounded) return. For example, a two-year period with a 50 percent gain in one year and a 50 percent loss in the other would represent a zero percent average return, but the investor would actually realize a 25 percent loss (150% × 50% = 75%). The average annual compounded return of −13.4 percent, however, would reflect the reality (86.6% × 86.6% = 75%).
2. **The Sharpe ratio does not distinguish between upside and downside volatility.** The risk measure inherent in the Sharpe ratio—the standard deviation—does not reflect the way most investors perceive risk. Investors care about loss, not volatility. They are averse to downside volatility, but actually like upside volatility. I have yet to meet any investors who complained because their managers

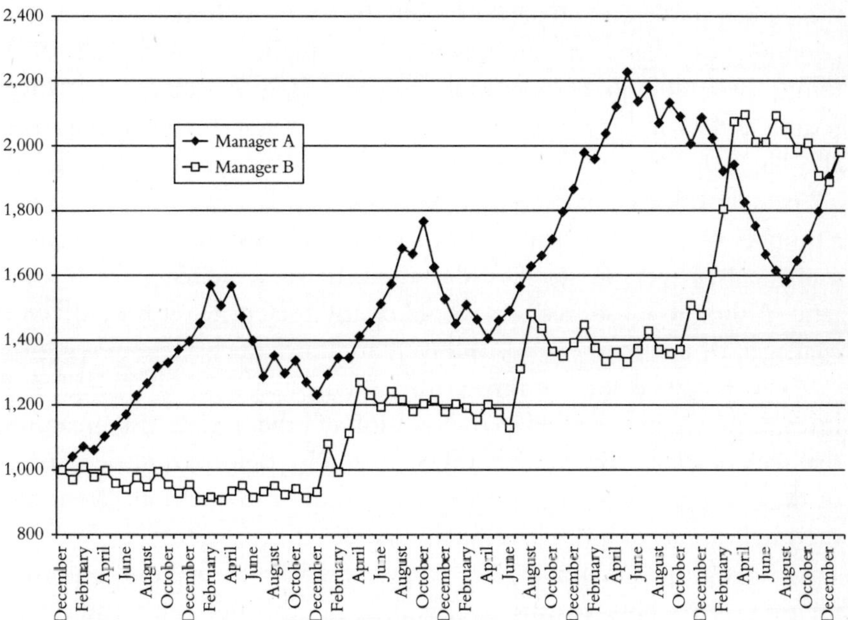

Figure 8.3 Which Manager Is Riskier?

made too much money in a month. The standard deviation, and by inference the Sharpe ratio, however, is indifferent between upside and downside volatility. This characteristic of the Sharpe ratio can result in rankings that would contradict most investors' perceptions and preferences.[4]

Figure 8.3 compares two hypothetical managers that have identical returns over the period depicted, but very different return profiles. Which manager appears riskier? Decide on an answer before reading on.

Most likely you chose Manager A as being riskier. Manager A has three episodes of drawdowns in excess of 20 percent, with the largest being 28 percent. In contrast, Manager B's worst peak-to-valley decline

[4]To be fair, in some cases, high upside volatility can be indicative of a greater potential for downside volatility, and in these instances, the Sharpe ratio will be an appropriate measure. The Sharpe ratio, however, will be particularly misleading in evaluating strategies that are designed to achieve sporadic large gains while strictly controlling downside risk (that is, right-skewed strategies).

is a rather moderate 11 percent. Yet the standard deviation, the risk component of the Sharpe ratio, is 30 percent higher for Manager B. As a result, even though both Managers A and B have equal cumulative returns and Manager A has much larger equity retracements, Manager A also has a significantly higher Sharpe ratio: 0.71 versus 0.58 (assuming a 2 percent risk-free rate). Why does this occur? Because Manager B has a number of very large gain months, and it is these months that strongly push up Manager B's standard deviation, thereby reducing the Sharpe ratio. Although most investors would clearly prefer the return profile of Manager B, the Sharpe ratio decisively indicates the reverse ranking.

The potential for a mismatch between Sharpe ratio rankings and investor preferences has led to the creation of other return/risk measures that seek to address the flaws of the Sharpe ratio. Before we review some of these alternative measures, we first consider the question: What are the implications of a negative Sharpe ratio?

Although it is commonplace to see negative Sharpe ratios reported for managers whose returns are less than the risk-free return, negative Sharpe ratios are absolutely meaningless. When the Sharpe ratio is positive, greater volatility (as measured by the standard deviation), a negative characteristic, will reduce the Sharpe ratio, as it logically should. When the Sharpe ratio is negative, however, greater volatility will actually increase its value—that is, the division of a negative return by a larger number will make it less negative. Comparisons involving negative Sharpe ratios can lead to absurd results. An example is provided in Table 8.3. Manager B has double the deficit to a risk-free return (–10 percent versus –5 percent) and four times the volatility as Manager A. Despite the fact that Manager B is much worse than Manager A in terms of both return and volatility, Manager B has a higher (less

Table 8.3 A Comparison of Two Managers with Negative Sharpe Ratios

	Average Annual Return	Risk-Free Return	Excess Return	Annualized Standard Deviation	Sharpe Ratio
Manager A	–3%	2%	–5%	5%	–1.0
Manager B	–8%	2%	–10%	20%	–0.5

negative) Sharpe ratio. This preposterous result is a direct consequence of higher volatility resulting in higher (less negative) Sharpe ratios when the Sharpe ratio is in negative territory. What should be done with negative Sharpe ratios? Ignore them.[5] They are always worthless and frequently misleading.

Sortino Ratio

The Sortino ratio addresses both the problems previously cited for the Sharpe ratio. First, it uses the compounded return, which is representative of the actual realized return over any period of time, instead of the arithmetic return. Second, and most important, the Sortino ratio focuses on defining risk in terms of downside deviation, considering only deviations below a specified minimum acceptable return (MAR) instead of a standard deviation (used in the Sharpe ratio), which includes all deviations, upside as well as downside. Specifically, the Sortino ratio is defined as the compounded return in excess of the MAR divided by the downside deviation. The MAR in the Sortino ratio can be set to any level, but one of the following three definitions is normally used for the MAR:

1. **Zero.** Deviations are calculated for all negative returns.
2. **Risk-free return.** Deviations are calculated for all returns below the risk-free return.
3. **Average return.** Deviations are calculated for all returns below the average of the series being analyzed. This formulation is closest to the standard deviation, but considers deviations for only the lower half of returns.

Frequently, the fact that a manager has a higher Sortino ratio than Sharpe ratio is cited as evidence that returns are positively skewed—that is, there is a tendency for larger deviations on the upside than on the

[5]What if some value must be used, as in an application such as ranking a list of managers based on the ratio? In this case, a dual rank criterion makes much more sense: ranking managers based on the Sharpe ratio when excess returns are positive and on excess returns when they are negative.

downside. This type of comparison is incorrect. The Sortino and Sharpe ratios cannot be compared, and as formulated, the Sortino ratio will invariably be higher, even for managers whose worst losses tend to be larger than their best gains. The reason for the upward bias in the Sortino ratio is that it calculates deviations for only a portion of returns—those returns below the MAR—but uses a divisor based on the number of *all* returns to calculate the downside deviation. Because it distinguishes between upside and downside deviations, the Sortino ratio probably comes closer to reflecting investor preferences than does the Sharpe ratio and, in this sense, may be a better tool for comparing managers. But the Sortino ratio should be compared only with other Sortino ratios and never with Sharpe ratios.

Symmetric Downside-Risk Sharpe Ratio

The symmetric downside-risk (SDR) Sharpe ratio, which was introduced by William T. Ziemba,[6] is similar in intent and construction to the Sortino ratio, but makes a critical adjustment to remove the inherent upward bias in the Sortino ratio vis-à-vis the Sharpe ratio. The SDR Sharpe ratio is defined as the compound return minus the risk-free return divided by the downside deviation. The downside deviation is calculated similarly to the downside deviation in the Sortino ratio with one critical exception: a multiplier of 2.0 is used to compensate for the fact that only returns below a specified benchmark contribute to the deviation calculation.[7] The benchmark used for calculating the

[6]William T. Ziemba, "The Symmetric Downside-Risk Sharpe Ratio," *Journal of Portfolio Management* (Fall 2005): 108–121.

[7]Ziemba used the term *benchmark* instead of MAR in defining downside deviation. If the median were used as the benchmark, only half the returns would be used to calculate the downside deviation, and a multiplier of 2.0 would then provide an exact compensating adjustment. For other choices for the benchmark (e.g., zero, risk-free return, average), the number of points below the benchmark would not necessarily be exactly half, and a multiplier of 2.0 would provide an approximate adjustment.

downside deviation can be set to any level, but the same three choices listed for the MAR in the Sortino ratio would apply here as well: zero, risk-free return, and average return. (In his article, Ziemba uses zero as the benchmark value.) Unlike the Sortino ratio, the SDR Sharpe ratio (with the benchmark set to the average) can be directly compared with the Sharpe ratio.[8]

The SDR Sharpe ratio (with any of the standard choices for a benchmark value) is preferable to the Sharpe ratio because it accounts for the very significant difference between the risk implications of downside deviations versus upside deviations as viewed from the perspective of the investor. The SDR Sharpe ratio is also preferable to the Sortino ratio because it is an almost identical calculation,[9] but with the important advantage of being directly comparable with the widely used Sharpe ratio. Also, by comparing a manager's SDR Sharpe ratio versus the Sharpe ratio, an investor can get a sense of whether the manager's returns are positively or negatively skewed.

---

[8]To be perfectly precise, there would be a tendency for the SDR Sharpe ratio to be slightly lower for a symmetric distribution of returns because the SDR Sharpe ratio uses the compounded return rather than the arithmetic return used in the Sharpe ratio, and the arithmetic return will always be equal to or higher than the compounded return. If, however, zero or the risk-free return is used as the benchmark in the downside deviation calculation, assuming the manager's average return is greater than the risk-free return, there would be a tendency for the SDR Sharpe ratio to be higher than the Sharpe ratio for a symmetric distribution of returns for two reasons:

1. There will be fewer than half the returns below the benchmark, so the multiplication by 2.0 will not fully compensate.
2. Downside deviations from the risk-free return (and especially zero) would be smaller than deviations from the average.

These two factors would cause the downside deviation to be smaller than the standard deviation, implying a higher SDR Sharpe ratio than Sharpe ratio.

[9]Besides the essential introduction of the 2.0 multiplier term, which allows unbiased comparisons between the SDR Sharpe ratio and the Sharpe ratio, the only difference between the SDR Sharpe ratio and the Sortino ratio is that it subtracts the risk-free return from the compounded return instead of the MAR (which may or may not be the risk-free return).

Gain-to-Pain Ratio

The gain-to-pain ratio (GPR) is the sum of all monthly returns divided by the absolute value of the sum of all monthly losses.[10] This performance measure indicates the ratio of cumulative net gain to the cumulative loss realized to achieve that gain. For example, a GPR of 1.0 would imply that, on average, an investor has to experience an equal amount of monthly losses to the net amount gained. The GPR penalizes all losses in proportion to their size, and upside volatility is beneficial since it impacts only the return portion of the ratio.

A key difference between the GPR and measures such as the Sharpe ratio, the SDR Sharpe ratio, and the Sortino ratio is that the GPR will be indifferent between five 2 percent losses and one 10 percent loss, whereas the other ratios discussed so far will be impacted far more by the single larger loss. This difference results because the standard deviation and downside deviation calculations used for the other ratios involve squaring the deviation between the reference return level (e.g., average, zero, risk-free) and the loss. For example, if the reference return is zero percent, the squared deviation for one 10 percent loss would be five times greater than the squared deviation for five 2 percent losses ($10^2 = 100$; $5 \times 2^2 = 20$). In the GPR calculation, by contrast, both cases will add 10 percent to the denominator. If an investor is indifferent as to whether a given magnitude of loss is experienced over multiple months or in a single month, then the GPR would be a more appropriate measure than the SDR Sharpe ratio and Sortino ratio. However,

---

[10]The gain-to-pain ratio (GPR) is a performance statistic I have been using for many years. I am not aware of any prior use of this statistic, although the term is sometimes used as a generic reference for return/risk measures or a return/drawdown measure. The GPR is similar to the profit factor, which is a commonly used statistic in evaluating trading systems. The profit factor is defined as the sum of all profitable trades divided by the absolute value of the sum of all losing trades. The profit factor is applied to trades, whereas the GPR is applied to interval (e.g., monthly) returns. Algebraically, it can easily be shown that if the profit factor calculation were applied to monthly returns, the profit factor would equal GPR + 1 and would provide the same performance ordering as the GPR. For quantitatively oriented readers familiar with the omega function, note that the omega function evaluated at zero is also equal to GPR + 1.

an investor who considers a single larger loss worse than multiple losses totaling the same amount would have the opposite preference.

Although the GPR would typically be applied to monthly data, it can also be calculated for other time intervals. If daily data is available, the GPR can provide a statistically very significant measure because of the large amount of sample data. The longer the time frame, the higher the GPR, because many of the losses visible on a shorter time interval will be smoothed out over a longer period. In my experience, on average, daily GPR values tend to be about one-sixth as large as the monthly GPR for the same manager. For monthly data, roughly speaking, GPRs greater than 1.0 are good and those above 1.5 are very good. For daily data, the corresponding numbers would be approximately 0.17 and 0.25.

One advantage of the GPR over the other ratios is that rankings remain consistent even for negative returns—that is, a smaller negative GPR is always better than a larger negative GPR (a relationship that is not necessarily true for the other ratios). A GPR of zero means that the sum of all wins is equal to the sum of all losses. The theoretical minimum GPR value is −1.0 and would occur if there were no winning months. The closer the GPR is to −1.0, the smaller the ratio of the sum of all wins to the sum of all losses.[11]

Tail Ratio

An important question for the investor is whether a manager's extreme returns tend to be larger on the upside or the downside. Managers with frequent small gains and occasional large losses (negatively skewed managers) are more risky and less desirable than managers with frequent small losses and occasional large gains (positively skewed managers). Although there is a statistic that measures skewness—the degree to which a return distribution has longer tails (extreme events) on the right (positive) or left (negative) side than the symmetric normal distribution—

[11]The ratio of the sum of wins to the sum of losses is equal to GPR +1. So, for example, a GPR of −0.25 would imply that the ratio of the sum of wins to the sum of losses is 0.75.

it is difficult to attach intuitive meaning to specific values (beyond the value of the sign).

The tail ratio measures the tendency for extreme returns to be skewed to the positive or negative side in a statistic whose value is intuitively clear. The tail ratio requires one parameter input: the upper and lower percentile threshold used to calculate the statistic. If the threshold is set to 10, for example, the tail ratio would be equal to the average of all returns in the top decile of returns divided by the average of all returns in the bottom decile of returns. If returns were normally distributed, the tail ratio would equal 1.0. A ratio significantly less than 1.0 would indicate a tendency for the largest losses to be of greater magnitude than the largest gains, while a ratio significantly greater than 1.0 would indicate the reverse tendency. For example, if the tail ratio was equal to 0.5, it would imply that the magnitude of the average loss in the bottom decile was twice as large as the average gain in the top decile—a reading indicative of a potentially very risky manager.

MAR and Calmar Ratios

The MAR ratio is the annualized compound return divided by the maximum drawdown. The Calmar ratio is exactly the same except the calculation is specifically restricted to the past three years of data. Although these ratios are useful in that they are based on a past worst-case situation, the fact that the risk measure divisor is based on only a single event impedes their statistical significance. Also, if applied over entire track records, the MAR will be strongly biased against managers with longer records, because the longer the record, the greater the potential maximum drawdown. (This bias does not exist in the Calmar ratio because, by definition, it is based on only the past three years of data.) As we detailed in Chapter 6, manager comparisons should be limited to common time periods, a restriction that is especially critical when using the MAR.

Return Retracement Ratio

The return retracement ratio (RRR) is similar to the MAR and Calmar ratios in that it is a measure of the average annual compounded return divided by a retracement measure. The key difference, however, is that instead of being based on a single retracement (the maximum retracement), the RRR divides return by the average maximum retracement (AMR), which is based on a maximum retracement calculation for each month. The maximum retracement for each month is equal to the greater of the following two numbers:

1. The largest possible cumulative loss that could have been experienced by any existing investor in that month (the percentage decline from the prior peak NAV to the current month-end NAV).
2. The largest loss that could have been experienced by any new investor starting at the end of that month (the percentage decline from the current month-end NAV to the subsequent lowest NAV).

The reason for using both metrics to determine a maximum retracement for each month is that each of the two conditions would be biased to show small retracement levels during a segment of the track record. The first condition would invariably show small retracements for the early months in the track record because there would not have been an opportunity for any large retracements to develop. Similarly, the second condition would inevitably show small retracements during the latter months of the track record for analogous reasons. By using the maximum of both conditions, we assure a true worst-case number for each month. The average maximum retracement is the average of all these monthly maximum retracements. The return retracement ratio is statistically far more meaningful than the MAR and Calmar ratios because it is based on multiple data points (one for each month) as opposed to a single statistic (the maximum drawdown in the entire record).

Comparing the Risk-Adjusted Return Performance Measures

Table 8.4 compares Managers A and B shown in Figure 8.3 in terms of each of the risk-adjusted return performance measures we discussed. Interestingly, the Sharpe ratio, which is by far the most widely used return/risk measure, leads to exactly the opposite conclusion indicated by all the other measures. Whereas the Sharpe ratio implies that Manager A is significantly superior in return/risk terms, all the other performance measures rank Manager B higher—many by wide margins. Recall that

Table 8.4 A Comparison of Risk-Adjusted Return Measures

	Manager A	Manager B	B as Percent of A
Sharpe ratio	0.71	0.58	82%
Sortino ratio (zero)	1.27	1.44	113%
Sortino ratio (risk-free)	1.03	1.15	112%
Sortino ratio (average)	0.87	0.94	107%
SDR Sharpe ratio (zero)	0.75	0.85	113%
SDR Sharpe ratio (risk-free)	0.73	0.81	112%
SDR Sharpe ratio (average)	0.62	0.66	107%
Gain-to-pain ratio (GPR)	0.70	0.71	101%
Tail ratio (10%)	1.13	2.86	253%
Tail ratio (5%)	1.10	2.72	247%
MAR ratio	0.41	1.09	265%
Calmar ratio	0.33	1.70	515%
Return retracement ratio (RRR)	0.77	1.67	218%

both Managers A and B had identical cumulative returns, so the only difference between the two was the riskiness implied by their return paths. The Sharpe ratio, which uses the standard deviation as its risk metric, judged Manager B as being riskier because of higher volatility, as measured across all months. Most of Manager B's volatility, however, was on the upside—a characteristic most investors would consider an attribute, not a fault. Although Manager A had lower volatility overall, the downside volatility was significantly greater than Manager B's—a characteristic that is consistent with most investors' intuitive sense of greater risk. The Sharpe ratio does not distinguish between downside and upside volatility, while the other risk-adjusted return measures do.

Although all the risk-adjusted return measures besides the Sharpe ratio penalize only downside volatility, they do so in different ways that have different implications:

- **Sortino ratio and SDR Sharpe ratio.** These ratios penalize returns below a specified level (e.g., zero) with the weight assigned to downside deviations increasing more than proportionately as their magnitude increases. Thus, one larger downside deviation will reduce the ratio more than multiple smaller deviations that sum to the same amount. These ratios are unaffected by the order of losing months. Two widely separated losses of 10 percent will have the same effect as two consecutive 10 percent losses, even though the latter results in a larger equity retracement.

- **Gain-to-pain ratio (GPR).** The GPR penalizes downside deviations in direct proportion to their magnitude. In contrast to the Sortino and SDR Sharpe ratios, one large deviation will have exactly the same effect as multiple smaller deviations that sum to the same amount. This difference explains why Managers A and B are nearly equivalent based on the GPR, but Manager A is significantly worse based on the Sortino and SDR Sharpe ratios: Manager A has both larger and fewer losses, but the sum of the losses is nearly the same for both managers. The GPR is similar to the Sortino and SDR Sharpe ratios in terms of being indifferent to the order of losses; that is, it does not penalize for consecutive or proximate losses.
- **Tail ratio.** The tail ratio focuses specifically on the most extreme gains and losses. The tail ratio will be very effective in highlighting managers whose worst losses tend to be larger than their best gains. In terms of the tail ratio, Manager B, who achieves occasional very large gains but whose worst losses are only moderate, is dramatically better than Manager A, who exhibits the reverse pattern.
- **MAR and Calmar ratios.** In contrast to all the foregoing performance measures, these ratios are heavily influenced by the order of returns. A concentration of losses will have a much greater impact than the same losses dispersed throughout the track record. Both these measures, however, focus on only the single worst equity drawdown. Therefore losses that occur outside the interim defined by the largest peak-to-valley equity drawdown will not have any impact on these ratios. Because the maximum drawdown for Manager A is much greater than for Manager B, these ratios show a dramatic difference between the two managers.
- **Return retracement ratio (RRR).** The RRR is the only return/risk measure that both penalizes *all* downside deviations and also penalizes consecutive or proximate losses. In contrast to the MAR and Calmar ratios, which reflect only those losses that define the maximum drawdown, the RRR calculation incorporates all losses.

Table 8.5 summarizes and compares the properties of the different risk-adjusted return measures.

Which Return/Risk Measure Is Best?

To some extent, the choice of which return/risk measures to use depends on the performance measure properties favored by the individual investor. The major advantages and disadvantages of these performance measures can be summarized as follows:

- **Sharpe ratio.** Although the Sharpe ratio is the most widely used risk-adjusted metric, it provides rankings that are least consistent with most people's intuitive sense of risk because it penalizes upside gains.
- **Sortino ratio.** This ratio corrects the main deficiency of the Sharpe ratio by focusing on downside risk instead of total volatility as the measure of risk. In addition, the Sortino ratio uses a compounded return, which matches actual return over the entire period, whereas the Sharpe ratio uses an arithmetic average return, which does not. One disadvantage of the Sortino ratio is that it is not directly

Table 8.5 Properties of Risk-Adjusted Performance Measures

Properties	Sharpe Ratio	SDR Sharpe Ratio	Sortino Ratio	GPR	Tail Ratio	MAR and Calmar	RRR
Is impacted by upside volatility	X						
Is impacted by downside volatility only		X	X	X	X	X	X
Reflects *all* downside volatility	X	X	X	X			X
More than proportionate weight to large losses	X	X	X		X		
Is impacted by proximity of losses						X	X
Focuses on extreme returns only					X		
Rankings remain consistent for net negative returns				X	X		

comparable with the Sharpe ratio because its calculation is biased to delivering higher values.

- **SDR Sharpe ratio.** This ratio provides the same fix as the Sortino ratio, and it has the advantage of an additional adjustment that allows for direct comparisons of its values with Sharpe ratio values. Similar to the Sortino ratio, the SDR Sharpe ratio also uses the compounded return instead of the arithmetic average return. Since the SDR Sharpe ratio will provide nearly identical rankings as the Sortino ratio and has the advantage of allowing for comparisons with the Sharpe ratio for the same manager, it seems the better choice for any investor. Using both ratios would be redundant.
- **Gain-to-pain ratio (GPR).** Similar to the Sortino and SDR Sharpe ratios, the GPR penalizes a manager only for losses (zero percent is also a common choice for minimum acceptable return or benchmark in the Sortino and SDR Sharpe ratios). The GPR weights losses proportionate to their magnitude, while the Sortino and SDR Sharpe ratios magnify the weight of larger losses. Investors who view one 10 percent monthly loss the same as five 2 percent losses might prefer the GPR, whereas investors who consider the single 10 percent monthly loss to be worse might prefer the SDR Sharpe ratio.
- **Tail ratio.** Since, by definition, the tail ratio considers only a small percentage of all returns (20 percent or less), it is not intended as a stand-alone risk-adjusted return measure. Its focus on extreme returns, however, makes it a very useful supplemental metric to one of the other measures.
- **MAR and Calmar ratios.** These ratios will penalize for losses that occur with sufficient proximity to be part of same drawdown. The other ratios (with the exception of the RRR) are unaffected by the sequence of returns. The drawback of these ratios is that the risk is defined by only a single event (the maximum drawdown), impeding their statistical significance and representativeness.
- **Return retracement ratio (RRR).** This ratio is both based on downside deviations and impacted by proximate losses. Its big advantage vis-à-vis the MAR and Calmar ratios is that it reflects all retracements, with the risk number based on all monthly numbers,

rather than just a single event and single statistic: the maximum drawdown. Although the MAR and Calmar ratios might still be consulted as supplemental measures reflecting a worst-case situation, the RRR is preferable as a return/drawdown ratio.

Visual Performance Evaluation

Most people will find that the performance charts in this section provide a better intuitive sense of relative performance (in both return and risk terms) than do performance statistics.

Net Asset Value (NAV) Charts

An NAV chart, such as was illustrated in Figure 8.3, provides an extremely useful way of evaluating a track record. The NAV chart depicts the compounded growth of $1,000 over time. For example, an NAV of 2,000 implies that the original investment has doubled from its starting level as of the indicated time. The NAV chart can offer a good intuitive sense of past performance in terms of both return and risk. In fact, if an investor were to examine only a single performance gauge, the NAV chart would probably be the most informative.

The way we visually perceive conventionally scaled NAV charts that depict longer-term periods, however, may result in misleading inferences. Consider Figure 8.4, and answer the following three questions before reading on:

1. Was return higher in the first half of the track record or the second?
2. Was the manager riskier during the first half of the track record or the second?
3. Was the return/risk performance better during the first half of the track record or the second?

If you picked the first half as the answer to any of these three questions, you are wrong. If you picked the second half for any answer, you are also wrong. The two halves are exactly the same. In fact, all four quarters of the track record are the same. Figure 8.4 was created by copying the returns of Manager A in Figure 8.3 and pasting the sequence

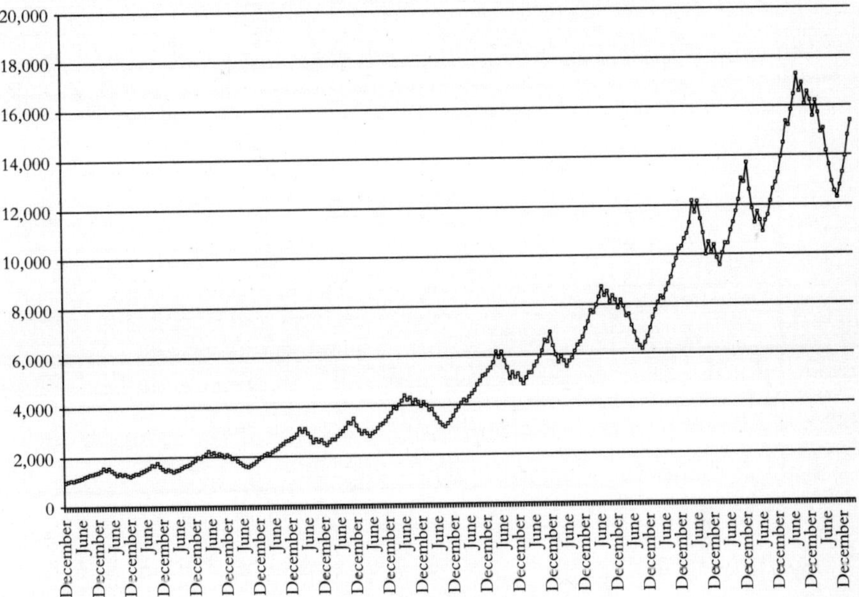

Figure 8.4 How Has Performance Changed over Time?

three times to the end to create an extended NAV that repeats the same return pattern, displaying it four times in all. Looking at Figure 8.4, however, it seems as if both the return and the volatility are increasing sharply over time. They are not. The illusion is an artifact of depicting NAV charts on a conventional arithmetic scale. On an arithmetic scale, an NAV decline of 1,000 when the NAV is at 16,000 looks the same as an NAV decline of 1,000 when the NAV is 2,000. The two declines, however, are radically different: a modest 6 percent decline in the first instance and a huge 50 percent drop in the second. The distortion on an arithmetic scale chart will get magnified when the NAV range is wide, which is frequently a serious problem for long-term charts.

The ideal way to depict an NAV chart is on a logarithmic scale. On a log scale chart, the increments for a fixed amount of movement (e.g., 1,000) become proportionately smaller as the level increases, and as a result, equal percentage price moves will appear as equal size moves on the vertical scale. Figure 8.5 depicts the same NAV as Figure 8.4, but on a log scale. The self-replicating nature of the chart is now evident as

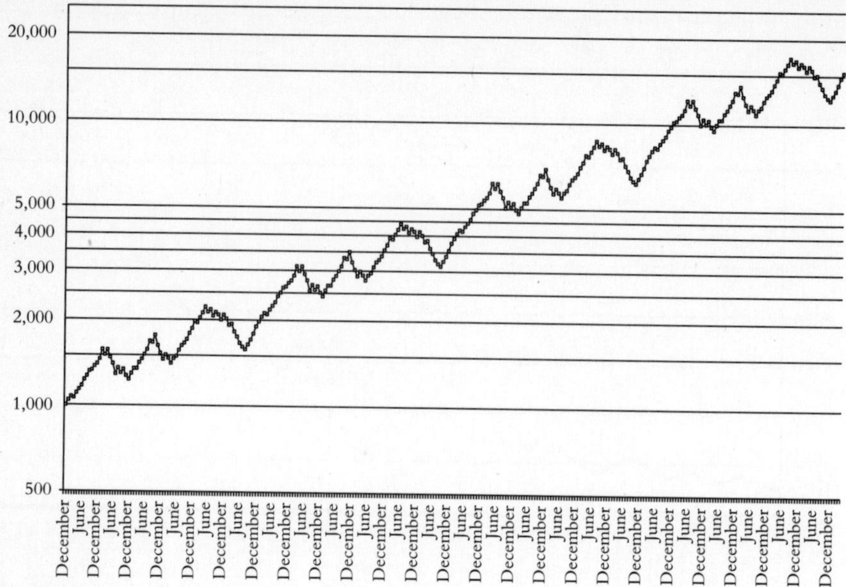

Figure 8.5 Log Scale: Equal Percentage Price Moves Appear Equal

equal percentage changes now look identical wherever they appear. The moral is that a log scale is always the correct way to represent an NAV chart and is especially critical when there is a wide NAV range (more likely on long-term charts). A log scale was used for Figures 8.1 and 8.2 earlier in this chapter to allow for an accurate representation of relative volatility across time.

Rolling Window Return Charts

The rolling window return chart shows the return for the specified time length ending in each month. For example, a 12-month rolling window return chart would show the 12-month return ending in each month (beginning with the 12th month of the track record). The rolling window return chart provides a clear visual summary of the results of investing with a manager for a specified length of time and answers such questions as: What would have been the range of outcomes with a manager for investments held for 12 months? 24 months? What was the worst loss for investments held for 12 months? 24 months?

For any December, the rolling 12-month return would be the same as the annual return. The important difference is that the rolling window return chart would show the analogous returns for all the other months as well. There is only a one-out-of-12 chance that December will be the worst 12-month return for the year. By showing all 12-month returns ending in any month, the rolling window chart will encompass worst-case events likely to be missed by annual returns and will provide a much more representative performance picture for one-year holding periods. The rolling window return chart can be calculated for other time intervals as well (e.g., 24 months, 36 months).

To illustrate the use of the rolling window return chart as a graphic analysis tool, we compare the two managers shown in Figure 8.6, who differ only moderately in terms of return (Manager E's annual compounded return is 1.3 percent higher), but differ widely in terms of the stability of returns. As shown in Figure 8.7, Manager E's 12-month returns range enormously from a severe loss of 49 percent to a spectacular gain of 142 percent. In contrast, manager F's 12-month returns are contained in a far more moderate range of –10 percent to +29 percent (see Figure 8.8). Investors who were patient enough to stay with

Figure 8.6 Small Difference in Return; Wide Difference in Stability of Return

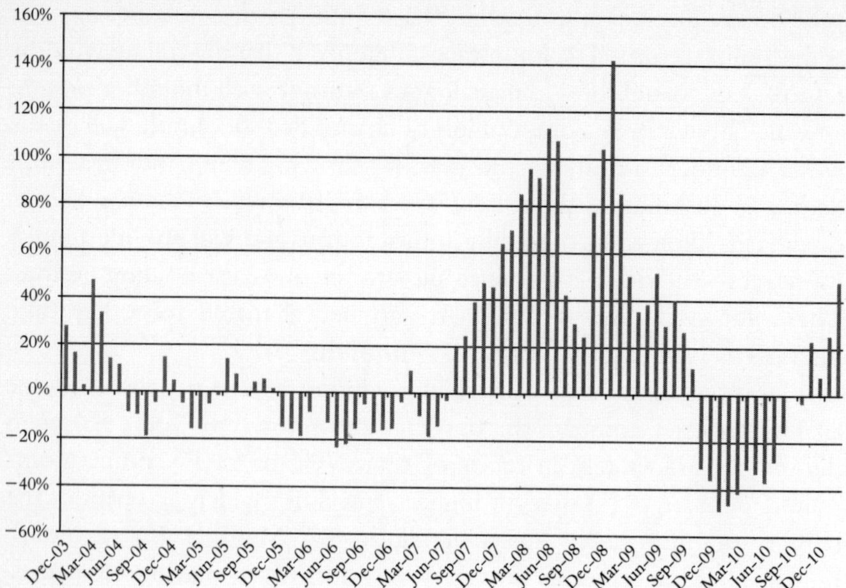

Figure 8.7 12-Month Rolling Return: Manager E

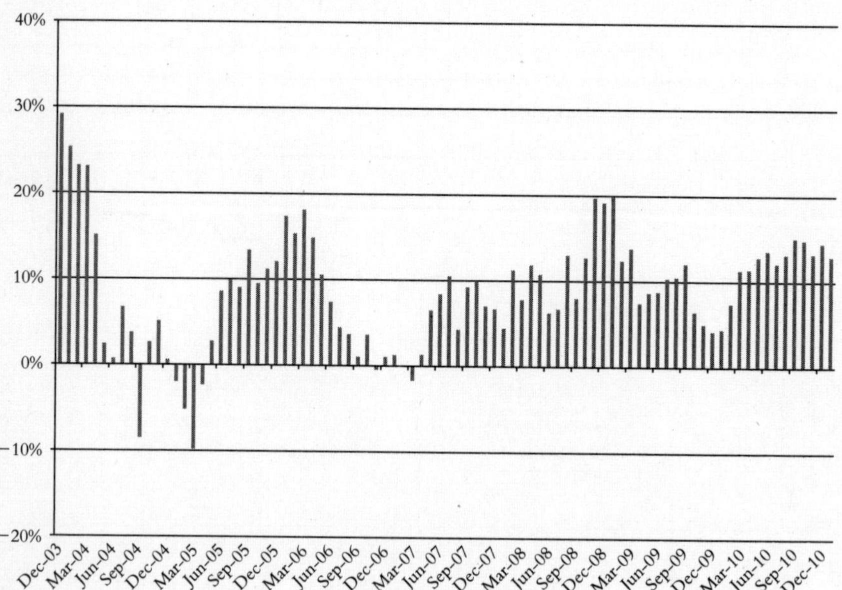

Figure 8.8 12-Month Rolling Return: Manager F

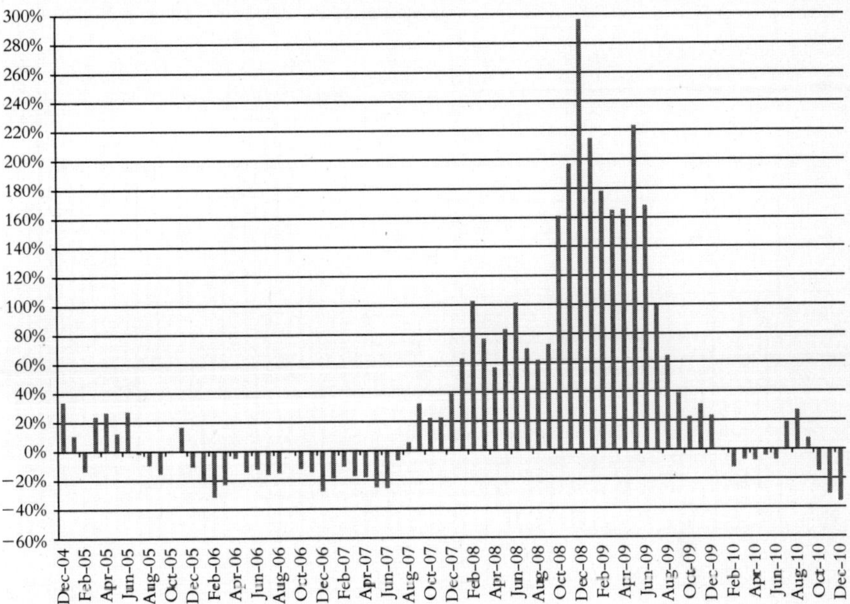

Figure 8.9 24-Month Rolling Return: Manager E

Manager F for at least 12 months would have experienced only a handful of investment initiation months that would have resulted in a net loss. Such patience, however, would not have provided any solace to investors with Manager E, who would have witnessed more than one-quarter of all 12-month holding periods resulting in net losses exceeding 15 percent, with several in excess of 40 percent. Even investors who committed to a 24-month holding period with Manager E would still have been subject to nearly one-fifth of all intervals with losses in excess of 15 percent (see Figure 8.9). In contrast, the worst-case outcome for investors with Manager F for a 24-month holding period would have been a positive return of 4 percent (see Figure 8.10).

Investors can use the rolling window return chart to assess the potential frequency and magnitude of worst-case outcomes as an aid in selecting investments consistent with their holding period tolerance for a losing investment. For example, an investor who is unwilling to maintain a losing investment for more than 12 months should avoid managers who have a meaningful percentage of negative 12-month returns, regardless of how favorable all the other performance statistics may be.

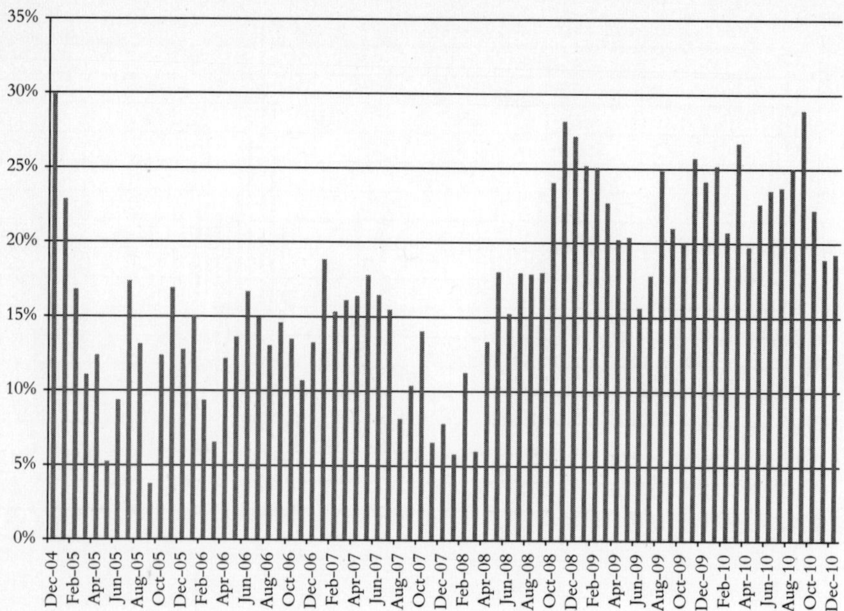

Figure 8.10 24-Month Rolling Return: Manager F

Rolling charts can also be used to depict other statistics besides return. For example, a rolling chart of annualized volatility (using daily data and a window of several months) can be used as a tool to monitor both managers and portfolios for early evidence of a possible increase in risk.

Underwater Curve and 2DUC Charts

The underwater chart shows the worst possible cumulative percentage loss any investor could have experienced as of the end of each month—an assumption that implies an investment started at the prior NAV peak. The low point in the NAV chart is the maximum retracement (the risk measure used in the MAR and Calmar ratios). The underwater chart, however, provides far more information because it not only shows the worst possible loss for the entire track record (the maximum retracement), but the worst possible loss as of the end of every other month in the track record as well. Figure 8.11 illustrates the underwater chart for the same two managers with widely disparate

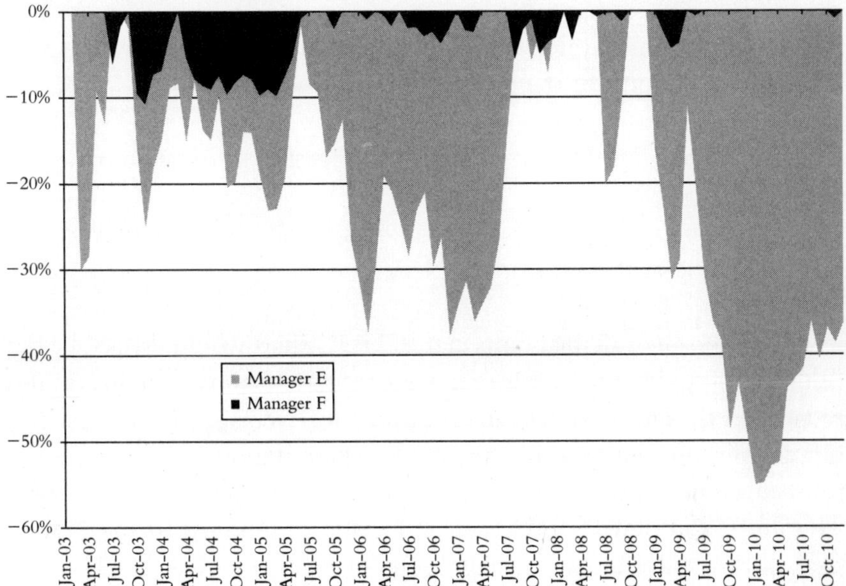

Figure 8.11 Underwater Curve: Manager E versus Manager F

stability of returns depicted in Figure 8.6. The difference between the two could hardly be starker. Manager F's retracements are very shallow and relatively short-lived (a rise to the 0 percent level indicates a new NAV high); Manager E's retracements are both deep and protracted. The underwater chart provides an excellent visual representation of an investment's relative risk in a way that is very consistent with the way most investors perceive risk.

One shortcoming of the underwater curve is that it will understate risk for months in the early portion of the track record because there is an insufficient look-back period for a prior NAV peak. For these earlier months, there is no way of assessing a true worst-case loss representation, because a prior track record of sufficient length simply does not exist. Also, the underwater curve is constructed from the perspective of the worst cumulative loss that could have been experienced by an existing investor. Arguably, the worst loss suffered by new investors may be an even more relevant measure. One solution to these inadequacies in the underwater curve calculation is to also consider the worst loss that could have been experienced by any investor starting in each month, assuming they exited at the subsequent lowest NAV point. We can then create a two-direction underwater curve (2DUC) that for each month would show the maximum of the following two losses:

1. The cumulative loss of an existing investor starting at the prior NAV peak.
2. The cumulative loss of an investor starting that month-end and liquidating at the subsequent NAV low.

The average of all the points in the 2DUC chart would, in fact, be the risk measure used in the return retracement ratio (the average maximum retracement). The underwater excursions for Manager E become significantly more extreme in the 2DUC chart (Figure 8.12), widening from an average monthly value of 21 percent to 30 percent (the AMR). The underwater curve for Manager F remains subdued in the 2DUC chart with a still very low average value of 3 percent. The 2DUC chart implies that the average worst-case scenario for investors with Manager E is 10 times worse than with Manager F; that is a lot of extra risk for a

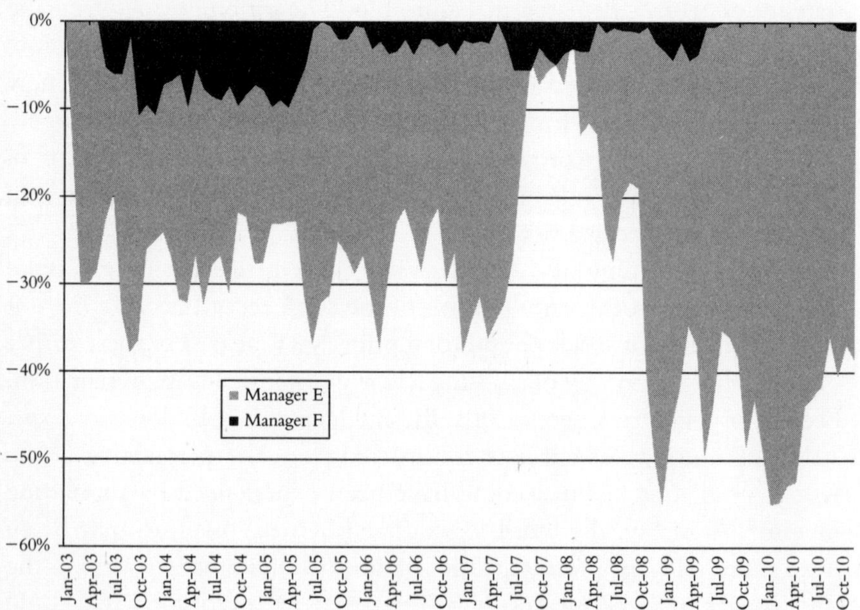

Figure 8.12 2DUC: Manager E versus Manager F

1.3 percent difference in the average annual compounded return. Based on performance, it would be difficult to justify choosing Manager E over Manager F, even for the most risk-tolerant investor.

Investment Misconceptions

Investment Misconception 23: *The average annual return is probably the single most important performance statistic.*

Reality: Return alone is a meaningless statistic because return can always be increased by increasing risk. The return/risk ratio should be the primary performance metric.

Investment Misconception 24: For a risk-seeking investor considering two investment alternatives, an investment with expected lower return/risk but higher return may often be preferable to an equivalent-quality investment with the reverse characteristics.

Reality: The higher return/risk alternative would still be preferable, even for risk-seeking investors, because by using leverage it can be translated into an equivalent return with lower risk (or higher return with equal risk).

Investment Misconception 25: The Sharpe ratio is the best choice for a return/risk measure.

Reality: The Sharpe ratio is the most widely used return/risk measure, but because it does not distinguish between upside and downside volatility, many of the alternative return/risk measures detailed in this chapter are more consistent with the way most investors perceive risk.

Investment Misconception 26: If the Sortino ratio is higher than the Sharpe ratio, it implies that the manager's return distribution is right-skewed (wide upside deviations are more probable than wide downside deviations).

Reality: The formula for calculating the Sortino ratio is biased to yielding a higher value than the Sharpe ratio. The return/risk measure based on downside risk that can be directly compared with the Sharpe ratio is the symmetric downside-risk (SDR) Sharpe ratio (using the average return as the benchmark). An SDR Sharpe ratio that is significantly higher than the Sharpe ratio would imply that returns are right-skewed.

Investment Misconception 27: The maximum drawdown is one of the most important risk measures.

Reality: The main drawback of the maximum drawdown is that it is based on only a single event. A retracement measure based on all data points, such as the average maximum retracement (AMR), would be far more meaningful than the maximum drawdown. For this reason, the return retracement ratio (RRR) is preferred to return/risk measures based on the maximum drawdown (e.g., MAR, Calmar).

Investment Misconception 28: The magnitude of the declines on an NAV chart are directly related to the magnitude of the equity drawdowns.

Reality: The conventional NAV chart is drawn on an arithmetic scale that exactly reflects dollar changes but not percentage changes. Consequently, as the value of an investment increases, the same percentage decline appears larger. For long-term charts that show a substantial value increase from start to end, recent-period price moves will appear greatly exaggerated relative to equal price moves in earlier periods. To avoid this distortion, long-term NAV charts should be plotted on a log scale.

Investment Insights

Many investors place too much emphasis on return. Since return can always be improved by increasing exposure (that is, taking on greater risk), the return/risk ratio is a far more meaningful performance measure.

An investment with higher return/risk and lower return than an alternative investment with the reverse characteristics can be brought up to the same higher return level with lower risk by using leverage. The Sharpe ratio is by far the most widely used return/risk metric. The Sharpe ratio, however, penalizes upside volatility the same as downside volatility, which is not consistent with the way most investors view risk. Other return/risk measures detailed in this chapter, which focus on losses as the proxy for risk, more closely reflect the way most investors perceive risk. Investors can use Table 8.5, which summarizes the properties of different return/risk measures, to select the performance measures that best fit their criteria. Return/risk statistics can be supplemented with the performance charts detailed in this chapter, which provide a tremendous amount of information in an intuitive and accessible format and should be at the core of any performance analysis. I recommend using the following performance charts in any manager or fund evaluation:

- An NAV chart.
- Both 12-month and 24-month rolling window return charts.
- A 2DUC chart.

■ ■ ■

Note: Some of the statistics and chart analytics described in this chapter are my own invention and hence not yet available on any existing software. I am currently consulting on the development of online performance evaluation software that will contain all the statistics and analytical chart tools detailed in this chapter. The product, the Schwager Analytics Module, is expected to be available in second quarter 2013 as a module for the Clarity Portfolio Viewer system developed by Gate 39 Media. The Schwager Analytics Module will be in a format designed to analyze both portfolios and the constituent investments (e.g., managers, funds, or any other investments). Interested readers can get more information at www.gate39media.com/schwager-analytics. For the sake of disclosure, I have a financial interest in this product.

Chapter 9

Correlation: Facts and Fallacies

In Chapter 4 we discussed correlation as an important tool in identifying and assessing hidden risk (event risk not evident in the track record). There is, however, considerable misunderstanding about what correlation does and does not show. In this chapter, we take a closer look at correlation and some of the ways it is often misinterpreted.

Correlation Defined

The *correlation coefficient*, typically denoted by the letter *r*, measures the degree of linear relationship between two variables. The correlation coefficient ranges from −1.0 to +1.0. The closer the correlation coefficient is to +1.0, the closer the relationship is between the two variables.

A perfect correlation of 1.0 would occur only in artificial situations. For example, the heights of a group of people measured in inches and the heights of the same group of people measured in feet would be perfectly correlated. The closer the correlation coefficient is to –1.0, the stronger the inverse correlation is between the two variables. For example, average winter temperatures in the U.S. Northeast and heating oil usage in that region would be inversely related variables (variables with a negative correlation coefficient). If two variables have a correlation coefficient near zero, it indicates that there is no significant (linear) relationship between the variables. It is important to understand that the correlation coefficient only indicates the degree of correlation between two variables and does not imply anything about cause and effect.

Correlation Shows Linear Relationships

Correlation reflects only *linear* relationships. For example, Figure 9.1 illustrates the returns of a hypothetical stock index option selling strategy (selling out-of-the-money calls and puts) versus Standard & Poor's (S&P) returns. Calls that expire below the strike price and puts that expire above the strike price would generate profits equal to the premium collected. Options that expire sufficiently beyond the strike price levels would result in net losses—the wider the price move, the larger the loss. When the S&P is unchanged, the strategy will realize maximum returns. The strategy will be profitable as long as the S&P does not change substantially; in our example (Figure 9.1) the strategy returns are positive in a range of monthly S&P returns between –6 percent and +6 percent.[1] As price changes exceed +6 percent or fall below –6 percent, returns become increasingly negative. Although Figure 9.1 clearly reflects a strong relationship between the strategy and S&P returns, the correlation between the two is actually zero! Why? Because correlation reflects only linear relationships, and there is no linear relationship between the two variables.

---

[1]Figure 9.1 is a hypothetical, simplified illustration. In actual markets, the pattern would not be symmetrical, since declining prices would likely increase implied volatility, further exacerbating losses, while rising prices would likely reduce implied volatility, mitigating losses.

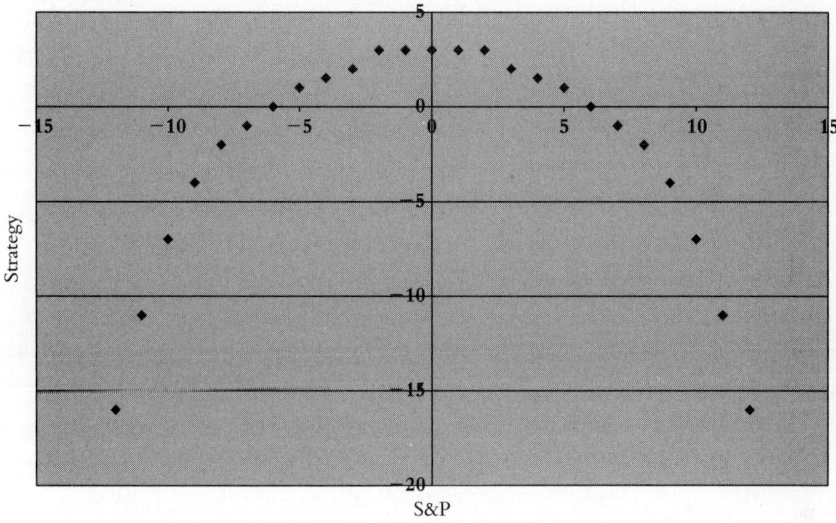

Figure 9.1 Strategy Returns versus S&P Returns

The Coefficient of Determination (r^2)

The square of the correlation coefficient, which is called the *coefficient of determination* and is denoted as r^2, has a very specific interpretation: It represents the percentage of the variability of one variable explained by the other. For example, if the correlation coefficient (r) of a fund versus the S&P is 0.7, it implies that nearly half the variability of the fund's returns is explained by the S&P returns ($r^2 = 0.49$). For a mutual fund that is a so-called closet benchmarker—a fund that maintains a portfolio very similar to the S&P index with only minor differences—the r^2 would tend to be very high (e.g., above 0.9). In other words, for such a fund, variation in the S&P would explain almost all the variation in the fund.

Spurious (Nonsense) Correlations

It is important to understand that the correlation coefficient (r) and the coefficient of determination (r^2) say nothing about cause and effect. The way we interpret the cause-and-effect relationship of the statistics emanates only from our theoretical understanding of the underlying process. It's quite obvious that if there is a significant correlation between electricity

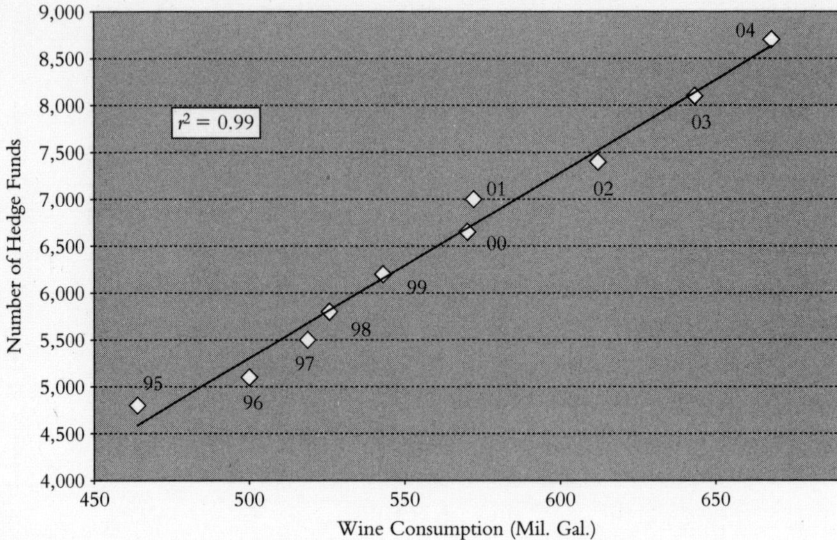

Figure 9.2 Number of Hedge Funds versus U.S. Wine Consumption

usage in New York City during July and temperature there, it is the temperature that is affecting electricity consumption and not vice versa. However, if, enshrouded in ignorance, we set out to determine whether summer temperatures in New York were affected by the city's electricity usage, the same correlation analysis would seem to support that absurd contention. Thus the r^2 value reflects only the degree of correlation between two variables; it in no way proves a cause-and-effect relationship.

The potential folly of drawing cause-and-effect inferences from an r^2 value is demonstrated by Figure 9.2. Note what appears to be a striking relationship between the number of hedge funds and U.S. wine consumption. In fact, the r^2 value between the number of hedge funds and U.S. wine consumption during the period depicted is a remarkably high 0.99! What conclusions are we to draw from this chart?

- Increased wine consumption encourages people to invest in hedge funds.
- Hedge funds drive people to drink.
- The hedge fund industry should promote wine consumption.
- Wine growers should promote hedge fund investing.
- All of the above.
- None of the above.

Actually, the striking correlation between wine consumption and the number of hedge funds is very easily explained. Both variables were affected by a common third variable during the period depicted: time. In other words, both the number of hedge funds and wine consumption witnessed pronounced growth trends during this time period. The apparent relationship arises from the fact that these trends were simultaneous. This type of coincident linear relationship is called "spurious" or "nonsense" correlation. Actually, the correlation is real enough; only the interpretation of cause and effect is nonsense.

The foregoing is intended to emphasize that one should be cautious in interpreting the implications of correlations. The fact that a fund has a significant correlation to an index doesn't necessarily imply that the fund's strategy is dependent on that index, but rather that it *may* be dependent. It is entirely possible that the correlation is simply due to a common third variable, or even chance. The shorter the track record, the greater the possibility that an apparent correlation may not be meaningful. Similarly, the fact that two funds have a significant correlation doesn't necessarily imply that they are employing similar strategies or are exposed to the same risks, but rather that this *may* be the case. Since many hedge funds have very short track records, the chances of encountering at least some spurious correlations are quite substantial. Therefore, correlations should be viewed as serious flags of possible similar risk exposures rather than conclusive evidence that this is the case.

Misconceptions about Correlation

Correlation often does not show what people think it does, and the use of correlation in filtering investments may not provide the intended effect. Figures 9.3 and 9.4 show two sets of hypothetical fund returns versus the S&P returns.[2] Which fund appears to have a higher correlation to

---

[2]The hypothetical fund returns examples (Funds A, B, and C) used in this chapter are artificial and not meant to be representative of any actual funds. The return statistics have been created specifically to highlight some key concepts related to the properties of correlation.

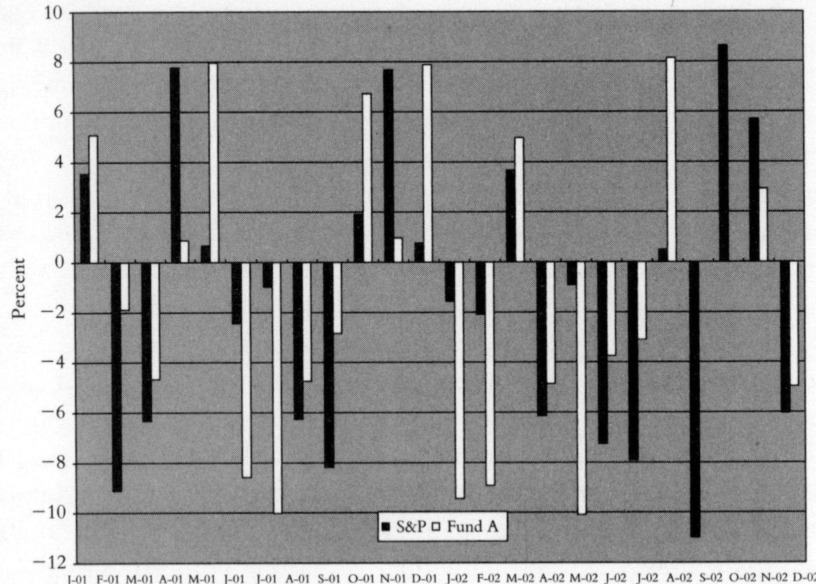

Figure 9.3 Fund A versus S&P 500

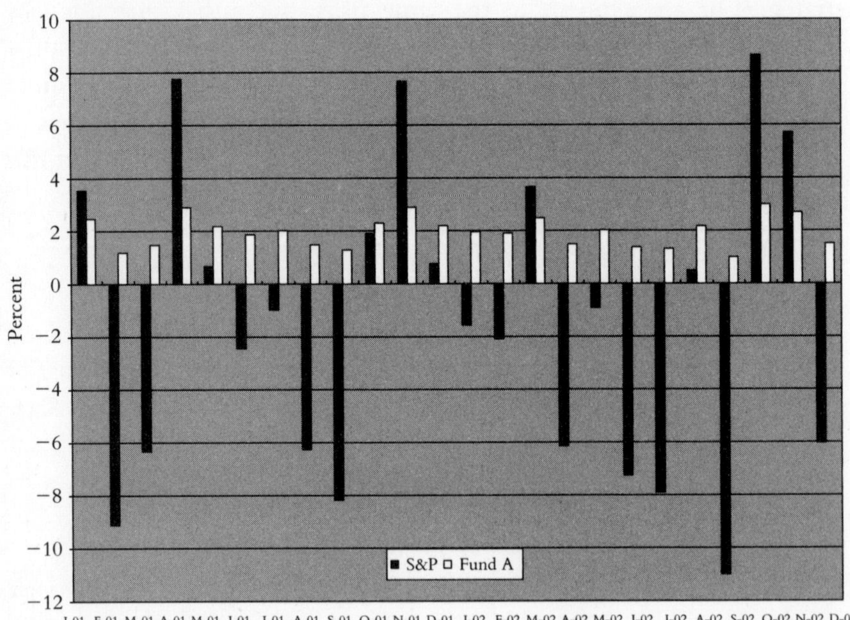

Figure 9.4 Fund B versus S&P 500

the S&P? (Hint: Note that Fund A is always up when the S&P is up and always down when the S&P is down.) Stop: Decide on your answer before reading on.

If you thought Fund A was correlated to the S&P, you're correct: $r = 0.41$. This correlation level, however, is relatively moderate and probably a lot lower than might have been assumed looking at the chart. The real surprise, though, relates to Fund B, which has a correlation of 1.0 to the S&P. How can this be? How can Fund B be perfectly correlated to the S&P when it never declines when the S&P does?

Figure 9.5, which plots the returns of Fund B versus the returns of the S&P in ascending order of S&P returns, makes clear what is happening. Here we can see that the returns of Fund B move progressively higher as S&P returns increase. This is the reason why Fund B is perfectly correlated to the S&P. But here's the thing to note: Even perfect correlation doesn't necessarily imply that a fund is likely to go down when the S&P goes down. It is entirely possible for a fund with lower correlation to the S&P (or any other equity index) to be more vulnerable to stock market declines than funds with much

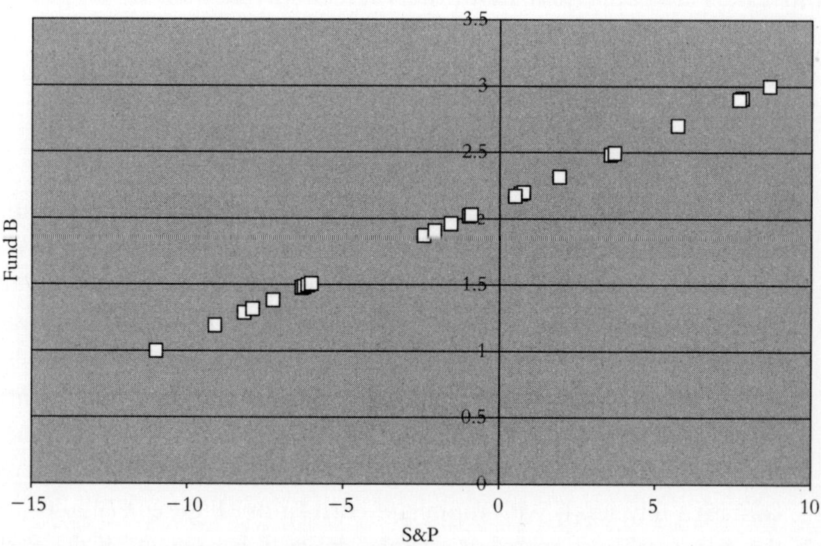

Figure 9.5 Fund B Returns versus S&P Returns

higher correlation. Our illustration, using two sets of hypothetical returns (Fund A and Fund B), simply provides an extreme example to make this point in its most stark fashion—namely, that it is even possible for a fund that is down every time the S&P is down to have a lower correlation to the S&P than one that is up every time the S&P is down.

In effect, while investors are concerned about a fund doing poorly when the S&P is down, this is not what correlation measures. Rather, correlation measures the linear relationship of returns across *all* months. Although investors would have little concern about a fund registering gains whenever the S&P was up—and in fact would prefer that this be the case—such a pattern would only serve to raise the correlation value, which ironically investors would view negatively. These observations lead to the following important investment conclusion:

> **Investment Principle:** If you are concerned about bear market months, then focus on bear market months.

Focusing on the Down Months

If investors are concerned about the vulnerability of their holdings to a bear market, for reasons illustrated in the prior section, correlation to a stock index is an insufficient statistic. The following statistics provide a useful supplement to correlation in assessing the degree of vulnerability of an investment to a market index:

- **Percentage of up months in down markets.** This statistic indicates the percentage of months in which a given fund has a positive return using only the negative months in the index to derive the measurement. A high winning percentage in down markets can vitiate the significance of correlation. For example, Figure 9.6 illustrates the correlation values of funds in a hedge fund portfolio versus the S&P. Although this particular portfolio does not contain any funds that have a high correlation to the S&P, it does contain a few funds with moderate correlation. Figure 9.7 illustrates the percentage of winning months *during down months of the S&P* for the same portfolio. The fact that all but one of the funds was up

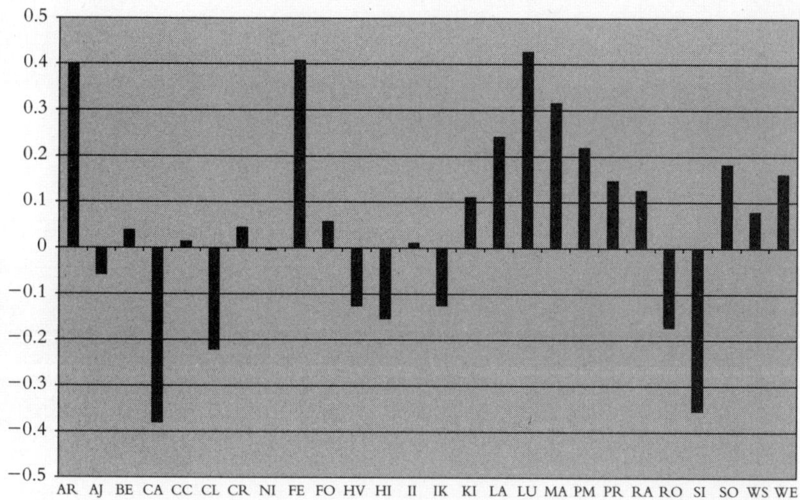

Figure 9.6 Correlation of Portfolio Funds versus S&P 500

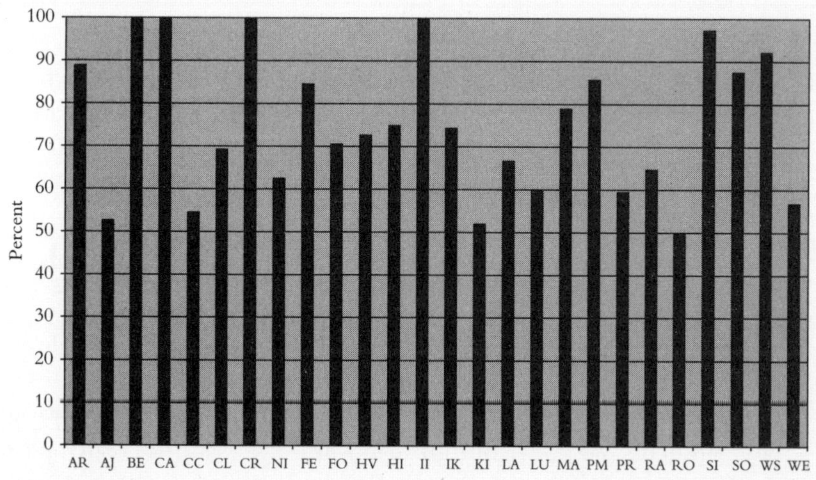

Figure 9.7 Portfolio Funds: Percentage Up during Negative S&P Months

more than 50 percent of the time during down months for the S&P mitigates the moderate correlation exhibited by a few of the funds.

As illustrated previously, it is even possible for a fund to be significantly correlated to the S&P and still be up in every month in

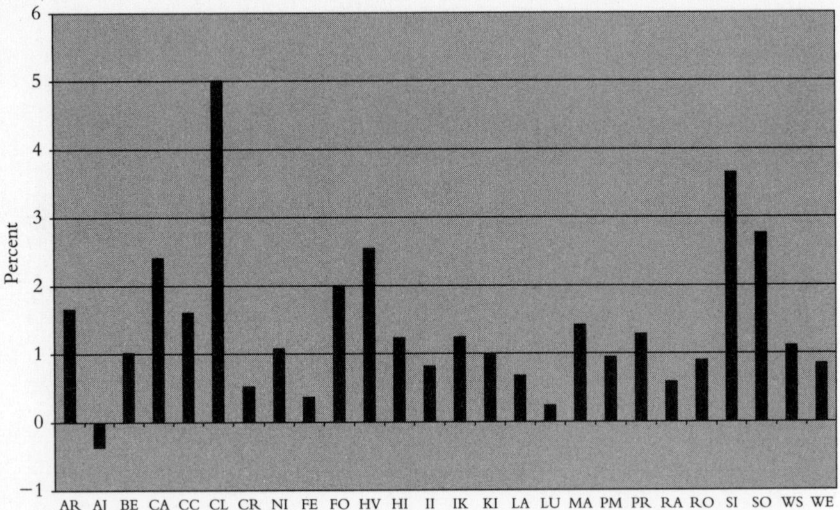

Figure 9.8 Portfolio Funds: Average Return in Negative S&P Months

which the S&P is down. If a fund is up most of the time when the S&P is down, a moderate or even high correlation is of no consequence, since the investor seeking diversification is concerned about losses occurring at the same time other equity-dependent investments are down, not whether returns tend to be higher in up months of the S&P than in down months, which is closer to what correlation actually measures.

- **Average return in down markets.** This statistic, in combination with the percentage of up months in down markets, provides a comprehensive picture of how a fund performs during bear market environments. Also, in combination, these two statistics really get to the heart of investor concerns much more closely than the far more widely used correlation. Figure 9.8 illustrates the average return for the funds contained in the portfolio depicted in Figure 9.6 during down months of the S&P. As can be seen, all but one of the funds have a net positive average return during these down market months. In this context, the moderate correlations between some of these funds and the S&P are of less concern.

Correlation versus Beta

Another consideration is that correlation does not tell us anything about the relative importance of one variable to changes in another variable. Figure 9.9 illustrates the hypothetical example of a fund that invests 1 percent of its assets in an S&P index and uses a strategy that earns a constant 1 percent per month on the remaining 99 percent of assets.[3] Such a fund would have perfect correlation to the S&P ($r = 1.0$) because all of its variation is explained by changes in the

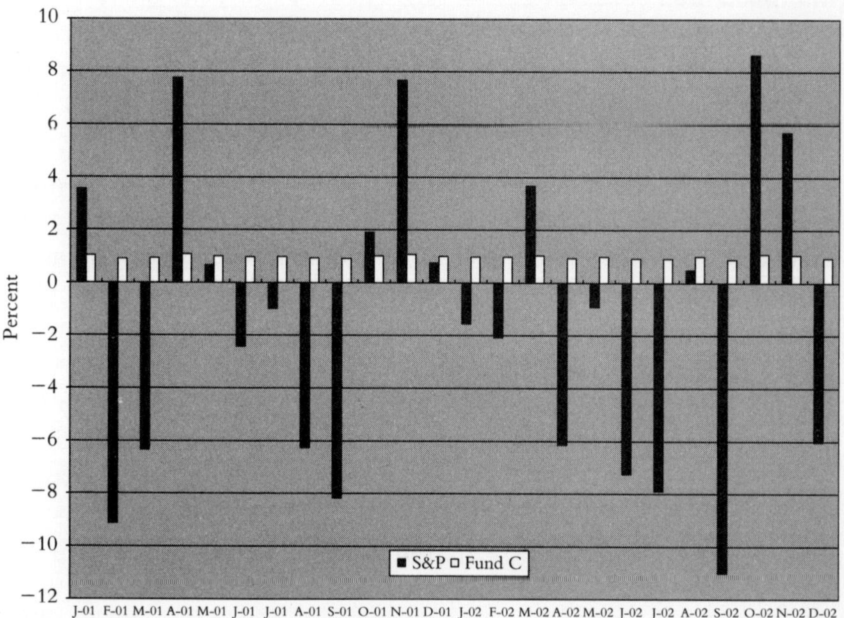

Figure 9.9 Fund C versus S&P 500

[3]Although this is an artificial and unrealistic return series, it is useful in helping to illustrate the concept that high correlation does not necessarily imply a large price impact.

S&P. Despite this perfect correlation, fluctuations in the S&P have very little effect on the fund's returns: Each 1 percent change in the S&P would imply only a 0.01 percent change in the fund. Correlation does not reflect the importance of one variable (e.g., S&P returns) to variations in another variable (e.g., returns of the fund considered for investment), but beta does.

Beta indicates the magnitude of change expected in an investment given a 1 percent change in the selected benchmark. For example, if a fund has a beta of 2.0 versus the S&P, it would imply that each 1 percent change in the S&P would be expected to lead to a 2 percent change in the same direction in that fund. Figure 9.9 provides an example of a fund with maximum correlation ($r = 1.0$), but very low beta (beta = 0.01). Beta actually comes much closer to reflecting an investor's true concerns—the expected impact of price changes in the benchmark on the price of the prospective investment—than does correlation. For example, an investor wishing to avoid funds that are likely to have vulnerability in bear market months should be far more concerned about an investment that has a correlation of 0.6 and a beta of 2.0 than one that has a correlation of 0.9 and a beta of 0.1. Even though movements in the former are less correlated to movements in the stock market, the implied magnitude of the impact of stock market price moves is 20 times greater for the former than for the latter.

Beta and correlation are mathematically related and provide two different ways of examining similar information. Correlation indicates the degree to which price changes in two variables (e.g., an investment and an index benchmark) are linearly related, while beta indicates the estimated percentage change in the investment for each 1 percent change in the benchmark.[4]

[4]Mathematically, beta is equal to correlation times the ratio of the investment standard deviation to the benchmark standard deviation. So, for example, if the correlation equals 0.8 and the investment has a standard deviation half as large as the benchmark, the beta would be equal to 0.4; that is, the investment would be expected to lose 0.4 percent for a 1 percent decline in the benchmark.

Investment Misconceptions

Investment Misconception 29: Low correlation between the returns of a strategy and a market implies there is no relationship between the two.

Reality: Although this conclusion will often be valid, all we can assume is that there is no *linear* relationship between the strategy and the market. We cannot rule out the possibility that the two are related in a nonlinear way (as would be the case, for example, in an option selling strategy).

Investment Misconception 30: High correlation between two variables implies that there is a cause-and-effect relationship between the two.

Reality: It is possible for two variables to be highly correlated yet completely unrelated to each other, if both variables are correlated to a third variable, such as a time trend during the survey period.

Investment Misconception 31: Investments that are more highly correlated to the market are more likely to decline in bear market months.

Reality: In comparing two investments, it is entirely possible for the one less prone to lose money when the market is down to have the higher correlation if it is more highly correlated during up market months, which is actually an attribute. Also, an investment could exhibit significant correlation to the market because its returns are lower in down market months than in up months, even if returns are still net positive during down market months. Investors are really only concerned about correlation on the downside: They don't want their investment to go down when the market goes down, but they are perfectly happy if it goes up when the market goes up. Because correlation doesn't distinguish between up and down months, it should be supplemented with statistics that focus specifically on performance in down market months.

Investment Misconception 32: The higher the correlation between an investment and a market, the more it will be impacted by moves in the market.

Reality: The percentage change expected in an investment per 1 percent change in a market (the beta) is a function of both correlation and the relative volatility of the investment to the market. In comparing two investments, the one less correlated to the market could be expected to be impacted more by market price changes if its volatility is sufficiently higher. To gauge the expected impact of market price changes on an investment, investors should focus on beta rather than correlation.

Investment Insights

The susceptibility of an investment to losses at the same time as equity markets and other holdings are declining is an important risk factor to consider, especially for investments chosen to provide diversification with other portfolio holdings. Correlation is an important metric that can be used to flag this risk. Moderate to high correlation, however, does not assure this risk is present, nor does low correlation assure its absence. If an investor is concerned about selecting a fund that is prone to losses when equity markets decline, correlation alone is an insufficient statistic. Instead of using only correlation for this task, investors should base their decisions on the following more comprehensive and descriptive combination of four statistics:

1. Correlation.
2. Beta.
3. Percentage of up months in down markets.
4. Average return in down markets.

Part Two

HEDGE FUNDS AS AN INVESTMENT

Chapter 10

The Origin of Hedge Funds*

Hedge funds entered the financial world's consciousness in April 1966 when an article by Carol J. Loomis appeared in *Fortune*. The article, titled "The Jones Nobody Keeps Up With," revealed that the fund with the best five-year record and the fund with the best 10-year record were the same fund—a fund that despite its remarkable performance achievement was virtually unknown. The fund that Loomis heralded was not a mutual fund, but rather a limited partnership, founded by Alfred Winslow Jones, that charged its investors a 20 percent incentive fee and utilized hedging and leverage. Jones's

*Unless otherwise noted, the material in this chapter is based on four sources: (1) A.W. Jones & Co., *A Basic Report to the Partners on the Fully Committed Fund*, May 1961; (2) Alfred Winslow Jones, "Fashions in Forecasting," *Fortune*, March 1949; (3) Carol J. Loomis, "The Jones Nobody Keeps Up With," *Fortune*, April 1966; (4) Carol J. Loomis, "Hard Times Come to the Hedge Funds," *Fortune*, January 1970.

fund with its unusual structure and strategy absolutely trounced the entire field of mutual funds. For the prior five-year period, the fund had a cumulative return of 325 percent versus 225 percent for the best-performing mutual fund (Fidelity Trend Fund). For the prior 10-year period, the fund had a cumulative return of 670 percent, almost double the corresponding 358 percent return for the top-performing mutual fund (Dreyfus). Moreover, these comparisons understated the magnitude of Jones's outperformance, since the figures cited by Loomis were net returns after deducting the 20 percent incentive fee.

Today's $2 trillion hedge fund industry has its origins in the $100,000 general partnership started by Alfred Winslow Jones in 1949,[1] which operated in virtual obscurity despite its stellar performance until its anonymity was shattered by the Carol Loomis's article 17 years later. The irony is that Jones, the undisputed founding father of modern hedge funds, was not even part of the financial community. He came to investing through a circuitous path that saw multiple careers, none of which had anything to do with finance or markets.

Jones graduated from Harvard in 1923. In his young adult years, he was a diplomat in Berlin and subsequently worked as an observer monitoring relief operations in the Spanish Civil War. He returned to academics to earn a PhD in social science from Columbia University in 1941. His thesis, *Life, Liberty and Property: A Story of Conflict and a Measurement of Conflicting Rights*, was also published as a book and later adapted by Jones into an article he wrote for *Fortune*. This article led to a journalistic career as a writer for *Fortune* and *Time*. Jones wrote articles on a wide range of topics, but not finance.

It was not until Jones was 48 that he wrote an article related to the market—an article that subsequently led to a relatively late career in investing. The article, "Fashions in Forecasting," was essentially a tour of new methods in technical analysis, which Jones thought showed promise as tools for avoiding the brunt of periodic market sell-offs that seemed to have little to do with prevailing fundamentals. As Jones wrote, "In late summer of 1946, for instance, the Dow Jones stock average dropped in five weeks from 203 to 163, part of the move a

[1]The general partnership was restructured as a limited partnership in 1952 to accommodate investors who were charged a 20 percent incentive fee on profits.

minor panic. In spite of the stock market, business was good before the break, remained good through it, and has been good ever since."

Jones thought that the Dow Theory,[2] which had been useful in its earlier years, had largely lost its effectiveness in the most recent decade, a deterioration that Jones attributed largely to the indicator's increasing popularization over the years. As Jones wrote, "Since the system's adherents are so numerous that they exert their own effect on the market, shrewd traders now buy and sell in anticipation of the Dow signals. Then when, say, a buy signal comes, unless they have their own good reasons for thinking that the uptrend will continue, they are likely to sell their stocks to the Dow followers stampeding in to buy." Jones also believed that this older technical approach was well suited only to markets witnessing protracted trends. It is fascinating that Jones, without benefit of practical market or investing experience, had the insight to understand that the excessive popularity of any approach would lead to its own demise.

Jones readily acknowledged that the field of technical analysis had its share of charlatans and pseudoscience, but he also seemed to believe that some of the new methodologies being developed held promise. Based on the research Jones conducted for the *Fortune* article, he concluded that it was possible to get an edge in investing and that he could stand a better chance at success than most market participants who remained wedded to older and ineffective approaches. The extensive research he conducted for the "Fashions in Forecasting" article inspired Jones to launch a partnership to trade the stock market in January 1949, funding it with $40,000 of his own money.

As a novice to investing, it is remarkable that the methodology Jones chose was entirely unique. One might have thought that, being inspired into his new career by the article he wrote surveying new methods of technical analysis, he would have chosen an approach that significantly incorporated such analysis. Instead, the method Jones chose effectively

---

[2]Roughly speaking, the Dow Theory held that when both the Dow Jones industrial and railroad averages exceeded their prior relative highs in a downtrend (a sequence of lower relative highs), it signaled a reversal from a bear to a bull trend. An analogous definition applied to the reversal of uptrends.

made stock selection the essential element, a characteristic that will become clear once the key components of his strategy are explained.

Jones felt that one of the flaws of conventional long-only investing was that it made it difficult for investors to hold on to their positions through steep market corrections. He saw that short selling could be used as a risk control tool. Jones referred to short selling as a "speculative technique for conservative ends." For Jones, the attractiveness of short selling was not the potential gains it provided from stock market declines, but rather its role as a market hedge that made it more feasible to hold on to and profit from good long positions, since the short positions provided the investor with some protection on market declines. Jones's ability to grasp that when used to counterbalance long positions, short selling was a risk-reducing rather than speculative tool demonstrated remarkable insight for a financial novice.

Although short selling was an essential component of Jones's strategy, he felt that short trades were inherently inferior to long trades for many reasons. These reasons included the inability to get long-term gains on short trades, the necessity of paying dividends while holding shorts, the restriction of not being able to go short except on an uptick, and the paucity of research on short-selling ideas because of Wall Street's almost exclusive focus on buy recommendations. For these reasons, Jones clearly preferred the long side, but his short trades were useful as an aid in profiting from his long positions. In a report Jones wrote to investors, he took aim at the prevailing notion that short selling was somehow "immoral or antisocial"—some things never change. Jones called this perspective "an illusion." As Jones explained, "The successful short seller is performing a useful market function in that he arrests an unjustified market rise in a stock by selling it, and then later cushions its fall by buying it back, thus moderating its fluctuations."

Jones's use of short selling to offset the risk of long positions gave him the ammunition to increase the magnitude of his long position vis-à-vis what it would have been without the short hedge, while still reducing the risk on balance. For example, instead of being 80 percent long, he might be 130 percent long and 70 percent short, with the shorts selected representing stocks that were expected to underperform. The net position would then be smaller (60 percent versus 80 percent in this example), but the gross long position would be considerably larger. It should now be clear why Jones's approach placed such a premium on stock selection. If Jones could select longs that went up more than his shorts in a bull market (or down less in a bear market), he could do very well. If the performance spread between his longs and shorts was sufficiently wide, he could, in fact, earn more than long-only funds despite having a lower net exposure—and indeed this proved to be the case. Ironically, while Jones's inspiration for launching a career in fund management had its roots in his research on new methodologies in technical analysis, the approach he developed was the epitome of a fundamentally focused strategy—that is, individual stock selection.

Jones may have started his fund with the thought that using technical analysis would allow adjusting exposures to benefit performance, but in reality it was the relative stock selection that provided the edge, while the directional market calls often proved disappointing. Jones readily acknowledged this shortcoming, as evidenced by the following excerpt from a lengthy retrospective report issued to investors in May 1961, in which Jones's disappointment in the failure of the firm's efforts in using technical analysis as a timing tool is evident both explicitly and between the lines:

> In the early years of our fund, in our stock selection, we gave weight to technical action, street sentiment, popularity of groups of securities, special situations, six-month tax selling and its effect on prices, pressure of additional issue of stock, and a host of other factors. Some of these we still believe are pertinent, to some degree. But we continue to think with increasing conviction that the really important fact for us is the intimate and fundamental knowledge of the management, problems, and prospects of the companies whose securities we take a position. Such knowledge is the only kind of wisdom that permits large and patient holding of stocks and is by far the most important factor in stock selection. Concerning judgment of the market, we know that dealing with any phenomenon in which mass emotion plays a part is a difficult art and that results are sure to be uneven.

In the same report, Jones was also clear in attributing the source of the firm's profits to its stock-selection capability and not to the hedging approach:

> Even the important and unique hedging operation is merely the means for greater profit with equal risk, or equal profit with less risk than in conventional investment programs, not the guarantee that such profits will develop. The guarantee is found only in good stock selection and good market judgment.

The innovative combination of hedging (through shorts) and leverage pioneered by Jones shifted the determinant of an equity fund's success from market direction to the skill in selecting relatively outperforming and underperforming stocks. The superlative performance of Jones's fund was a testament to the stock-selection capability of the fund's managers, especially since, as we have seen, market timing had little to do with the fund's success.

Who was responsible for this stock-picking capability? Certainly not Jones, who was a novice in the equity markets and reputedly held no great passion for financial analysis. Jones's talent was picking people, not picking stocks. This talent came from both external brokers and internal portfolio managers. Jones had an arrangement wherein the executing broker gave up 50 percent of brokerage commissions to those brokers who provided Jones with the best recommendations. These brokerage payouts provided strong incentives for brokers to provide Jones and his co-managers with pertinent news and trading ideas. The better the information and trading ideas provided by brokers, the more commissions they could expect to earn from Jones's operation.

Jones also hired individuals who demonstrated strong stock-picking ability as internal managers. These co-managers were each responsible for a portion of the entire portfolio and were compensated by sharing in incentive fees in proportion to their trading success. The most successful managers were also allocated the largest share of the assets under management. In effect, the management structure of Jones's fund anticipated not only hedge funds but also multimanager hedge funds.

Although, to a major extent, the success of Jones's fund reflected the stock-selection skill of the internal managers and external brokers employed by Jones, there is some controversy as to what extent insider information influenced the results. The line between legal and illegal insider information is often not clear-cut. In some cases, this line was clearly crossed. In 1966, Merrill Lynch, which was the underwriter for a convertible bond issued by Douglas Aircraft, learned that the company would be reducing its earnings estimate from the approximate $3.75 per share level anticipated by the market to zero—news that would be devastating for the stock. Although it is illegal for the investment bank to divulge privileged information, the details of the impending disastrous news for Douglas Aircraft made its way to the broker handling the A.W. Jones account, who promptly relayed it to his contact at Jones (and then at least one other hedge fund as well). The Jones manager who received the tip went short, well ahead of the avalanche of sell orders that hit the market in subsequent days when the news became known. The incident led to a Securities and Exchange Commission (SEC) investigation and fines.[3] Given the potential corrupting power of the incentives provided by Jones to brokers for profitable advice, it seems plausible that there were other undiscovered incidents of illegal insider information being passed on. So some portion of the wide outperformance of Jones's fund vis-à-vis all other funds may have reflected access rather than skill.

Jones's pioneering efforts in regard to risk management extended beyond the use of shorts as a hedge against long exposure. Jones also anticipated the modern-day concept of beta as a measure of relative risk. A stock's beta indicates the amount its price moves given a 1 percent change in the selected benchmark (e.g., S&P 500 index). For example, a stock with a beta of 2.0 would be expected to experience an approximate 2 percent price change (in the same direction) if the benchmark index moved by 1 percent, whereas a stock with a beta of 0.5 would be expected to move by only an estimated 0.5 percent in the similar event. Beta depends on both the correlation of the stock to the benchmark index and its relative volatility to the index. The higher the correlation and the higher the relative volatility, the larger the beta. Higher-beta stocks are

[3]This episode is detailed in Sebastian Mallaby, *More Money Than God* (New York: Penguin Press, 2010): 373–374.

riskier than low-beta stocks because they will experience larger percentage changes for the same given percentage change in the index.

Beta is the slope of the best-fit regression line between daily price changes in the selected stock versus daily price changes in the index. In Figure 10.1, which illustrates a stock with a beta of 1.0 the daily price change of the stock is shown on the vertical axis and the corresponding daily price change of the index is shown on the horizontal axis. Each day is represented by a point on the chart whose placement is determined by the percentage change in the stock and the index on that day. The slope of the statistically determined best-fit line for these points represents the beta. For example, a 45-degree slope, which is equivalent to a beta of 1.0, would indicate that any given daily percentage change in the index implies an equal daily percentage change in the stock price (as the best-fit estimate).

Jones's precursor to beta was a concept he called *relative velocity*. The relative velocity for a stock was computed by comparing its percentage changes to the corresponding percentage changes of the index (Jones used the S&P for comparison) during major market swings. For example, if a stock had a relative velocity of 200, this implied that its

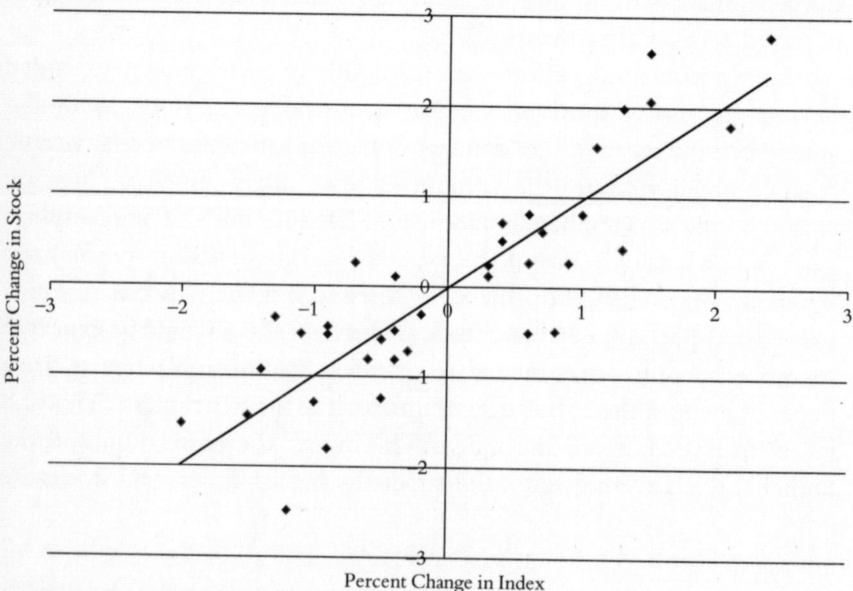

Figure 10.1 Stock with Beta of 1.0

percentage price swings tended to be approximately twice as large as those of the index. Jones advocated incorporating a stock's relative velocity in measuring market exposure. Thus, a $50,000 position in a stock with a relative velocity of 200 would be equivalent to a $100,000 position in a stock with a relative velocity of 100. From a trading perspective, Jones's relative velocity concept is actually a more sophisticated relative risk measure than beta in that it focuses on market swings rather than day-to-day fluctuations. For example, if a stock has a beta of 2.0 (its daily price changes tend to be twice as large as the index changes) but its relative velocity is only 1.5 (its price swings tend to be about 1.5 times as large as the index), a 1.5 ratio (index to stock) would probably come closer to balancing portfolio risk than a 2.0 ratio. While it is not used today, it seems that Jones's relative velocity concept is worth dusting off and analyzing as a possible alternative to the ubiquitous beta as a relative risk measure. Quite conceivably, traders and investors might find that relative velocity (a largely forgotten measure) actually does a better job than beta in gauging relative risk.

Jones's combination of hedging and leverage to provide the potential for superior return/risk is the hallmark of the modern equity long/short hedge fund model. Although, as we will explore in the next chapter, there are a wide range of hedge fund strategies, equity long/short is the dominant hedge fund style and the Jones model—hedging through shorts and combining with moderate leverage—is the dominant approach. So more than 60 years after Jones launched his fund, his basic strategy remains the most representative hedge fund style and still provides an excellent starting point for understanding hedge funds.

Another critical element of the modern-day hedge fund structure utilized by Jones was the reliance on profit incentives (as opposed to asset-size-based management fees) as the key component of manager compensation. The incentive fee compensation formula tends to draw the best portfolio management talent into hedge funds. Although others had previously employed the tools of hedging or leverage, Jones was probably the first to combine the three essential characteristics of most modern-day hedge funds—hedging, leverage, and incentive fee compensation—into a single fund. It is for this reason—and probably also for the extraordinarily successful execution of the strategy and structure—that Jones is widely regarded as the founding father of hedge funds.

Incidentally, Jones referred to his fund as a "hedged fund," which is certainly a more accurate description than "hedge fund," which sounds like a fund that invests in landscaping companies. My guess is that most people who probably had no understanding of what "hedged" referred to simply misheard the term as "hedge," and the erroneous name prevailed. I am reminded of a comment by Ed Seykota (one of the pioneers of computerized trend following) regarding his use of an exponential moving average instead of an arithmetic moving average: "It was so new at the time that it was being passed around by word of mouth as the 'expedential system.'"[4] I suspect a similar bastardization occurred in Jones's case. Jones viewed the popularized term with disdain, reportedly telling friends, "I still regard 'hedge fund,' which makes a noun serve for an adjective, with distaste."[5]

---

[4]Jack D. Schwager, *Market Wizards* (New York: New York Institute of Finance, 1989).

[5]John Brooks, *The Go-Go Years*, p. 142, as quoted by Mallaby, *More Money Than God*, p. 413.

Chapter 11

Hedge Funds 101

What exactly is a hedge fund? My favorite definition was provided by Cliff Asness, one of the founding partners of the hedge fund AQR:

> Hedge funds are investment pools that are relatively unconstrained in what they do. They are relatively unregulated (for now), charge very high fees, will not necessarily give you your money back when you want it, and will generally not tell you what they do. They are supposed to make money all the time, and when they fail at this, their investors redeem and go to someone else who has recently been making money. Every three or four years they deliver a one-in-a-hundred-year flood. They are generally run for rich people in Geneva, Switzerland, by rich people in Greenwich, Connecticut.[1]

[1]Clifford Asness, "An Alternative Future: Part 2," *Journal of Portfolio Management* (Fall 2004): 8–23.

This definition is humorous precisely because it is true, or at least more true than most hedge fund managers would care to admit.

There is no absolutely precise definition of a hedge fund because they are so heterogeneous. Most definitions focus on hedge fund structure and fee arrangement rather than the composition of the investments. Perhaps the best way to get a basic understanding of hedge funds is to compare their primary characteristics with the plain-vanilla investment structure of long-only mutual funds.

Differences between Hedge Funds and Mutual Funds

The following are the essential differences between mutual funds and hedge funds:

- **Dependency on market direction.** By virtue of being near 100 percent long, mutual fund performance is almost totally dependent on market direction. In a mutual fund, the influence of the portfolio manager's investment decisions is typically only slight compared with the impact of market direction. In contrast, many hedge funds are more dependent on the portfolio manager's investment decisions than the direction of the market. Even hedge funds that are significantly correlated to market direction will normally still have a meaningful portion of their performance determined by the individual portfolio manager's investment decisions.
- **Static versus dynamic exposure.** Whereas mutual funds maintain a static near 100 percent long exposure, most hedge funds will vary their market exposure based on the manager's perception of current trading opportunities, as well as expectations regarding future market trends.
- **Homogeneous versus heterogeneous.** Whereas mutual funds are highly homogeneous, consisting primarily of long equity or long bond investments (or a combination of the two), hedge funds encompass a broad range of strategies—a diversity made possible by the wide spectrum of financial instruments in which hedge funds can invest, combined with an ability to use the tools of short selling and leverage. The next section provides a synopsis of the major categories of hedge fund strategies.

- **Ability to diversify a multifund portfolio.** Creating a diversified mutual fund portfolio is virtually impossible, as nearly all mutual funds are highly correlated to either the stock market or the bond market. In contrast, the large number of different hedge fund strategies makes it possible to create a portfolio with significant internal diversification. The ability to meaningfully diversify a portfolio is the key reason why equity drawdowns in hedge funds of funds are muted compared with the magnitude of retracements witnessed in mutual funds.
- **Shorting.** Short selling is an integral component of most hedge funds. The incorporation of short selling means that the success of the hedge fund manager is no longer necessarily tied to a rising market (although it may be if the manager so chooses). In an equity hedge fund, particularly one with low net exposure, stock selection is a more important driver of return than it is for long-only mutual funds, where returns are much more influenced by market direction than stock selection. The net exposure of hedge funds to the market can range from heavily net long to heavily net short or anything in between. While some managers will maintain net exposure within a moderate range consistent with their approach (e.g., net long, market neutral, short bias), other managers will dynamically adjust their net exposures over a wide range over time, depending on their broad market views and the opportunities they perceive in individual securities.
- **Leverage.** Hedge funds commonly use leverage as a tool to offset the return-dampening effect of the reduced net exposure that results from short selling. For example, while the returns of a market neutral fund would be constrained by its near-zero market exposure, leverage can be used as an offsetting tool to enhance returns. For example, a market neutral fund with one-fourth the volatility of the market could use 3× leverage and still have lower volatility than the market.
- **Relative return versus absolute return objective.** Mutual funds normally have a relative return objective of beating their benchmark (e.g., S&P 500). A mutual fund that is down 20 percent in a year when the benchmark index is down 23 percent can and will herald its "superior performance." Hedge funds, in contrast, have

an absolute return objective—a goal of delivering positive returns regardless of market performance. A hedge fund manager cannot excuse losses as being the fault of a declining market, because the manager could just as well have chosen to be net short and in so doing have profited from the decline.

- **Incentive fee.** Mutual fund fees are based on assets managed. Hedge funds are paid in a combination of management fees (fixed per annum level) and performance incentive fees (fixed percentage of profits above the high-water mark[2]). Typically, most of the management fee will be used to offset the operating costs of the hedge fund, which means the managing firm's profitability will be highly dependent on performance incentive fees. Although hedge fund fees are much higher than mutual fund fees, the performance-based fee structure will align manager and investor interests and will draw the best talent to hedge funds. Of course, high fees will also attract a lot of mediocre and unskilled managers to hedge funds, and in much larger numbers, but the key point is that the best managers will typically be found in hedge funds, not mutual funds. (There will be occasional striking exceptions to this general rule, such as Peter Lynch.)
- **Portfolio manager incentive.** A mutual fund manager who tries to outperform by creating a portfolio that is significantly differentiated from the benchmark may enjoy only moderate benefits if the fund surpasses the benchmark by a wide margin, but be out of a job if it lags by a similar margin. Mutual fund managers are thus incentivized not to rock the boat. In contrast, hedge fund managers have a strong incentive to excel because of the incentive-based fee structure. Moreover, many hedge fund managers invest a substantial

[2]Almost all hedge fund documents will specify that incentive fees are charged only on the portion of the gain that exceeds the prior high net asset value (NAV) on which an incentive fee was paid (the high-water mark). This restriction is necessary to avoid a manager getting paid twice on the same gain. For example, assume a manager collects an incentive fee when the NAV is at 2,000, and in the next two periods the NAV falls to 1,800 and then rises to 2,100. At the end of the second period, an incentive fee would be charged only on one-third of the 300 gain (the portion above the prior NAV high of 2,000). Investors should avoid any hedge fund that does not include a high-water mark provision.

portion of their own net worth in their own funds, further aligning manager and investor interests.

- **Minimum investment size.** Hedge funds require larger minimum investment levels, typically $1 million or more. The high minimum investment size means that most individuals would not be able to invest directly into single hedge funds, let alone construct their own hedge fund portfolios. For most people, the only viable means of investing in hedge funds will be via funds of hedge funds, which typically have much lower investment minimums and allow for accessing a portfolio of hedge fund managers with a single allocation.
- **Investor requirements.** Mutual funds are public offerings. Hedge funds open to U.S. investors are typically structured as limited partnerships open only to accredited investors ($1 million net worth or $200,000 income in the past two years) or qualified investors ($5 million net worth). Hedge funds that accept accredited investors are limited to 99 investors, and those that use the more restrictive qualified investor requirement are permitted to have 499 investors.
- **Liquidity.** Mutual fund investments can be redeemed daily. Hedge funds are far less liquid, with multiple restrictions and impediments to redemptions:
  - **Redemption frequency.** Most hedge fund redemption frequencies range between monthly and annual. Some hedge funds even restrict redemptions to a multiyear cycle.
  - **Redemption notice.** Most hedge funds require 30 to 90 days' advance notice of redemptions.
  - **Lockups.** Many hedge funds enforce a lockup period, wherein an investor cannot redeem an investment for an initial fixed interval (e.g., one or two years) or can do so only at a substantial early redemption penalty.
  - **Gates.** Hedge funds that experience large redemptions can impose gates that limit the maximum total amount that can be redeemed by all investors combined in one redemption period. If the total of investor redemptions exceeds the gating threshold (e.g., 10 percent), then investors would receive only a pro rata portion of their redemption, with the remainder deferred to subsequent redemption periods. It is not unusual for it to take as long as two or three years for investor redemptions to be fully paid out if a gate is imposed.

- **Side pockets.** Managers who hold illiquid assets may choose to place these assets in a so-called side pocket if they are unable to liquidate the positions at acceptable prices to meet redemptions. If a side pocket is imposed, redeeming investors would be paid out on only the portion of the fund not in the side pocket. It is not unusual for it to take years for managers to fully liquidate side-pocketed assets.

Types of Hedge Funds

There is a wide range of hedge fund strategies, but absolutely no consensus on how they should be categorized. Even the number of hedge fund strategy categories differs widely among different hedge fund data providers. The fact that hedge funds can trade virtually any type of financial security and in any combination complicates their classification into strategy styles. Also, many managers use strategies that overlap several classifications, while other hedge funds don't fit neatly into any classification.

The most basic, as well as most prevalent, hedge fund strategy is the **equity hedge** fund, which takes both long and short equity positions. The typical equity hedge fund is similar to the classic Jones model described in Chapter 10. Figure 11.1 illustrates how the exposure of an equity hedge fund differs from the exposure of the standard mutual fund. For simplicity of exposition, we ignore the small percentage of cash held by mutual funds to meet normal redemptions or anticipated near-term purchases. Mutual funds are essentially 100 percent long and 0 percent short, implying that both the gross (long plus short) and net (long minus short) exposures are also equal to 100 percent. In the example in Figure 11.1, the equity hedge fund is 110 percent long and 60 percent short. The gross exposure is much greater than the mutual fund (170 percent versus 100 percent), but the net exposure is much smaller (50 percent versus 100 percent). This comparison illustrates a very important point: although most equity hedge funds have total exposure significantly higher than 100 percent, their risk is usually much lower than mutual funds because of the smaller net exposure.

Similar to the fund depicted in Figure 11.1, most equity hedge funds will usually have a larger long than short exposure (i.e., a positive net

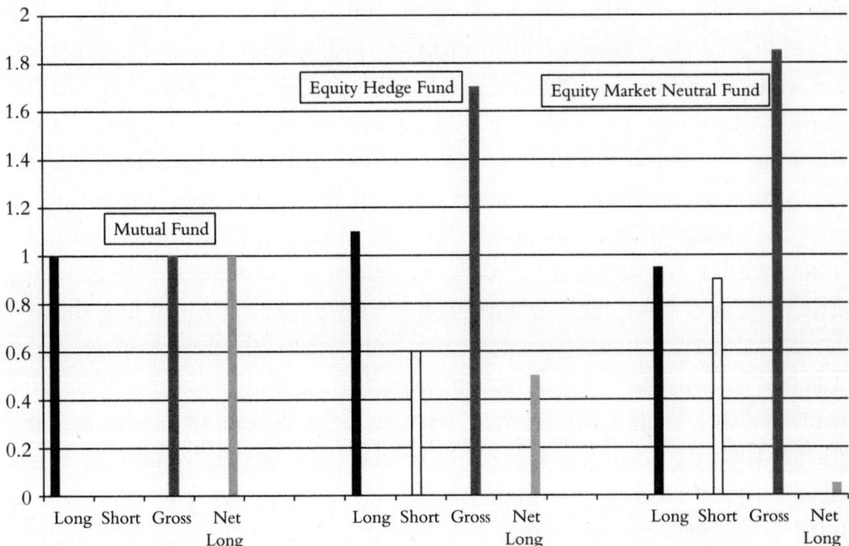

Figure 11.1 Exposure: Mutual Funds versus Equity Hedge Funds

exposure). The ranges for both gross and net exposures can vary widely between different equity hedge funds and also within the same fund over time. Some hedge funds will keep their net exposure within a moderate range (e.g., between 20 percent and 60 percent net long), whereas others may shift their net exposure in a much broader range, increasing to near 100 percent (or even higher) if they are very bullish on the market and shifting to net short if they are bearish. The performance of an equity hedge fund will be a function of both the manager's market-timing skill (the ability to vary net exposure in a beneficial way) and stock-selection skill.

Figure 11.1 also illustrates the **equity market neutral** fund, which is a close cousin of the equity hedge fund. In the equity market neutral fund, the long and short exposures will be near equal, but not necessarily exactly equal, leading to a net exposure near zero. The equity market neutral hedge fund completely removes the market as a performance-determining factor and instead makes performance entirely dependent on stock-picking skill—the ability to select longs that will go up more or down less than the selected short positions. Since it is common for shorts to be more volatile than longs, most market neutral funds will neutralize the portfolio in beta-adjusted terms rather than dollar terms. For example, if the beta of the short position (the ratio of expected percentage change in value relative to the percentage price move in the market) is equal to 1.25 times the beta of the long position, then the long exposure will be 25 percent larger, simply to target neutrality.

Some equity hedge funds are **long only** or consistently maintain a large net **long bias**. A long-only hedge fund is a bit of an oxymoron. These funds are "hedge" funds in name and structure (e.g., legal structure, incentive fees, redemption terms, etc.), but more like mutual funds in investment composition and strategy. Presumably, one investment strategy difference between long-only hedge funds and mutual funds is that the former strive to be different from the indexes (hopefully in a positive way), whereas the latter generally seek to avoid deviating too far from the benchmark index. An investor would need to have a fairly strong conviction about the skill of a long-only equity manager to justify paying much higher fees and accepting far worse investor terms for an investment that is similar in composition to an equity mutual fund. Some hedge fund databases define long bias equity hedge funds as a separate category. Although long-only equity hedge funds are unambiguously long biased, there is no specific definition of what minimum percentage net long exposure constitutes a fund as being long biased. The line between equity hedge and long bias equity hedge can be murky and differ between the different data sources.

Short bias equity hedge funds either implement only short equity hedge positions or always maintain a net short equity exposure. Because the equity market has a long-term secular uptrend, it is difficult for hedge funds of this type to compile good stand-alone track records, and performance can be particularly poor during protracted bull markets. For this reason, many hedge funds in this category tend to fail, and their percentage representation in the hedge fund universe is small. Sophisticated investors, however, view these funds as potent portfolio diversifiers rather than stand-alone investments. Short and short-biased funds will typically do best when equity markets and hedge funds as a group are witnessing their largest losses. They will do worst when other investments are doing best. In this context, the inclusion of short bias funds can be used to smooth portfolio performance, exchanging windfall profits in strong months for loss mitigation in the most negative months.

For this reason, the inclusion of a fund in this strategy group in a portfolio is likely to increase the portfolio's return/risk ratio, even if the fund itself is not profitable, and in some cases, even if it generates a net loss. Some investors will use short bias funds opportunistically, adding them to a portfolio when they believe the risk of an equity market decline is greater than normal and liquidating these holdings when their concern over declining equity prices is low.

The **sector** fund is a hedge fund strategy category that is very similar to the equity hedge fund (long and short positions combined with leverage), with the one defining exception that the manager specializes in a specific sector (e.g., technology, health care). Although the sector fund sacrifices the benefits of diversification and a broader universe of opportunities, the idea is that managers who focus on a single sector will obtain a greater level of expertise and investment accuracy in their group of stocks than equity hedge managers, who invest across a broader spectrum of equities. Some fund of funds managers prefer to apportion their equity-based strategy allocation to multiple sector funds (selecting one manager for each major sector) rather than to multiple equity hedge funds.

In addition to the foregoing equity long/short strategies (i.e., equity hedge, market neutral, long bias, short bias, and sector), there is a broad range of other hedge fund strategy categories. These include:

- **Merger arbitrage.** In a merger, the acquiring company will pay for the acquired company stock either with cash or in a fixed-ratio exchange for its own stock. When a merger is announced, the acquired company's stock will gap higher, but will trade at a discount to the announced price in a cash acquisition or to the implied ratio to the acquiring company's stock in a stock exchange acquisition. The discount exists because there is some uncertainty as to whether the merger will be completed. Merger arbitrage funds will seek to profit by buying the acquired company's stock in a cash acquisition or buying the acquired company's stock and selling the acquiring company's stock in the appropriate ratio in a stock exchange deal and earning the discount. Since a large majority of announced mergers are completed, most such trades will be profitable. The risk in the strategy is that if the deal breaks, the resulting loss can be many multiples of the discount that would have been earned. To be successful, merger arbitrage managers need to have the expertise and skill to select those mergers that will end up being completed. Some merger arbitrage managers will also occasionally seek to profit by doing a reverse merger arbitrage trade on announced mergers they believe will fail to be successfully concluded.

- **Convertible arbitrage.** Convertible bonds are corporate bonds that pay a fixed interest payment but also include a built-in option to exchange the bond into a fixed number of shares before maturity. A rising stock price would push up the convertible bond price by increasing the bond's conversion value. In effect, a convertible bond is a hybrid investment that combines a bond and a call option. Trading opportunities can arise if the implied option value in a convertible bond is mispriced. In the most typical trade, a convertible bond hedge fund would buy a convertible bond and hedge the implied equity exposure by selling the appropriate number of shares. This position would then have to be risk-managed by dynamically changing the hedge to maintain a neutral equity exposure as the stock price changed, a process called *delta hedging*. The profits in the strategy will be a combination of interest income, trading profits derived from mispricings, and short rebate income. The major risk in the strategy arises from the fact that virtually all convertible bond hedge funds are net long convertible bonds. If, as occurred in 2008, they need to liquidate at the same time because of a flight-to-safety psychology in the market, the huge imbalance between supply and demand can result in managers being forced to liquidate positions at deeply discounted prices.
- **Statistical arbitrage.** The premise underlying statistical arbitrage is that short-term imbalances in buy and sell orders cause temporary price distortions, which provide short-term trading opportunities. Statistical arbitrage is a mean-reversion strategy that seeks to sell excessive strength and buy excessive weakness based on statistical models that define when short-term price moves in individual equities are considered out of line relative to price moves in related equities. The origin of the strategy was a subset of statistical arbitrage called *pairs trading*. In pairs trading, the price ratios of closely related

stocks are tracked (e.g., Ford and General Motors), and when the mathematical model indicates that one stock has gained too much versus the other (either by rising more or by declining less), it is sold and hedged by the purchase of the related equity in the pair. Pairs trading was successful in its early years, but lost its edge as too many proprietary trading groups and hedge funds employed similar strategies. Today's statistical arbitrage models are far more complex, simultaneously trading hundreds or thousands of securities based on their relative price movements and correlations, subject to the constraint of maintaining multidimensional market neutrality (e.g., market, sector, etc.). Although mean reversion is typically at the core of this strategy, statistical arbitrage models may also incorporate other types of uncorrelated or even inversely correlated strategies, such as momentum and pattern recognition. Statistical arbitrage involves highly frequent trading activity, with trades lasting between seconds and days.

- **Fixed income arbitrage.** This strategy seeks to profit from perceived mispricings between different interest rate instruments. Positions are balanced to maintain neutrality to changes in the broad interest rate level, but may express directional biases in terms of the yield curve—anticipated changes in the yield relationship between short-term, medium-term, and long-term interest rates. As an example of a fixed income arbitrage trade, if five-year rates were viewed as being relatively low versus both shorter- and longer-term rates, the portfolio manager might initiate a three-legged trade of long two-year Treasury notes, short five-year T-notes, and long 10-year T-notes, with the position balanced so that it was neutral to parallel shifts in the yield curve. Fixed income arbitrage normally requires the use of substantial leverage because the relative price aberrations it seeks to exploit tend to be small. Therefore, although the magnitude of potential adverse price moves in fixed income arbitrage trades is normally small, the fact that these trades tend to be heavily leveraged can lead to occasional large losses.
- **Credit arbitrage.** This strategy can involve long and short positions in all types of credit instruments (e.g., corporate bonds, bank loans, credit default swaps, collateralized debt obligations). In its most basic form, the strategy is the credit counterpart of an equity

hedge strategy: The manager will buy corporate bonds whose prices are expected to rise (rates expected to fall) and sell corporate bonds whose prices are considered vulnerable, with a net long bias being typical. As is the case of equity hedge funds, the net exposure held by credit arbitrage managers can vary widely. Although some managers run a true arbitrage strategy, approximately balancing long and short positions, most credit-based hedge funds will routinely maintain significant net long exposure. A common approach is for credit arbitrage managers to borrow money at the London interbank offered rate (LIBOR) plus and buy corporate bonds or other debt instruments with the proceeds, earning the interest rate differential on the borrowed assets. As long as credit spreads move sideways or narrow, this approach will be very profitable with minimal downside volatility. The risk, however, is that if credit spreads widen significantly, the combination of leverage and the assumption of credit risk (through net long positions) can lead to substantial losses. Net long credit exposure is a much better indicator of a credit arbitrage manager's inherent risk than is historical downside volatility.

- **Capital structure arbitrage.** Hedge funds that specialize in capital structure arbitrage look for situations in which different securities of the same company appear to be mispriced relative to each other. Examples of capital structure arbitrage include taking opposite positions in a firm's bonds versus its stock, or in a firm's senior debt versus its subordinated debt.
- **Distressed.** Many institutional investors are subject to investment guidelines that prohibit holding debt securities below a certain grade. The forced selling that accompanies the bond downgrades of a company under threat of bankruptcy or in bankruptcy may depress the prices of its debt securities below expected recovery values. This selling creates buying opportunities for hedge funds with the expertise to evaluate the probabilities and valuations implied by different restructuring scenarios. Although some short positions might be taken, distressed is primarily a long-only strategy style. The assets held by distressed funds are primarily debt-based securities (e.g., bonds, bank loans, trade claims), but may also involve the equity of post-bankruptcy reorganized companies.

- **Event driven.** Hedge funds in this strategy category focus on trading the equities and debt of companies affected by significant corporate events, such as mergers, acquisitions, spin-offs, restructurings, and bankruptcies. The investment domain of event driven funds includes the same trading opportunities covered by two of the aforementioned hedge fund strategy groups—merger arbitrage and distressed—as well as trades related to corporate events other than mergers and bankruptcies.
- **Emerging markets.** The unifying theme of funds in this category is that they execute their trades in markets of emerging economies. This category can include many different types of strategies: equity hedge, credit, distressed, and various types of arbitrage. Historically, emerging markets have been more volatile than developed markets, a characteristic that has generally carried over to hedge funds involved in these markets.
- **Global macro.** Managers in this strategy category seek to profit from correctly forecasting future trends in major global markets, including equities, bonds, and foreign exchange (FX). Trades are by definition directional, but are not inherently biased to the long or short side. A global macro fund is not inherently more likely to be long equity exposure than short equity exposure; the net equity position will reflect the manager's expectations for the equity market at that point in time. Trades may reflect single market trend expectations (e.g., long U.S. bonds) or relative strength market expectations (e.g., long U.S. bonds/short German bonds). Some global macro managers will confine their trades to macro-level instruments (e.g., futures, exchange-traded funds [ETFs]), while others may include specific securities in a market group (e.g., selecting stocks with the best perceived potential to express a bullish equity bias). The success of a global macro fund is dependent on the manager's ability to correctly analyze the probable price direction of major global market trends and to successfully time implied trades.
- **Managed futures and FX (CTAs).** This group of managers executes all their trades in the futures or FX markets, or both. These types of managers are typically referred to as CTAs, a term that stands for commodity trading advisors, the official designation for managers registered with the Commodity Futures Trading Commission (CFTC)

and members of the National Futures Association (NFA). The term is a misnomer on at least two counts. First, a CTA is a fund or account manager with direct investment responsibility and not an advisor as the name appears to suggest. Second, CTAs do not necessarily trade only commodities as the name implies; the vast majority of CTAs also trade futures contracts in one or more financial sectors, including stock indexes, fixed income, and FX. Ironically, many CTAs do not trade any commodities at all, but trade only financial futures.

The majority of CTAs, and especially a majority of the CTAs who manage the most assets, utilize systematic trend-following approaches. This strategy employs systems that generate buy signals when an uptrend is defined and sell signals when a downtrend is defined. As implied by the word *following*, these systems will enter the market after the trend is already under way. The advantage of the systematic trend-following approach is that it is likely to capture sustained long-term trends in markets, which can be very profitable. A major drawback of the approach is that it can experience many false signals when markets are in wide-swinging trading range patterns, leading to large cumulative losses. Another drawback is that these systems are often prone to surrendering large open profits before a liquidation or reversal signal is triggered. System modifications designed to mitigate the surrender of open profits will usually come at the expense of increasing premature exit signals from unfinished trends.

Although there is a perception that managed futures or CTAs are synonymous with systematic trend following, this view is wrong. There are many CTAs who use a discretionary rather than systematic approach. Also, many CTAs use strategies that have nothing to do with trend following. A partial sampling of alternative approaches includes:

- Countertrend approach (or mean reversion).
- Pattern recognition.
- Fundamental systematic approach (systems that are based on fundamental inputs rather than price movements).
- Fundamental discretionary approach.
- Spread trading (long positions in one futures contract versus short positions in another contract in the same market or a related market).

- Multisystem (e.g., combination of trend-following, countertrend, and pattern recognition systems).

Managed futures are often categorized as a separate asset class rather than as a hedge fund category. One reason for this distinction is that managers who trade futures markets for U.S. clients are subject to mandatory registration and strict regulation, neither of which is true for hedge funds. Another factor is that many CTAs manage money only through managed accounts (see Chapter 16) and do not offer a fund structure. However, the line between hedge fund managers and CTAs has become increasingly blurred over the years. There is no difference between global macro managers who execute trades only in the futures and FX markets and CTAs. Although it is true that most CTAs pursue systematic, trend-following approaches and most global macro funds (including those that trade only futures and FX) are primarily discretionary, there are discretionary CTAs and systematic global macro funds. In this light, the distinction between the groups as separate asset classes appears artificial. If anything, it makes more sense to differentiate along strategy approaches, such as systematic macro versus discretionary macro (with each group containing both CTAs and global macro hedge funds), rather than between global macro managers and CTAs.

- **Fund of hedge funds.** As the name implies, these funds allocate to other hedge funds. Most funds of funds seek to allocate to a broad mix of hedge fund strategies in order to enhance portfolio diversification. Some funds of funds, however, create thematic portfolios (e.g., long/short equity, credit, managed futures, etc.) for investors seeking exposure to a specific strategy group. Funds of funds provide investors with multiple services related to prudent hedge fund investment, including manager selection, due diligence, portfolio construction, and manager monitoring. These services, however, entail an additional set of fees besides those charged by the managers.

This list is by no means exhaustive and it differs from the categorization used by hedge fund databases, as they differ from each other. The scope of the list, however, should demonstrate the wide variety of strategies available via hedge fund investment and illustrate why it is possible to achieve significant diversification by combining different hedge fund strategies in a single portfolio—a goal that is impossible to achieve by using traditional investments only.

Correlation with Equities

The degree of correlation between different hedge fund strategies and equities varies widely. At one extreme, long-only hedge funds would be highly correlated with equities, and at the other extreme, short-selling strategies would be negatively correlated. Some strategies, such as global macro managed futures, are completely unrelated to equities and tend to have near-zero correlation over the long term. Most hedge fund strategies would have only moderate positive correlation to equities across most months. There is, however, one important exception: During flight-to-safety market liquidations, most markets and most hedge fund strategies (with the exception of highly liquid strategies, such as managed futures) will witness significant losses simultaneously. A classic example of such an event was the financial panic that gripped world markets in late 2008. During such events, it is said that "correlations go to one."[3]

[3]One (1.0) is the highest possible correlation value and indicates that two variables are perfectly correlated. The phrase is not meant literally, but rather is a deliberate overstatement meant to imply that markets become very highly correlated.

Chapter 12

Hedge Fund Investing: Perception and Reality

What is a conservative investment? Figure 12.1 shows two investments over a 22-year investment horizon scaled so they are equal at the start of the period. The two series have tracked each other over the long term, with the lead changing several times. As of the end of 2011, the investment represented by the solid line had a modestly higher average annual compounded return of 8.2 percent for the entire period versus 7.4 percent for the investment represented by the dotted line, although as recently as three months earlier the two long-term returns were near equal. Which would you label as the more conservative investment? Choose before reading on.

Presumably, you picked the dotted line as being more conservative. Congratulations—you have just identified a hedge fund index as being more conservative and, by implication, an equity index as being riskier. The solid line is the S&P 500 Total Return index (that is, including

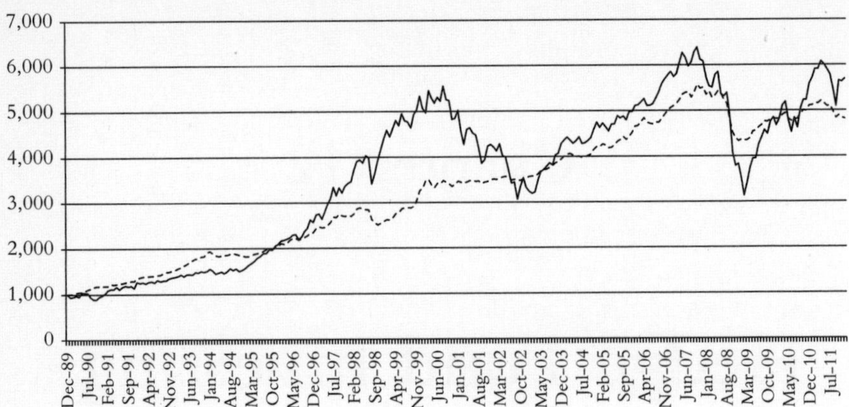

Figure 12.1 Which Is the Conservative Investment?

dividends) and the dotted line is the Hedge Fund Research (HFR) Fund of Funds index.[1] These lines were deliberately left unlabeled in the chart to assure reader objectivity.

The most striking contrast between the two indexes is in the magnitudes of the equity drawdowns. The S&P 500 Total Return index experienced two periods of massive declines: a 51 percent loss during the period from November 2007 to February 2009 and a 45 percent loss during the period from September 2000 to September 2002. In contrast, the HFR Fund of Funds index witnessed only one large loss: a 22 percent decline during the period from November 2007 to February 2009. Thus the worst decline that would have been encountered by the average diversified investor in hedge funds would have been less than one-half the magnitude of the second-worst loss that would have been experienced by mutual fund investors (using the S&P 500 as a proxy).

The lower risk of a diversified hedge fund investment (e.g., fund of funds) versus a diversified equity investment (e.g., equity index exchange-traded fund [ETF], mutual fund) is not simply a matter of the largest equity drawdowns being less severe. As Figure 12.1 illustrates, the HFR Fund of

[1]We use the fund of funds index rather than the composite index of individual funds to represent hedge fund performance because, as will be explained in Chapter 14, hedge fund indexes based on individual funds are significantly biased.

Funds index has consistently been far smoother than the S&P 500. The standard deviation (the most commonly used measure of volatility) of the HFR Fund of Funds index during the illustrated period was under 6 percent annualized, far less than the corresponding S&P 500 standard deviation of over 15 percent. Thus by any measure—worst drawdowns, standard deviation, smoothness of net asset value (NAV) curve—hedge funds have demonstrated considerably lower risk than equities.

Hedge fund returns, on average, have been only moderate. During the 22-year period depicted in Figure 12.1, the HFR Fund of Funds index realized an average annual compounded return of 7.4 percent—0.8 percent less than achieved by the S&P 500 Total Return index.

The conventional wisdom about hedge funds has it exactly backwards. The common perception is that hedge funds provide the potential for high returns for those willing to take high risk. The reality, however, is that hedge funds (using a fund of funds approach) offer only moderate returns, but with much lower risk than conventional equity investments. The question should not be "Would you put your grandmother in hedge funds?" but rather "Would you put her in mutual funds?"

The Rationale for Hedge Fund Investment

As illustrated by Figure 12.1, counter to widely held perceptions, hedge funds as an investment class have exhibited considerably less volatility and smaller drawdowns than traditional long-only equity investments. But why is this true? The answer to this question also provides the raison d'être for hedge fund investment.

The one basic concept that all investors should understand about hedge funds is the key rationale for why they are not merely a legitimate investment, but even a compelling one. Begin by considering the standard alternative of a purely traditional portfolio. An investor in traditional funds has a choice of equity funds and bond funds. There is very limited potential for diversification. Within each of these categories—equities and bonds—the funds will be very highly correlated. In other words, selecting multiple equity and multiple bond funds will provide only modest additional diversification over a portfolio consisting of a single diversified fund of each kind.

In contrast, one major advantage of hedge funds versus traditional investments is that they encompass an extremely diverse range of strategies. This much richer palette of investment colors makes it possible to construct a diversified hedge fund portfolio that offers considerably better return/risk performance than can possibly be achieved by a traditional portfolio—as long as the hedge fund investor allocates to multiple hedge funds (ideally, at least 10 to 20) or alternatively, and far more easily, a fund of funds. Diversification may be the only free lunch on Wall Street, but it is served at a diner accessible only to hedge fund investors.

Although it can be reasonably argued that the hedge fund arena draws the most talented managers because of the incentive fee structure of hedge funds, the rationale for hedge fund investment does not depend on such an assumption. Hedge fund investment would make sense even if hedge fund managers as a group had no skill advantage over their traditional fund counterparts. Even if individual hedge funds, on average, had the same return/risk characteristics as mutual funds or equity indexes, it would still be possible to create a portfolio with significantly better return/risk characteristics by utilizing hedge funds because of their heterogeneous nature. The fact that there are so many different types of hedge fund strategies, some with moderate to low correlation with each other, makes it possible to create a portfolio that has much greater diversification and hence lower risk. Consequently, a diversified portfolio of hedge funds has an intrinsic important advantage over traditional mutual fund investments simply because there are so many more tools to work with.

Advantages of Incorporating Hedge Funds in a Portfolio

There are two key reasons why a hedge fund allocation should be added to traditional long-only investment portfolios:

1. **Hedge funds are a better-performing asset in return/risk terms.** Table 12.1 summarizes some of the key performance statistics based on the data depicted in Figure 12.1. Although the S&P 500 Total Return index achieved a 0.8 percent higher average annual

Table 12.1 Performance Comparison: Hedge Funds versus S&P 500, 1990–2011

	Average Annual Compounded Return	Annualized Standard Deviation	Maximum Drawdown	Return/ Standard Deviation Ratio	Return/ Maximum Drawdown Ratio
S&P 500	8.2%	15.2%	51.0%	0.54	0.16
HFR Fund of Funds	7.4%	5.9%	21.9%	1.25	0.34

compounded return than the HFR Fund of Funds index, the hedge fund index had far lower risk levels: a 61 percent lower standard deviation and a 57 percent lower maximum drawdown. As a result of having only modestly lower return but much lower risk, the hedge fund return/risk ratios were more than double the corresponding S&P 500 levels. And, as we saw in Chapter 8, return/risk rather than return is the most meaningful performance measure.

2. **Hedge funds provide a diversification benefit.** Although hedge funds don't fully live up to their first name—they are significantly correlated with equities, especially during market liquidation episodes—they still provide much greater diversification than can be achieved within the long-only world, where different equity investments are usually extremely highly correlated.

The Special Case of Managed Futures

Managed futures are sometimes considered a subset of hedge funds and sometimes categorized to as a separate investment class. Managed futures refer to investments where the manager trades the futures and foreign exchange (FX) markets (FX is traded both through futures and the interbank markets). Managers who trade futures are referred to as commodity trading advisors (CTAs). CTAs are subject to separate and more rigorous regulation and oversight (by the CFTC and NFA) than are hedge funds. The lines between CTAs and other hedge funds have become increasingly blurred. Many CTAs also manage hedge funds.

Many global macro hedge funds execute trades entirely in futures and FX and, in this sense, are indistinguishable from CTAs, especially if they are registered with the CFTC and NFA.

The one reason why it may be useful to think of managed futures as a separate investment class is that it is by far the most liquid hedge fund strategy. Liquidity refers to both the portfolio level and the investor level:

- **Portfolio level.** Most CTAs can easily liquidate their entire portfolio in a day, and often in minutes.
- **Investor level.** Redemption terms are usually the most investor friendly in the hedge fund spectrum, with monthly redemption (or better) the norm and investor gates[2] a rarity.

The liquidity of futures provides managed futures with a characteristic that differentiates it from most hedge fund strategies: Managed futures (including FX) are the one investment category that is immune to the "correlations going to one" phenomenon. In times of financial panic and sharply declining equity markets, widespread risk aversion among investors can trigger liquidation across virtually the entire range of hedge fund strategies. This simultaneous, broad-based liquidation across all types of investments results in nearly all hedge fund strategies experiencing losses at the same time—even strategies that in most market environments have low to moderate correlation to equities and other hedge fund strategies. These type of events are referred to as "correlations going to one," implying all investments are moving in lockstep fashion. A classic example of such an episode was the financial panic and market collapse in late 2008 to early 2009. During such

[2]Many hedge funds contain gate provisions that allow the managers to severely limit redemptions if total investor redemptions for any given redemption period exceed a specified threshold. If gates are applied and not lifted, it could take investors years to fully redeem their investments. If managers trade securities that are prone to be illiquid during crisis situations, there is at least a rationale for the gate—to avoid the manager from being forced to liquidate positions at extremely wide bid/ask spreads in a market where there is a paucity of buyers. Futures, however, are extremely liquid (with the exception of less traded contracts and markets), and therefore there is no valid reason for a futures manager to require gate provisions.

periods of widespread investor fear, anticipated diversification in multistrategy portfolios can disappear exactly at those times when diversification is most needed.

Managed futures are not subject to the correlations going to one effect because even if there are heavy investor redemptions, futures and FX portfolios can be liquidated easily without significant slippage. Moreover, the liquidity of these markets allows CTAs to easily reverse positions and potentially gain advantage from the fear-based moves in many markets. Consequently, if anything, futures managers are more likely to benefit than be hurt by financial crisis periods. The tendency for managed futures to provide diversification even at those times when virtually all other investments (including most hedge funds) are experiencing losses warrants viewing it as a separate investment category that merits inclusion in most portfolios.

Another advantage provided by managed futures is that it is the strategy most amenable to a managed account structure, and a far larger percentage of futures and FX managers provide managed accounts than managers in any other hedge fund category. The advantages of managed accounts are fully detailed in Chapter 16.

Single-Fund Risk

Even though as a group hedge funds have clearly been a less risky investment than stocks—or by inference mutual funds, which as a group tend to underperform equity indexes—some might counter by questioning the degree of risk inherent in individual hedge fund investments. What about those periodic hedge fund horror stories? Isn't it true that some hedge funds blow up because of fraud, lax risk controls, or grossly flawed strategies? Yes to all of the above. And the risk cannot be ignored simply because such hedge fund disasters occur infrequently. Severe consequences can outweigh low probabilities. So it is no more advisable to rely on probability to be spared the one or two hedge fund frauds in a thousand than it would be to forgo insurance on your home because the odds of a fire are very low. The risk of a single hedge fund disaster, however, can be greatly reduced by investing in hedge funds via a fund of funds.

A properly managed fund of funds greatly mitigates the chances of experiencing a large loss in a hedge fund investment in two ways:

1. The investment analysis and due diligence typically performed by the managers of these funds make it less likely that they will pick a fraudulent or seriously flawed fund.
2. Even if a disastrous fund is selected, diversification will greatly limit the damage (typically, funds of funds hold between 10 and 50 individual investments). For example, even in the extreme case where a 30-investment fund of funds selects a fund that loses 100 percent of investors' money, assuming equal allocations, the impact at the fund of funds level would be a 3.3 percent loss—far less than the loss in the typical mutual fund during a bad month for equities.

Some investors object to investing in funds of funds because of the double fee structure. The underlying funds charge their own management and incentive fees, and then the fund of funds charges an additional layer of management and incentive fees. Circumventing funds of funds in hedge fund investment is not a feasible alternative for the individual. Most hedge funds have very high minimum investment levels. Typically, the minimum investment for a hedge fund is $1 million. Thus investing in a well-diversified portfolio of hedge funds could require $20 million or more, a number that is clearly out of range for virtually all individual investors.

As for institutional investors, a decision to directly invest in hedge funds to save the additional fees charged by funds of funds often represents a false saving. The institution that decides to directly invest in hedge funds has two choices:

1. **Doing it right.** This alternative implies establishing an internal investment team that has the expertise to evaluate, select, conduct due diligence on, and monitor investments across a wide spectrum of hedge fund strategies. The in-house solution may be the appropriate choice for institutions making very large hedge fund allocations. For most institutional investors, however, establishing such a team and related infrastructure will be more expensive than the fees that would have been charged by a fund of funds, especially since institutions will typically be able to negotiate a steeply discounted fee structure.

2. **Doing it on the cheap.** In this alternative, the institution simply selects hedge fund investments on the basis of database searches or other means without establishing an internal department with the appropriate expertise. This approach may be easy and inexpensive, but the investment errors committed by novices to hedge fund investment can well be far more costly than fund of funds fees.

Also, it is important to note that fund of funds results are reported net of fees. Thus, the historical experience of this investment generating long-term returns in line with equity indexes at much lower volatility is based on results that have already subtracted the dual layer of fees.

Investment Misconceptions

Investment Misconception 33: Hedge funds provide a *risky* investment with the possibility of very *high returns*.

Reality: A well-diversified hedge fund portfolio provides a *conservative* investment with *moderate return* potential.

Investment Misconception 34: Investors in hedge funds run the risk of losing much or even all of their money.

Reality: Although this statement is certainly valid for investors placing their entire hedge fund investment with a single manager, the analogous statement would hold for equity investors placing their entire investment in a single stock. Think Enron. The risk alluded to is one that can arise because of a lack of diversification, rather than one that is intrinsic to the investment. The idiosyncratic risk in hedge funds, which raises the specter of a total or near-total loss, can easily be eliminated by confining hedge fund investments to diversified, professionally managed funds of funds, as opposed to single hedge fund investments.

Investment Misconception 35: Hedge fund investment is appropriate only for high-net-worth, sophisticated investors.

> ***Reality:*** An analytical, rather than emotional, evaluation of portfolio alternatives would indicate that hedge funds are a desirable investment even for unsophisticated, lower-net-worth individuals—that is, via a fund of funds vehicle, which provides both professional management and diversification. In fact, it could be argued that these are the investors who most need to include a diversified hedge fund investment in their portfolios, as they can least afford the risk implicit in investing all their money in a typical traditional portfolio, which is inherently poorly diversified.
>
> **Investment Misconception 36:** Although hedge fund investments may provide some diversification in normal market conditions, during major market sell-offs and panics, virtually all major hedge fund categories except short biased will lose money at the same time (i.e., the "correlations going to one" effect).
>
> ***Reality:*** Managed futures tend to be immune to the "correlations going to one" effect because of the excellent liquidity in the futures and FX markets.
>
> **Investment Misconception 37:** Hedge fund investments should be limited to a maximum of 5 percent to 10 percent of portfolio allocations.
>
> ***Reality:*** In most cases, an objective assessment based on return, risk, and correlation levels would point to a higher allocation to hedge funds than 10 percent.

Investment Insights

Hedge funds have one important advantage over traditional stock and bond investments: They encompass a heterogeneous range of investments, which allows for a much greater degree of diversification than is achievable within the traditional investment world. This feasibility for creating well-diversified portfolios is the key reason why hedge fund portfolio return/risk levels are significantly higher than equity index or mutual fund return/risk levels. The combination of the higher return/risk ratios of hedge fund portfolios and their moderate diversification with equities implies that adding a hedge fund allocation component can usually be expected to enhance the return/risk performance of traditional portfolios.

Although historically it has been advantageous to add a hedge fund allocation to portfolios, there is an important caveat regarding the sustainability of this benefit in the future. An increasing number of institutional investors are allocating to hedge funds. If the arguments made in this chapter become more widely accepted, and institutions significantly further increase their current level of allocations to hedge funds, then inflows into hedge funds may surpass the hedge fund industry's ability to absorb these larger assets under management efficiently, leading to a diminution of returns. Hedge fund managers, as a group, have been more skilled than mutual fund managers and the investing public and have been able to profit from market inefficiencies created by these less skilled market participants, as well as by participants who are not motivated by making a profit, namely hedgers. As long as there are not too many hedge funds trying to exploit the same inefficiencies, they can do well. But if hedge funds grow to the point where they are primarily competing with each other, then a performance decline is inevitable. In this context, it should also be noted that because of their much more greater frequency of trading, hedge funds account for a much larger portion of each market's trading activity than is implied by their share of total assets under management. Big fish can do very well in a small pond, but if there are too many of them, they will starve. So the advice in this chapter that investors should include hedge fund allocations in their portfolios will remain valid, *as long as this advice does not become too popular.*

There is a wide chasm between facts and perception in regard to hedge funds as an investment alternative. Hedge funds are perceived to be high-risk investments that offer high return potential. The empirical evidence, however, indicates that hedge funds are considerably less risky than traditional equity investments, while offering roughly similar return levels. Why then are equity mutual funds considered conservative investments appropriate for most investors, while hedge funds are considered high-risk investments? The answer brings us to the next chapter.

Chapter 13

Fear of Hedge Funds: It's Only Human

A Parable

In the kingdom of Financia, the automobile was invented. After a number of years and numerous improvements, this new invention became practical and grew in popularity. More and more of the kingdom's citizens purchased automobiles. Although the automobile improved their lives, there was a problem: As the roads grew more crowded, accidents mushroomed. Many Financians were being seriously injured and even killed because of this new invention.

An inventor in Financia made it his mission to find a solution to this problem. After a few false starts, he came up with the idea of a strap that would be attached to the car seat and wrapped around the driver (with similar straps for passengers). He called this new invention the "seat belt." One manufacturer of luxury automobiles began installing these new seat belts in all his vehicles.

The prince of Financia, who was much loved and respected by his countrymen, purchased one of these new automobiles. He very much liked the idea of having the protection of the seat belt in case of an accident. The prince, although sensible in most respects, was a bit of a reckless driver. Now, with the feeling of security provided by the seat belt, he thought he could drive even faster.

One day, as he drove down one of Financia's steep, winding mountain roads at breakneck speed, the prince lost control of his automobile, crashing at over 80 miles per hour. The automobile was smashed to pieces, and the prince was killed.

The news went round the land: The prince had been killed in an automobile with one of those new seat belts. Soon automobile purchasers shunned automobiles with seat belts. Manufacturers stopped putting seat belts in their automobiles. The seat belt all but disappeared except for the small percentage of automobiles that already contained this now disparaged innovation. The inventor of the seat belt was devastated.

Years later, a researcher found that the passengers in automobiles with seat belts who used them experienced dramatically fewer deaths and injuries in accidents than other passengers. The seat belt worked after all! He took his research to the seat belt inventor, who was thrilled by the evidence. "Now I shall be able to revive my wonderful invention," he said.

Armed with this new evidence, the inventor tried to convince Financia's automobile manufacturers of the wisdom of installing seat belts in their vehicles. But he couldn't sway them.

"Remember what happened to the prince," they all said, confident that this fact proved the folly of seat belts.

"I loved the prince as much as you did," said the exasperated inventor, "but he died because of his careless driving, not because of the seat belt." He then showed them the indisputable evidence demonstrating that seat belts saved lives.

The automobile manufacturers listened skeptically. "Perhaps you are right" was the typical response, "but we are a conservative company, and we could never sell such a risky product to our customers."

Fear of Hedge Funds

Following their March 2000 peak, stock prices moved sharply lower in the following two and a half years, with the Standard & Poor's (S&P) 500 index losing 45 percent of its value, and the NASDAQ plunging by an even more dramatic near 75 percent. Mutual funds fared no better than the stock indexes. Hedge funds, however, largely escaped the damage. During the same cataclysmic period for equities, the HFR Fund of Funds index[1] approximately broke even. Yet astoundingly, even after this episode, most institutions and individual investors kept repeating the mantra that hedge funds were a high-risk investment that were not appropriate for the average investor. Apparently, only investments that could lose half to three-quarters of their value were suitable for "conservative" investors.

Hedge funds, however, did not escape unscathed during the financial meltdown later in the decade. During the period from November 2007 to February 2009, the HFR Fund of Funds index witnessed its worst loss ever by a wide margin, falling 22 percent. Although hedge funds experienced a substantial decline, during the exact same period both the S&P 500 and NASDAQ indexes lost more than half their value. How is it that an investment with a one-time worst loss of 22 percent is considered much riskier than one that has lost more than double that amount on two separate occasions during the same time frame?

Perhaps no single event contributed more to the lasting distorted perception of the risk in hedge fund investment than the collapse of Long-Term Capital Management (LTCM), no doubt the most famous hedge fund failure in history.[2] In its first four years of operation, this multibillion-dollar hedge fund generated steady profits, quadrupling

---

[1]We use the fund of funds index rather than the composite index of individual funds to represent hedge fund performance because, as will be explained in Chapter 14, hedge fund indexes based on individual funds are significantly biased.

[2]Bernie Madoff may have been even more prominent, but his was a Ponzi scheme rather than a hedge fund. Madoff simply made up performance results and never did any trading. Also, Madoff lacked all the normal structural checks of a hedge fund, such as an independent broker and administrator.

the starting net asset value. Then in a five-month period (May to September 1998), it all unraveled, with the net asset value of the fund plunging a staggering 92 percent. Moreover, LTCM's positions had been enormously leveraged, placing the banks and brokerage firms that provided the credit at enormous risk. Fears that LTCM's failure could have a domino effect throughout the financial system prompted the Federal Reserve to orchestrate (but not pay for) a bailout for the firm.

What made LTCM such a compelling story was not merely the magnitude of the failure and its threat to the financial system, but also the brainpower of those involved, a connection famously highlighted in the title of Roger Lowenstein's excellent book on the subject, *When Genius Failed*.[3] Prospective investors could well wonder, if a hedge fund with two Nobel Prize winners as principals, staffed with some of Wall Street's sharpest minds, and with a prestigious list of sophisticated investors could abruptly lose virtually all of its capital, what degree of comfort could anyone have about any hedge fund investment? Just as the car manufactures in our parable might reject seat belts with the refrain "What about the prince?," investors could dismiss hedge funds with the rejoinder "What about LTCM?"

The key question, however, is: How representative was LTCM of hedge fund investing? In fact, hedge fund blowups, such as LTCM, occur relatively infrequently. LTCM began by employing conservative arbitrage trades, which usually had limited and well-defined risks. These trades sought to extract profits from market inefficiencies, which led to relative mispricings between related market instruments.

As increased competition diminished the profit opportunities in its core trades, LTCM began to shift into far riskier trades. By the time of its collapse, the portfolio was filled with positions that were the very antithesis of the types of positions LTCM originally held (e.g., spread trades in which the loss of the long side versus the short side was theoretically unlimited). The risks were further exacerbated by the use of enormous leverage and the vulnerability of much of the portfolio to similar market events (e.g., weakening credit spreads). In short, LTCM, which began as a conservative arbitrage house,

[3]New York: Random House, 2000. This book was the source for the LTCM discussion in this section.

ultimately metamorphosed into a financial gunslinger, relying on models that did not account for the possibility of tail events, so-called black swans, like Russia defaulting in 1998, which triggered LTCM's unraveling. Judging the risk of hedge fund investment based on the LTCM experience is much like judging the risk of long-term equity investing based on Enron.

The impact of LTCM on the perception of hedge fund investment risk is a specific example of one of several behavioral biases that distort people's perception of risk (in this instance, the confusion of intensity of media coverage with the likelihood of an event). People are incredibly illogical when it comes to making risk judgments, and irrational perceptions regarding risk are hardly the exclusive domain of hedge fund investing.

To cite a few examples: Why, at one time, did so many Europeans avoid eating meat because of a fear of mad cow disease (one is considerably more likely to be struck by lightning than to contract this ailment), while continuing to smoke with abandon, an action with known devastating health consequences? Why did some African nations refuse to distribute U.S. donations of genetically altered grain, choosing to let their populations starve rather than eat foodstuffs that are routinely consumed by hundreds of millions of Americans?[4] Why do some people drive long distances to avoid the risk of flying when the chances of their being killed in an automobile per mile traveled are far higher? Why will the fear of shark attacks (a rarity) deter far more people from swimming than the fear of drowning, which is a far likelier event?

The foregoing examples illustrate certain behavioral biases in people's attitudes toward risk. First, there is an inverse relationship between familiarity (or knowledge) and fear. For example, the connection between smoking and cancer or heart disease has the ring of familiarity, whereas the mechanics of contracting mad cow disease are poorly understood. Similarly, genetically engineered foods are a new

[4]In 2003, President Levy Mwanawasa of Zambia banned the distribution of donated genetically modified food to his starving population. "I have been told it is not safe," Zambia's minister of agriculture, Mundia Sikatana, said in an interview quoted by the *New York Times*.

phenomenon—one about which most people have little if any knowledge—but there is not much mystery about starvation.

Second, ironically, the very rarity of an event enhances its potential for inducing anxiety, because rare events are more likely to receive prominent media coverage. The shark attack may make the evening news and might possibly even be the lead story. When was the last time you saw a news story on a drowning death? A plane crash is a news event; a car crash isn't. Publicity distorts people's assessment of risk by making the unusual seem common or by simply heightening the public's sensitivity to rare risks that would otherwise have been ignored. Either way, heightened media focus contributes to such anomalies as chain smokers panicking about mad cow disease.

The dichotomy of media coverage between traditional markets (e.g., equity markets) and hedge funds has a great deal to do with the divergent public perceptions of these investment sectors. Typically, hedge funds tend to make the news only when there is some disaster, such as a hedge fund fraud or blowup.[5] In contrast, equity market reporting is a routine daily affair. Imagine if the public's perception and knowledge of equities were based solely on stories of Enron and WorldCom. In such a world, mentioning to a friend that you were thinking of investing in the stock market might engender the response "Are you crazy? Don't you know you can lose all your money?"

Third, people appear to perceive greater risk in a rare event over which they have no control than in the more commonplace occurrence they can influence. Hence, shark attacks engender more anxiety than drowning, fatal plane crashes more fear than fatal car crashes.

These three inherent human biases in the perception of risk explain why people are fearful about investing in hedge funds, but not mutual funds, even though major declines occur more frequently and are much larger in equities than in hedge funds. First, people are unfamiliar with hedge funds and don't understand the broad range of strategies they employ, but are quite familiar with mutual funds and fully

[5]A blowup refers to a huge, often firm-destroying, loss due to the mismanagement of risk rather than a consequence of deceit. Blowups can occur either because the fund deliberately takes on excessive risk or because of inaccurate risk measurement, or both (as was the case with LTCM).

understand the concept of being long a portfolio of diversified stocks. Second, the hedge fund that loses more than 50 percent of its investors' capital is a colorful news story (e.g., LTCM); the mutual fund that does the same is one of hundreds or perhaps even thousands that have witnessed such declines in recent years. Third, investors have far more control over their mutual fund or direct equity investments, which can be redeemed daily, than over hedge fund investments, which are subject to a wide assortment of redemption impediments, including infrequent redemption periods, lengthy redemption notices, lockups or early redemption penalties, and gates.[6]

The fear of hedge funds is not entirely driven by psychological factors. There are also real substantive factors that provide some rational justification for the risk perceptions associated with hedge funds. Frauds and blowups, although infrequent, occur often enough to be a source of concern. The complexity of hedge funds makes it difficult for investors to gauge risk, especially hidden risk (discussed in Chapter 4). Redemption impediments have real, as well as psychological, repercussions. Still, with the exception of the redemption issue, these real risk factors can be substantially mitigated through fund of funds investing. Also, redemption impediments can be eliminated, and fraud and blowup risks can be greatly reduced, by using managed accounts as an alternative investment structure (see Chapter 16).

On balance, although there are some hedge-fund-specific risks, they do not adequately explain the widespread perception of hedge funds being a particularly high-risk investment. Inherent psychological biases lead investors to make distorted risk assessments and ultimately irrational investment decisions when comparing hedge funds with traditional investments.

---

[6]At one time, monthly redemption was the norm for hedge funds, but now quarterly or even less frequent redemption periods are more common. Many hedge funds also have lockups—a prohibition against redemption for some period after the initial investment (e.g., one or more years). Other funds impose penalties on redemptions made during some defined period after investment. Gate provisions, which have become virtually standard in hedge fund offering documents, permit funds to suspend additional investor redemptions if total redemptions exceed a specified threshold (e.g., 10 percent of assets under management).

Chapter 14

The Paradox of Hedge Fund of Funds Underperformance

Compare a hedge fund index constructed from single hedge funds with one constructed from funds of funds and you will notice an odd thing: The index based on funds of funds will tend to consistently underperform. Not only are the fund of funds returns lower in almost every year, but the magnitude of their underperformance is quite substantial, with annual performance lags of 5 percent or more commonplace in the historical record.

Is the apparent substantial underperformance of fund of funds managers another example of what might be termed "Eckhardt's dictum"? Bill Eckhardt is one of the managers I interviewed in *The New*

Market Wizards.[1] In that interview, Eckhardt asserted that human nature was so poorly attuned to trading and investing decisions that most people would do worse than random. To be clear, Eckhardt was not saying the equivalent of the proverbial academic claim that a monkey throwing darts at the *Wall Street Journal* stock quote page could do as well as fund managers; Eckhardt was saying that the monkey would do better! In his view, the innate human tendency to seek comfort, honed by evolution, will lead most people to make *worse than random* trading and investment decisions. Are we to conclude that fund of funds managers should exchange their fund selection, due diligence, portfolio construction, and monitoring processes for a good set of darts?

Part of the explanation for the underperformance of funds of funds is the extra layer of fees. If funds of funds realized the same return on their underlying investments as the average return for single funds, the results of the index based on funds of funds would be lower because of the second layer of fees charged by funds of funds. The fact that funds of funds charge fees does not necessarily imply that they are a poorer investment. On the contrary, these fees compensate for two essential services that funds of funds provide for investors:

1. **Diversification.** Very few individual investors are wealthy enough to adequately diversify hedge fund investments. Assuming an average minimum investment of $1 million for hedge funds and a portfolio of 20 hedge funds, an investor would need $20 million to construct a diversified hedge fund portfolio. Funds of funds, however, allow for much smaller minimum investments (minimums of $100,000 or less are common). Therefore, funds of funds make it possible for the individual investor to diversify. It can reasonably be argued that the value of the risk reduction provided by diversification more than compensates for any fund of funds fees.
2. **Professional management.** The selection, due diligence, portfolio construction, and monitoring processes conducted by funds of funds, which are all part of prudent hedge fund investing, are beyond the capabilities of most individual investors. Moreover, even in the case of institutions that may have the capability of

[1]New York: HarperBusiness, 1991.

establishing their own hedge fund investment departments, the cost of constructing and maintaining a fund of funds portfolio would simply replace an explicit fee with an internal cost, which could be even higher (especially since institutional fees are normally deeply discounted).

Fund of funds fees, however, do not come close to fully accounting for the performance gap between single-fund indexes and fund of funds indexes. Even if fund of funds indexes were restated in gross terms (that is, excluding fees), they would still lag single-fund indexes in a large majority of years. Roughly speaking, fund of funds fees account for less than one-third of the historical performance gap vis-à-vis single-fund indexes (the exact percentage will vary by data vendor). So the question of whether fund of funds managers do worse than random in their fund selections remains.

The real crux of the explanation for why indexes based on funds of funds underperform indexes constructed from single funds relates to hedge fund index biases, which are far more pronounced in single-fund indexes. These biases include:

- **Survivorship bias.** This effect is perhaps the best-known bias since it has been the subject of numerous academic articles written over many years. Essentially, if an index fails to retain defunct funds, it will tend to be upwardly biased because poorer-performing funds will have a greater tendency to cease operation. A number of indexes now correct for this bias, so while this bias is significant if present, it has become less important.
- **Selection bias.** Hedge funds decide whether to report their numbers to databases. Insofar as better-performing funds will be more likely to report their numbers, the self-selection process will create an upward bias. However, in this instance there is an offsetting effect in that funds that do particularly well and close to new investment may decide to stop reporting their numbers to avoid inquiries from new investors. Although it is difficult to say how these two offsetting effects balance out, from the perspective of a new investor, selection bias also creates an upward bias, since the universe of potential investments does not include closed funds.

- **Backfilling bias (or "instant history" bias).** When a fund begins reporting its numbers to an index, some indexes will backfill the fund's performance numbers from inception. Although these backfilled numbers represent actual returns, a bias is created because there is a much greater tendency for better-performing funds to decide to report their numbers. For example, assume 1,000 hedge funds begin operation in a given year and two years later 500 have done well and 500 have done poorly. The 500 that did well will be much more likely to report their numbers. Their numbers will be backfilled (in those indexes that backfill), whereas the numbers from the poorer-performing funds will not. Thus, historical numbers of indexes that backfill data will overstate the actual performance of prevailing funds at the time.
- **Termination bias.** When funds experience very poor performance, with losses sufficiently large to cause them to cease operation, the last thing they're going to be concerned about is reporting their numbers to the index databases. Therefore, for the most part, the very worst performance months for funds that go out of business tend to never see the light of day. Note that this problem will exist even if an index corrects for survivorship bias (although the fund may be retained in the database, the returns for the final months of its death throes may be unavailable).
- **Allocation bias.** Most indexes use an equal weighting assumption, which is statistically equivalent to monthly rebalancing. In actual portfolios, funds that do well will increase in size because of their gains, while those that lose will shrink in size. An equal weighting scheme implicitly assumes gains from winners are redistributed to losers. To the extent there may be patterns of reversion to the mean among the different strategies, monthly rebalancing (implied by equal weighting) would help performance. This monthly rebalancing advantage, however, cannot be realized in practice, given redemption and subscription lags and impediments.

Some indexes contain all the foregoing biases (for at least part of their track record), while some avoid backfilling and survivorship biases after a demarcation date. The key point, however, is that, as has been detailed by academic researchers William Fung and David Hsieh, fund of funds indexes eliminate or significantly mitigate hedge fund index biases.[2] We now reconsider the foregoing biases from a fund of funds perspective.

- **Survivorship bias.** This bias is eliminated for single funds at the fund of funds level because defunct fund results remain reflected in historical fund of funds data. If a fund of funds was invested in a fund that blew up, the fund may disappear from some databases, but the losses incurred by the fund will remain reflected in the fund of funds track record. Although there may still be a survivorship bias at the fund of funds level (that is, defunct fund of funds), the effect will be much more muted than for single funds because the difference between a defunct and an active fund of funds is much smaller.
- **Selection bias.** This bias is eliminated for single funds at the fund of funds level because a fund's result will be reflected in fund of funds data even if it chooses not to report. At the fund of funds level, both positive and negative selection bias effects are far more moderate. The negative bias effect is probably negligible for a fund of funds because most funds of funds will continue to report their numbers even if closed, in order to aid the marketing of other fund of funds products under the same umbrella.
- **Backfilling bias.** This bias is eliminated for single funds in fund of funds data because results for any underlying fund are reflected only from the point of investment. At the fund of funds level, this bias is far more moderate because backfill data for a fund of funds will not differ radically from the contemporaneous average of funds of funds.
- **Termination bias.** This bias is eliminated for single funds in fund of funds data because results remain reflected until the fund of funds redeems, regardless of whether the underlying fund ceases reporting its numbers. For example, if a fund loses 60 percent during a short

[2]William Fung and David Hsieh, "Benchmarks of Hedge Fund Performance: Information Content and Measurement Biases," *Financial Analysts Journal* 58 (2002): 22–34.

time frame and goes out of business, the 60 percent loss is unlikely to be reported to fund databases, but the loss will be reflected in the results of all the funds of funds that were invested in that fund. Termination bias is probably minimal at the fund of funds level because even unsuccessful funds of funds do not implode, but rather tend to fade into oblivion due to lackluster performance or inadequate marketing.

- **Allocation bias.** This bias is eliminated for single funds in fund of funds data because results are based on actual investment levels. Allocation bias at the fund of funds level is probably minimal because funds of funds are far more heterogeneous, mitigating any reversion to the mean effect.

Thus, the paradox of fund of funds underperformance is resolved. It is not that funds of funds underperform the average of single funds, but rather that fund of funds indexes contain far fewer upside biases than single-fund indexes.

Investment Misconception

Investment Misconception 38: Hedge fund indexes provide a reasonable proxy for hedge fund performance.

Reality: Hedge fund indexes based on single funds substantially overstate performance due to multiple biases. A comparison of a typical hedge fund index with traditional investment indexes (e.g., equity indexes) will tend to dramatically overstate hedge fund relative performance. In other words, true hedge fund performance is nowhere near as good as implied by typical indexes.

Investment Insights

Single hedge fund indexes tend to significantly overstate performance because of multiple database biases. The use of these indexes leads to unrealistic expectations for hedge fund returns. Fund of funds hedge fund indexes eliminate, or at least greatly mitigate, these biases and provide a much truer representation of hedge fund performance. Therefore, in evaluating the effects of including a hedge fund investment component in portfolios, investors should use fund of funds hedge fund indexes as a proxy for this investment sector. When should single hedge fund indexes be used? In my opinion: never.[3]

[3]The comments here pertain to broad-based hedge fund indexes. In regard to sector hedge fund indexes, these exist only as indexes based on single funds. Although biased for all the reasons we detailed, sector indexes can be used in comparisons with each other based on the implicit simplifying assumption that they will be about equally impacted by these biases. Indeed, we used such comparisons in the hedge fund performance analysis in Chapter 3.

Chapter 15

The Leverage Fallacy

Leverage can be dangerous. There is no shortage of hedge funds that have collapsed as a result of excessive leverage, with Long-Term Capital Management, detailed in Chapter 13, being the classic example. Investors have learned the lesson that leverage *is* dangerous rather than leverage *can be* dangerous. In this sense, they are much like the cat that sits on a hot stove. As Mark Twain observed, "She will never sit down on a hot stove-lid again—and that is well; but also she will never sit down on a cold one any more."

Investors always seem to ask hedge funds the question: "How much leverage do you use?" This question is flawed on two fundamental grounds. First, the question is meaningless, given that it ignores units of measurement: the underlying investment (that is, what is being leveraged). Second, it implicitly assumes that there is a direct connection between leverage and risk. Not only is this assumption false, but it is even possible—in fact, entirely common—for a higher-leverage investment to have lower risk.

Consider a comparison between two fixed income funds that are approximately equivalent in terms of credit risk, liquidity, and other relevant risk factors with the exception of exposure to interest rate changes. Assume Fund A's portfolio is unleveraged and has a net duration of 10 years, while Fund B's portfolio is leveraged 5:1 and has a net duration of one year. (Duration is the approximate multiple by which a bond's price will change, in percentage terms, given a small change in interest rates. So a seven-year-duration bond would decrease approximately 0.07 percent in response to a 0.01 percent increase in interest rates.) An investor comparing these two funds on the basis of leverage would conclude that Portfolio B was five times as risky. In fact, even at 5:1 leverage, Portfolio B is only about half as risky as Portfolio A because its holdings (on an equal dollar-invested basis) are only one-tenth as risky as Portfolio A's holdings.

Leverage can even be used as a tool to *lower* risk. As a simple example, consider a long-only fund that implements 2:1 leverage and uses all the leverage to fund short positions. In this instance, although the fund has gone from unleveraged to 2:1 leverage, it has transformed the portfolio from 100 percent long to market neutral in the process, clearly reducing risk.

In both these cases, focusing on leverage alone leads to totally erroneous risk perceptions because the holdings in the portfolios of the funds being compared are vastly different in terms of their risk. Risk is a function of both the risk of the underlying investment and leverage. Comparing investments only on the basis of leverage without considering the underlying investments leads to nonsensical risk-comparison conclusions. In essence, it makes sense to compare leverage only if the underlying investments are approximately equivalent. The underlying investment is, in effect, the unit of measurement.

When I worked for a fund of funds group, as part of our monitoring procedures we set up fund-specific flags related to such factors as gross and net exposures, size of monthly loss, significant changes in assets under management, and leverage. These flags were used to signal when we should take a closer look at a fund. One month, the leverage flag for a credit fund in our portfolio was triggered. The threshold level for the leverage flag had been set to 5:1 for this fund. When we examined the situation, we found that while leverage had increased to 5.2:1, its highest level ever, the leverage increase was entirely due to a substantial increase in the fund's short hedge. In fact, the gross short exposure was 1.7:1, while the gross long exposure was 3.5:1, resulting in a net long exposure of only 1.8:1, the lowest level in two years. Moreover, the beta of the fund versus the high yield index was only 0.6, meaning that the fund would be expected to decline by only a little more than half the decline in an unleveraged high yield bond portfolio (as implied by the index).

This real-world example, which represents a common situation, reflects two ironies.

1. Although the gross leverage of the fund increased to its highest level ever, the net exposure, which is much more reflective of risk, simultaneously declined to its lowest level in two years.
2. Although the gross leverage of the fund was over 5:1, its volatility was equal to only 0.6 times the volatility of an unleveraged portfolio, as represented by the index.

This actual example illustrates an important principle: If leverage is used for hedging, it actually *reduces* risk rather than increases it—exactly the opposite effect of leverage assumed by conventional wisdom.

Imagine a teller at a bank being told by her supervisor to count up the money in the till at the end of each day, but to calculate the sum based on the number of bills without regard to their denomination. Sound ridiculous? Well, that's exactly what investors do when they attempt to gauge risk in terms of leverage without considering the risk of the underlying portfolio.

The Folly of Arbitrary Investment Rules

Some investors operate with checklists of investment criteria. Frequently, one item on the checklist is the maximum permissible leverage level. For example, a pension fund might have a rule that says it will invest only in hedge funds that use no more than two times leverage. Such a rule might sound like a rational risk constraint and one particularly appropriate for a risk-averse institution such as a pension fund. Yet such a one-size-fits-all rule represents the height of folly, leaving the institution open to investing in highly risky funds that use less than the maximum leverage or even no leverage at all (e.g., long-only emerging market fund, long-only technology fund, etc.), while avoiding many low-risk funds (e.g., market neutral). A maximum leverage constraint applied uniformly to all prospective investments regardless of portfolio content is analogous to a traffic law that applies a 40 miles per hour speed limit to all roads, in all conditions. Such a speed limit would be both absurdly low for a highway in fair weather, but recklessly fast on an ice-covered, curvy mountain road. Certainly, it would be much safer to drive 65 miles per hour on the former and 15 miles per hour on the latter than 40 miles per hour on both.

In essence, leverage comparisons should be made only between *equivalent* portfolios. A corollary is that asking for the *average* leverage of the underlying assets in a diversified fund of funds portfolio makes no sense. How can you average leverage across completely different investments? Assume a simplified example of a fund of funds that has three holdings: a fixed income fund that uses 6:1 leverage, a market neutral fund that uses 2:1 leverage, and a long-only fund that doesn't use any leverage, all with equal allocations. What is the leverage of the portfolio? This is a nonsensical question that can't be answered any more than the question "What is the sum of two apples plus five baseballs?"

Leverage and Investor Preference

Imagine you receive a check for $1,000,000 from a very wealthy anonymous benefactor (just as in *The Millionaire* TV series of the late 1950s) with the one twist that the gift is conditional on it being invested in one of the two following investments *for exactly one year*. Which would you choose?

Investment A

Average annual return: 25 percent
Prior worst 12-month performance: –25 percent

Investment B

Average annual return: 50 percent
Prior worst 12-month performance: –50 percent

Compare the alternatives and pick the preferred investment before reading on.

Now assume the same scenario, but this time you are given a choice between the following two investments. Which would you choose?

Investment A

Average annual return: 10 percent
Prior worst 12-month performance: –2 percent

Investment B

Average annual return: 20 percent
Prior worst 12-month performance: –4 percent

Again, compare the alternatives and pick the preferred investment before reading on.

If you are like most people, you will have readily picked investment A in the first case and investment B in the second. But here is the odd thing: In both cases, both the return and worst loss of investment B are twice as high as those of investment A, or equivalently, investment B is twice as leveraged as investment A. Why then do most people have a strong preference for A in the first case (i.e., 25/–25 combination preferred over 50/–50) and the more leveraged B alternative in the second (i.e., 20/–4 combination over 10/–2), even though both involve the same leverage (2:1)?

The explanation for this apparent paradox is that people's desire for a more or less leveraged version of an existing strategy is influenced by the following two factors:

1. Return/risk ratio
2. Risk level

The higher the return/risk ratio and the lower the risk level, the more likely leverage will be preferred by an increasing portion of investors.

When Leverage Is Dangerous

There are certain circumstances when leverage can be especially dangerous. Leverage can imply high risk when any of the three following conditions apply:

1. The leveraged assets are illiquid.
2. The credit lines supporting leverage can be pulled. The combination of conditions 1 and 2 can be particularly lethal. Many funds that suffered severe losses in 2008 were exposed to this combination when their credit lines were cut and their relatively illiquid holdings could be liquidated only at steep discounts.
3. Leverage is used to *increase* exposure of a portfolio that already has moderate to high risk without leverage (e.g., leveraging a long-only portfolio of emerging market equities).

Investment Misconceptions

Investment Misconception 39: Leverage is a measure of risk.

Reality: Risk is a function of *both* the underlying portfolio and leverage. Leverage alone tells you nothing about the portfolio risk. In fact, leveraged portfolios can often have lower risk than unleveraged portfolios—it depends on the assets in the portfolio.

Investment Misconception 40: Increasing leverage increases risk.

Reality: It depends on what the leverage is being used for. Increasing leverage can increase risk if leverage is used to increase net exposure to the market. If, however, leverage is used for hedging to reduce the portfolio's net exposure, then it actually *reduces* risk.

Investment Misconception 41: Investors should never leverage an investment.

Reality: When an investment has a high return/risk ratio and a low risk level, most investors would prefer to uniformly increase return and risk. In these instances, leverage can be a prudent and useful tool to adjust the investment more closely to the investor's risk preference.

Investment Insights

Although leverage can be dangerous, the knee-jerk reaction many investors have to leverage can lead to nonsensical investment biases. Investors need to focus on risk, not leverage. Sometimes, leverage may indeed be a risk factor. But other times, such as when it is used for hedging, leverage can actually be a risk-reducing factor. In this sense, blanket prohibitions against leverage are shortsighted and misguided, as is the use of leverage as a risk measure—that is, the assumption that higher leverage implies greater risk.

Leverage is a tool that can aid more efficient investing. It allows for creating hedged portfolios with higher return/risk ratios than unhedged portfolios and for adjusting the return levels of low-risk investments to more closely match investor preferences. But like any tool, leverage can cause damage if misused. The solution is not to ban its use—any more than it would make sense to ban power tools because they are dangerous in the hands of intoxicated users—but rather to ensure that leverage is used appropriately. The guiding principle should be risk assessment, where risk is viewed comprehensively as a function of both the underlying investments and leverage, not naively as a function of leverage alone.

Chapter 16

Managed Accounts: An Investor-Friendly Alternative to Funds

Suppose you can buy the exact car of your choice at two different dealers. Both dealers will charge the same price. Dealer A has an unknown reputation and offers nothing extra. Dealer B has a stellar reputation, will give you a model with optional side air bags at no extra cost, and will also add a free extended guarantee for all parts and labor. This choice seems like a no-brainer, but in the world of hedge fund investments, the vast majority of investors are choosing the equivalent of Dealer A (read hedge funds) over Dealer B (read managed accounts). In the aftermath of the 2008 financial meltdown, when a large number of funds invoked redemption gates[1] or implemented side pockets[2] or both, an increasing number of investors are discovering the advantages of Dealer B. This trend is likely to continue.

The Essential Difference between Managed Accounts and Funds

Managed accounts allow parallel investments to counterpart hedge funds, while at the same time avoiding many of the negative investment features of the typical hedge fund structure. The key difference between a managed account and a fund can be summarized as follows:

- In a fund, the investor owns shares in a fund fully controlled by the manager.
- In a managed account, the investor (or the investor's proxy) has control of the account and grants *limited* power of attorney to the manager to execute trades.

A portfolio of managed accounts is quite similar to a fund of funds. Whereas the fund of funds holds a portfolio of hedge funds, the counterpart managed account structure holds a portfolio of managed

---

[1]As a reminder from Chapters 11 and 12: Many hedge funds contain gate provisions that allow the managers to severely limit redemptions if total investor redemptions for any given redemption period exceed a specified threshold. If gates are applied and not lifted, it could take investors years to fully redeem their investments. If managers trade securities that are prone to be illiquid during crisis situations, there is at least a rationale for the gate—that is, to avoid the manager being forced to liquidate positions at extremely wide bid/ask spreads in a market where there is a paucity of buyers.

[2]As a reminder from Chapter 11: If faced with large redemptions, hedge funds whose portfolios contain securities that are particularly illiquid and difficult to sell may decide to place those securities in a side pocket that is cordoned off from the rest of the portfolio. When investors redeem, they receive cash on only the pro rata portion of their investment that is not in the side pocket. The side pocket is liquidated over time by the manager as conditions allow. When side pockets are invoked, it can take years for investors to receive cash reimbursements for their portions of these assets, and the amounts received are often considerably less than the values assigned to these assets at the time the side pocket was implemented.

accounts in which each managed account corresponds to a fund. Typically, a hedge fund manager will hold a similar or identical portfolio in the managed account as in the fund.

The Major Advantages of a Managed Account

The major advantages of a managed account include:

- **Daily transparency.** A managed account allows for daily position level transparency and monitoring.
- **Daily independent pricing.** A managed account makes it possible to independently price a portfolio daily.
- **Better liquidity terms.** Managed accounts typically provide much more favorable liquidity terms than the counterpart funds. Monthly liquidity (or better) is the norm rather than the exception.
- **Control of cash movements.** If structured properly, a managed account will prohibit the manager from any involvement regarding cash movements in or out of the account; the manager's sole responsibility is limited to the investment of the portfolio.
- **Insulation of account from fraudulent linkages.** The managed account will belong to the investor or a proxy for the investor—a structure that makes it impossible for an unscrupulous manager to fraudulently link the account to any other account without investor knowledge and approval.
- **Minimal lag between liquidation of investment and return of cash.** In a managed account, funds are normally returned far more promptly upon redemption than they are in a hedge fund. There are also no audit holdbacks for managed accounts.
- **Elimination of investor-unfriendly terms characteristic of funds of funds.** The managed account structure does not allow for lockups, redemption penalties, gates, side pockets, and the like.
- **Accounts can be customized to minimize assets held in cash.** Some hedge fund strategies utilize only a fraction of their assets under management to meet margin requirements (e.g., commodity trading advisors [CTAs], foreign exchange [FX] managers). Managed accounts can be structured to be more cash efficient by allowing investors to provide a much smaller cash outlay than

required for an exactly equivalent fund portfolio. (In a fund, the extra cash is not needed by the manager for investments and is generally kept in Treasury bills.)

Individual Managed Accounts versus Indirect Managed Account Investment

There are three ways of investing in managed accounts:

1. **Individual managed accounts.** The investor opens a managed account directly with the manager. This avenue will typically be feasible only for large investors or institutions, since most hedge fund managers will require a high minimum investment for establishing a separate managed account ($10 million or higher, and sometimes much higher). CTAs as a group typically have lower minimum levels for managed accounts, but well-established CTAs will still require multimillion-dollar minimums for separate managed accounts. Consequently, for most investors, the managed account alternative will require investing via third-party intermediaries as in one of the two ways that follow.
2. **Fund of managed accounts.** This type of investment is the counterpart of a fund of funds except that the fund is structured so that the underlying holdings are managed accounts instead of funds.
3. **Managed account platforms.** Managed account platforms offer a list of approved managers with whom they have established managed accounts. Investors can allocate to these managed accounts through an investment structure created by the platform to allow pooled investments from multiple investors (e.g., separate funds that invest directly into the individual managed accounts).

Both funds of managed accounts and managed account platforms will conduct due diligence and risk monitoring of selected managers. The funds of managed accounts will also provide portfolio construction and management (similar to a fund of funds), whereas for managed account platforms, investors construct and manage their own portfolios by choosing managers from the approved list. Funds of managed accounts and managed account platforms will have all the advantages inherent in managed accounts—benefits that are passed on to investors via their role as investor proxies.

Why Would Managers Agree to Managed Accounts?

There is a common belief that hedge fund managers will object to managed accounts because they will be concerned about the confidentiality of their positions. This perception is based on faulty logic. How many hedge fund managers don't have a prime broker? Presumably zero. Obviously, by definition, the prime broker knows all the manager's positions. This full transparency is not a problem because there is a nondisclosure agreement between the prime broker and the manager. A managed account platform is entirely analogous. (*Note:* All the following comments regarding managed account platforms apply to funds of managed accounts as well.) Thus, the manager is not giving up any confidentiality, since a platform will not share position-level data with investors unless the manager agrees to such dissemination of information. Typically, the manager will agree to the platform providing investors with sector exposures without specific position-level detail. It is hard to come up with any legitimate reason for a manager to object to the disclosure of sector exposure to investors, and investors should probably be wary of any manager unwilling to provide such basic account information to them. For highly liquid strategies, such as those involving futures and FX, managers will often allow the platform to share even position-level information with investors. For most other strategies, however, position-level transparency will be available only to the platform and not to investors. (The exception would be large investors who can negotiate their own managed accounts with the manager and sign a nondisclosure agreement.) Since platforms will provide monitoring, and most investors will not have the resources to utilize position-level transparency even if available, the limitation of investor transparency to the sector level will typically not be a material issue.

Another misconception is that managers will avoid managed accounts because they require a lot of extra work. This might be true to some extent if a manager were providing a separate managed account for each investor. If, however, the manager instead opens one managed account on a managed account platform, or with a fund of managed accounts, which in practice is accessible to any prospective investor, the extra work implied is minimal. Typically, the manager would simply instruct the prime broker to split all orders proportionately between the existing funds and a managed account. For example, if a manager previously had an offshore fund with $200 million and an onshore fund with $100 million, the prime broker would have been instructed to split orders two-thirds to the offshore fund and one-third to the onshore fund. If the same manager now adds a managed account with $100 million, the manager would simply change the split instruction to be three ways (50 percent, 25 percent, and 25 percent) instead of two ways as before. There would also be one additional account to administer. This is hardly an onerous change.

Thus far, we have explained why a manager might not object to a managed account rather than why the manager would seek to do one. The reason for the latter is obvious: self-interest. Providing a managed account investment vehicle will allow a manager to raise assets that would otherwise be unavailable, as some investors will insist on the transparency, safety, and fairer investment terms intrinsic in the managed account structure as a precondition for investment. This sentiment was enhanced by the rash of gates and side pockets implemented in the aftermath of the 2008 financial crisis. Establishing a managed account on a platform or as a direct investment from a fund of managed accounts is a very efficient means of offering this structure of investment to investors, since it allows the manager to have one account accessible to many investors. In addition, having a managed account on one or more platforms will provide asset-gathering vehicles for the manager with the potential of raising assets beyond the scope of direct marketing efforts. Similarly, establishing an account with a fund of managed accounts will create an additional revenue source, drawing a percentage of assets raised by the fund from end investors directly seeking the benefits of a managed account structure.

Are There Strategies That Are Not Amenable to Managed Accounts?

While, theoretically, the managed account structure could be utilized for virtually any fund category, it is best suited to liquid or at least relatively liquid strategies. For portfolios holding difficult-to-price illiquid instruments, even best-effort independent pricing by a platform may not be sufficient to provide fully accurate valuations. In addition, if strategies containing illiquid or relatively illiquid holdings provide the type of redemption liquidity normally associated with managed account platforms (typically monthly or less), there will be a liquidity mismatch between the investment and the terms provided to investors. In such a case, investors in a managed account may be able to redeem more promptly, but this flexibility will come at the expense of the manager being forced to sell holdings at deeply discounted values (implicit in the assumption of illiquid holdings that must be liquidated promptly) in order to meet redemptions. As a general rule, investors should be wary of investing in a managed account that provides redemption terms significantly better than implied by the nature of the holdings. For the most part, managed accounts will not be available for most illiquid strategies, and this is just as well.

Evaluating Four Common Objections to Managed Accounts

1. Managed account investments incur an extra layer of costs.

For institutions or large investors who make direct managed account investments, this objection does not apply. As for investing via a fund of managed accounts, these funds are often able to negotiate some fee discounts with managers, which will serve as a partial offset to their own fees. Also, funds of managed accounts have similar fee structures to funds of funds, so there is no cost disadvantage using this mode of investment. In fact, the implicit monetary benefits of better redemption and cash repayment terms, as well as the ability to allocate to some investments with a smaller cash outlay, provide funds of managed accounts a cost advantage versus their fund of funds counterparts.

As for managed account platforms, while most do charge fees, there are a number of cost offsets:

- Some platforms earn most of their income via a fee share from managers rather than charges to the investor.
- Some platforms provide investors with discounted manager fees that offset the platform fee. (The platform can often negotiate a discounted fee by virtue of representing a large investment.)
- Large investors will often be able to negotiate discounts to any existing platform fees.
- Administrative fees for managed accounts are explicitly stated (or included in the platform fee), but these types of fees also exist in funds—they are just not typically broken out as they are for managed accounts.
- The typical more prompt repayment of cash upon redemption and the absence of audit holdbacks in managed account investments mitigate the cash drag inherent in fund redemptions, providing an implicit bottom-line advantage.
- Fund investments sometimes entail redemption penalties, whereas managed accounts do not.
- On some managed account platforms, the ability to finance the same investment in a managed account for a significantly smaller cash outlay than in the counterpart fund provides an advantage that has an implicit monetary value.
- In a sense, a managed account investment structure provides fraud insurance (in practical, not literal, terms), an attribute that has some monetary value, depending on the individual investor.

The combination of these factors means that the significant advantages of a managed account platform can often be obtained at a small, or even near zero, cost as compared with investing via the counterpart funds.

2. Managed accounts offer a far more limited choice of managers.

Insofar as not all hedge funds are available as managed accounts, it is a truism that the universe of managed accounts is much smaller than the universe of funds. This limitation, however, is not as much an impediment as might appear at first glance. First, a whole range of illiquid, and partially illiquid, strategies are not well suited to the managed account structure. Second, since even highly diversified portfolios will usually have less than 50 holdings, the difference between, say, a universe of 5,000 versus 1,000 managers may not be material. The only relevant question is whether there are enough diversified, high-quality managers accessible as managed accounts to form superior portfolios, and in this regard, there is no apparent shortage of hedge fund investments available as managed accounts. Moreover, the number of managers who offer managed accounts appears likely to continue to increase in response to institutional demand.

3. The best managers won't offer managed accounts.

Although there are certainly many high-quality managers who won't offer a managed account alternative, there are many who do. Also, many managers who may not have a managed account on any platform have managed accounts with large investors or would be amenable to a managed account at a sufficient account size. Thus, the absence of a publicly visible managed account does not automatically mean a manager will not offer one. Even when a manager is not accessible via a managed account, the investor may be able to identify equally attractive managers in the same strategy style who do offer managed accounts. In the event the investor judges that there is not an equal-quality managed account alternative, then a fund investment may be the preferable choice.

4. Managed accounts underperform their fund counterparts.

This criticism has some merit, but primarily for reasons that are not well appreciated. Empirically, there is some evidence that, on average, funds have a higher return than their counterpart investments on managed account platforms. Platform fees can explain part of this performance difference, especially since many of the implicit monetary benefits listed earlier in item 1 are not directly reflected in the managed account track record. The performance difference between funds and managed accounts, however, is probably more influenced by two reasons that have nothing to do with relative cost or relative merit:

1. **Exclusion of illiquid trades.** Managed account platforms will routinely structure the investment to exclude a segment of the less liquid trades that may be placed in the counterpart fund. Insofar as these investments tend to be net profitable, which is to be expected, since they should embed an illiquidity premium, the managed account will lag the counterpart fund. But what is often forgotten is that the exclusion of these trades enables some of the important advantages of managed accounts, such as better redemption terms and the avoidance of gates and side pockets—attributes that would not be possible if there were illiquid holdings in the portfolio.
2. **Ramp-up period underperformance.** Typically, a managed account will launch after the fund has been operating for some time. When starting a new account, many managers will choose to initiate only new trades rather that preexisting ones, especially if these trades already embed large open profits. During the ramp-up period when the newer managed account does not include trades still held by the preexisting fund, the performance can diverge significantly between the fund and managed account portfolios. Insofar as there will be a bias for existing trades to be net profitable, the managed account performance would lag the fund during this period.

Investment Misconceptions

Investment Misconception 42: Thorough due diligence can provide the same benefits as managed accounts.

Reality: No matter how thoroughly a fund of funds conducts due diligence, it cannot compete with the safety provided by the direct account ownership and full transparency inherent in the managed account structure. There have been a multitude of instances wherein organizations with solid review and monitoring processes have been caught out by a manager taking on unexpected risks, which don't become apparent until it is too late. Typically, when a manager deviates from the risk guidelines described to investors and suffers a large loss, investors find out after the loss has occurred. Unless there is full transparency and real-time monitoring directly tied to the portfolio, there is no way to protect against such unpleasant surprises.

In a fund structure, in the absence of full transparency, even thorough monitoring may fail to uncover ongoing frauds. As one example based on an actual fraud, a rogue broker working for the prime broker conspired with the fund manager to create a hidden account, which they linked to the visible fund account. The investors (including many large funds of funds and institutions), as well as the administrator and auditor (both leading service providers) received access and statements only for the visible account. Meanwhile, the linked hidden account was racking up huge losses. When the fraud broke, the hidden account losses wiped out three-quarters of the assets of the fund account in one swoop. Such an event could not have occurred in a managed account structure, because direct investor ownership of the account would have made an unauthorized account linkage impossible.

Investment Misconception 43: The number of hedge fund managers accessible via managed accounts is very limited.

Reality: By definition, there are considerably fewer managers available as managed accounts because only a portion of the universe of hedge fund managers offer managed accounts. There are, nevertheless, far more than enough quality managers available via managed accounts to allow both ample choice and wide diversification in building a portfolio. Also, the number of managers who have established managed accounts or would be willing to do so (for the right size of investment) is substantially larger than the sum of all managers on managed account platforms. Finally, for highly liquid strategies, such as futures and FX trading, which are the types of strategies best suited for managed accounts, a large percentage of the managers are available as managed accounts.

Investment Misconception 44: Only poor-quality managers will offer managed accounts.

Reality: While there are certainly many excellent managers who do not offer managed accounts, there are also many who do. Moreover, the number of managers who offer managed accounts is steadily growing, as large institutional investors demand better account control and transparency. Investors seeking the safety of a managed account structure will have a smaller universe of available managers (vis-à-vis funds), but there are more than enough top-quality managers accessible via managed accounts to form a well-diversified portfolio.

Investment Misconception 45: Managed account investing is more expensive than traditional hedge fund investing.

Reality: This perception is based on superficial comparisons and fails to account for all the relevant factors. We examine the assertion that managed accounts are more expensive than funds separately for each of the three types of managed account investment:

1. **Direct investment.** For direct managed account investments, there are no additional fees, and investors large enough to go this route are often able to get a discount to the fund fee levels.
2. **Funds of managed accounts.** Fees charged by funds of managed accounts are similar to those charged by funds of funds. In addition, some of the advantages of the managed account structure

provide benefits that have monetary value (e.g., more prompt repayment of redeemed assets, more efficient use of investment capital, etc.).

3. **Managed account platforms.** While platforms do add another layer of fees, these fees are at least partially offset by less directly visible monetary benefits. If all the monetary benefits of managed accounts (implicit as well as explicit) are taken into account, the net additional expense incurred by using platforms is generally small.

Investment Insights

Managed accounts have many substantial advantages for the investor versus the more standard fund structure. For liquid investments, especially those available both as managed accounts and as funds, the arguments for preferring managed accounts seem compelling (assuming no significant cost differential). Managed accounts should continue to gain market share versus funds in the liquid strategy sphere. Even managers who are currently resistant to offering managed accounts may find themselves economically compelled to become more flexible, as they find more and more competitors offering managed accounts and experience a loss of assets under management as a result. This manager self-incentive should drive the number of managers available via managed accounts steadily higher. Managed accounts, however, are not well suited for illiquid strategies. The intention is not to suggest that managed accounts are a universal solution to hedge fund investing, but rather that managed accounts are the preferable investment structure wherever feasible and are an investment alternative whose market share is likely to grow steadily.

Postscript to Part Two: Are Hedge Fund Returns a Mirage?

As this book was entering its copyediting phase, I came across the following startling quote:

> If all the money that's ever been invested in hedge funds had been put in treasury bills instead, the results would have been twice as good.
>
> —Simon Lack

This opening line from Simon Lack's book, *The Hedge Fund Mirage* (John Wiley & Sons, 2012), may well be the most damning sentence ever written or uttered about hedge fund investment. But is it true? Well, it's a true statement about the wrong question. The question that Lack chose to focus on was: *How many total dollars have investors earned in hedge funds?* The appropriate question, however, is: *How much would an individual investor have earned assuming hedge fund index returns?*[1] Measuring the performance of hedge funds based on total dollars earned, as Lack does, is deeply flawed for two reasons:

1. Investors are terrible in timing and redeeming investments, and measuring performance based on cumulative dollars earned by investors blames managers for the poor timing decisions of investors. Lack reaches his conclusion because hedge funds' worst-performing year by far, 2008, occurred with hedge fund assets under management (AUM) at a relative peak. Lack states that "in 2008, the hedge fund industry lost more money than all the profits it had generated during the prior 10 years." But whose fault is that? Who is to blame for investments in hedge funds peaking right before the industry's worst year? If an individual investor had been invested in a fund of funds with index-like returns all along, would the 2008 loss have wiped out the investor's returns of the prior 10 years? Of course not. The returns would not be impacted by the fact that a lot of new investors chose to allocate to hedge funds in the year preceding the funds' large decline.

   Imagine if equity returns were based on equity investor returns instead of equity index returns. We don't have to imagine. Every year Dalbar, Inc. releases a report that compares investor returns with the S&P 500 index return. Dalbar's 2012 report showed that for the 20-year period ending in 2011, equity investors earned an average annual compounded return of 3.49 percent versus 7.81 percent for the S&P 500 index—a 4.32 percent per annum difference. Should we therefore conclude that equity returns for this period were over 4 percent lower than reported? Of course not. Any individual investor or institution could have achieved the index return with an index investment. The fact that investors as a group fared worse because of their poor timing of additions and withdrawals is irrelevant to the individual index investor.

---

[1]By hedge fund index we assume a fund of funds index that would not be subject to the multiple biases of an index based directly on manager returns (as was explained in Chapter 14).

2. Since there has been dramatic secular growth in hedge fund assets under management (AUM), the more recent years have undue weight. This could cut both ways, but since the biggest AUM year until very recently was the extremely poor-performing 2008, it creates a downward bias by measuring results in cumulative dollars.

So how have hedge fund returns fared compared to Treasury bills? Using the same hedge fund index Lack used, the HFRX Global index, and the same starting year, 1998, the average annual compounded return through the end of 2011 would have been 5.49 percent for the hedge fund index versus 2.69 percent for T-bills. Thus the statistics show that hedge fund returns were more than double T-bill returns, not half as much as Lack contends. Admittedly, beating T-bill returns by 2.8 percent per annum is not terribly impressive. But consider that during the same period, the S&P 500 generated an average annual compounded return only 1.0 percent above T-bills with far greater volatility and drawdowns.

Although I believe Lack's evaluation of hedge fund performance is based on faulty assumptions and hence is incorrect, I do not want this commentary to be construed as a broad-based criticism of his book, *The Hedge Fund Mirage*. On the contrary, with the exception of the measurement of hedge fund performance—which admittedly is a pretty big exception—I am in general agreement with many of the other opinions Lack expressed in his book, which include:

- Hedge fund fees are too high relative to the value they deliver to investors (albeit this is an inevitable consequence of the laws of supply and demand).
- The early history of hedge fund returns is irrelevant to current investors because those returns were achieved when the hedge fund industry was much smaller. Now that hedge funds have grown so much, and there is much more competition to exploit the same inefficiencies and many hedge funds are too large to take advantage of less liquid trading opportunities, it is highly unlikely that the industry will again approach the returns of those earlier years.
- Although institutional investors almost invariably invest only in large hedge funds, the available data tends to suggest that small hedge funds perform better than large hedge funds.

Part Three

PORTFOLIO MATTERS

Chapter 17

Diversification: Why 10 Is Not Enough

The Benefits of Diversification

As long as investments are not highly correlated, increasing the number of holdings will reduce portfolio volatility and the magnitude of equity drawdowns, since low to moderately correlated assets will not necessarily witness losses at the same time. For highly correlated assets (e.g., mutual funds), however, more diversification will drive the portfolio toward index-like returns with minimal reduction in portfolio volatility.

Although the straightforward benefit of diversification is reduced risk, this benefit can be partially, or even totally, transformed into higher return. For example, assume that additional diversification leaves the expected return unchanged, but reduces risk levels by about 50 percent. There are three ways the portfolio manager can utilize this risk reduction:

1. Do nothing, which will result in a portfolio with approximately unchanged expected return, but half the risk of the starting portfolio.
2. Leverage the new portfolio 100 percent, which will double the expected return level and leave risk approximately unchanged.
3. Leverage between 0 percent and 100 percent, which will divide the diversification benefit between return and risk, with the relative proportions of each dependent on the degree of leverage.

Diversification: How Much Is Enough?

There is a perception fostered by academic literature that the benefits of diversification are mostly realized in the first 10 investments and further improvements beyond that point are modest.[1] The reason these results are obtained is that the effect of diversification is measured as the average over many tests (say 10,000 samples for each portfolio size), rather than as the impact on the worst cases.

As an illustrative example, assume that 5 percent of 10-manager portfolios contain one of a subset of very poorly performing funds that lose an average of 50 percent. The impact on any portfolio that contains one of these funds will be a 5 percent loss (one-tenth of 50 percent, assuming equal allocation). The impact on the *average* of all 10-manager portfolios, however, will be only 0.25 percent (zero impact on 95 percent of portfolios and 5 percent impact on the remaining 5 percent[2]). In a 30-manager portfolio, the average loss impact would still be 0.25 percent, as the probability of including one of the large losing funds would be tripled while the portfolio impact would be one-third as large.. Although the impact on the average might not change with portfolio size, for any fund of funds manager unfortunate enough to invest in one of these extremely

[1] In this chapter the term *investments* refers to manager portfolios rather than securities as is more typically the case.

[2] To be precise, if the probability of one poorly performing fund in a portfolio was 5 percent, the probability of no poor funds would be only about 94.9 percent because there would also be a small number of portfolios with two or more poorly performing funds. But because the probability of such two-or-more-poor-fund portfolios is relatively small (about 0.1 percent if the probability of one such fund in a 10-manager portfolio is 5 percent), as a simplifying assumption, we ignore this possibility to avoid unnecessarily complicating the exposition.

poorly performing funds, the loss impact would be three times greater in the 10-manager portfolio than in the 30-manager portfolio. So from the perspective of the individual fund of funds manager who is concerned about limiting the worst-case loss for the portfolio, there can be very appreciable benefits to diversification beyond 10 managers.

There are two ways in which insufficient diversification can increase risk:

1. **Randomness risk.** The smaller the number of funds, the greater the probability that a specified percentage of the funds will experience a loss in the same month *purely as a function of chance.*
2. **Idiosyncratic risk.** This is the implied portfolio loss due to a single investment experiencing a highly unrepresentative loss far in excess of worst-case expectations for that investment.

We will examine each of these effects in turn.

Randomness Risk

Of course, if investments in a portfolio are correlated, and especially if they are significantly correlated, months in which a large majority of holdings experience a loss would be common. However, we assume that investments are chosen so that they are uncorrelated, or nearly so. Even when this is done, though, months will occur when a substantial majority of the funds lose money, a phenomenon frequently referred to as "correlations going to one." Under certain tumultuous market conditions or events, even previously uncorrelated investments can lose money at the same time. A common thread is that such periods are exemplified by heavy liquidation phases that can distort normal market relationships and simultaneously affect normally unrelated markets.

What is less well recognized, however, is that even when the "correlations going to one" effect is not an issue and a portfolio consists of uncorrelated assets, a large percentage of holdings can exhibit losses for reasons of chance alone. Moreover, this randomness risk increases at an accelerated rate as the number of holdings is reduced.

Figures 17.1 and 17.2 illustrate the relationship between the number of funds in a portfolio and the probability that the percentage of

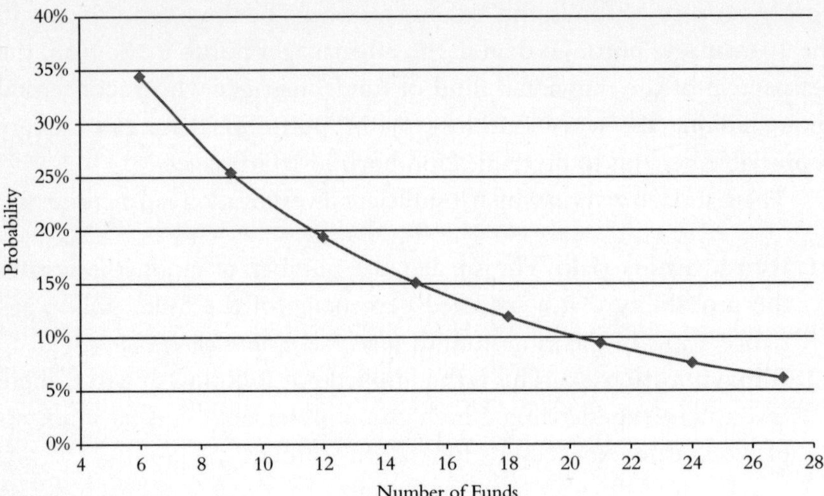

Figure 17.1 Probability of Two-Thirds or More of Funds in Portfolio Declining

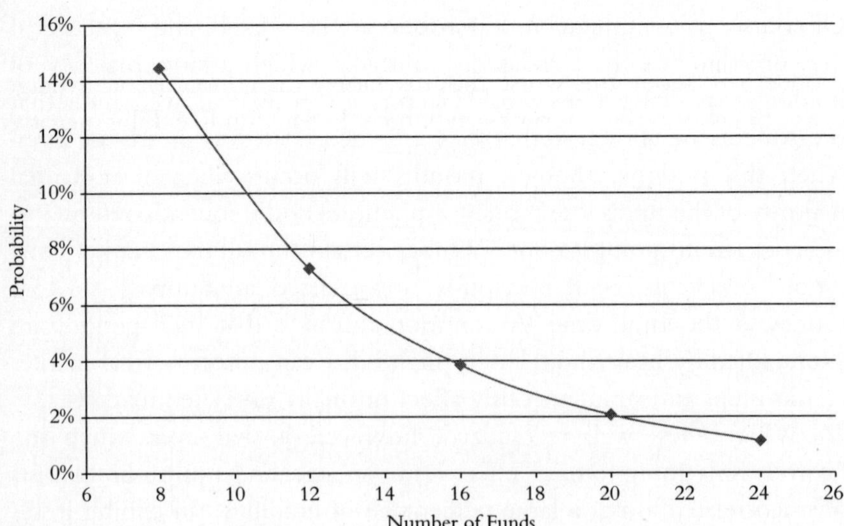

Figure 17.2 Probability of Three-Quarters or More of Funds in Portfolio Declining

losing funds will exceed the specified thresholds (two-thirds and three-quarters). The three assumptions used to calculate these probabilities are:

1. The individual holdings are completely uncorrelated.
2. There is an equal chance of each fund winning or losing in a given month.
3. For each fund, the sizes of wins and losses are equivalent.[3]

In regard to assumption 1, although most portfolios exhibit some correlation between holdings, this is not a problem, since any correlation will only increase the probabilities of exceeding some given percentage of losers for each specified number of funds. Thus the presence of any correlation would only serve to exacerbate the effect of reducing diversification as the number of funds decline. In effect, assumption 1 is a very conservative baseline assumption.

In regard to assumptions 2 and 3, they implicitly assume that funds in the portfolio will have a zero return on average. Insofar as funds in a portfolio are likely to have net positive returns, it may appear that these assumptions will exaggerate the implied probability of losses and the effect of reducing the number of funds. Although this may be true on balance across all months, it is important to emphasize that we are most concerned about the worst months rather than months on average. In difficult months—months in which hedge funds exhibit negative returns—it is reasonable to assume that there would be a bias toward negative returns for the funds in the portfolio as well. Thus, in these months in which hedge fund portfolios are most likely to exhibit a drawdown, the assumption of an average zero return for all funds may be a conservative assumption as well; that is, it will mitigate the potential impact of reduced diversification on the probability and magnitude of a loss.

As can be seen in Figure 17.1, under the aforementioned assumptions, when there are only six funds, the probability of at least two-thirds

[3]If this assumption were not true—for example, if wins were significantly larger than losses—then the percentage of losing funds would be an insufficient statistic upon which to draw conclusions, since a majority of losses might not necessarily imply an expected portfolio loss (that is, it could be offset by the differential between wins and losses).

being losers is over 34 percent. Also note that going from 10 funds to 18 funds halves the probability of getting two-thirds or more losing funds—hardly the minimal diversification benefit beyond 10 holdings generally implied by academic studies.

As can be seen in Figure 17.2, the probability of getting three-quarters or more losing funds—an outcome likely to be associated with a significant losing month for the portfolio—is a substantial 14 percent when there are only eight funds in the portfolio. This probability decreases by a factor of more than three (falling to under 4 percent) when the number of funds increases to 16. Once again, the diversification effect beyond 10 is highly substantial.

Idiosyncratic Risk

Individual hedge funds can sometimes witness much worse losses than might have been anticipated based on their prior track records or strategies. One of the most important benefits of diversification is diluting the impact of outlier losses in single funds. Clearly, the larger the number of funds in a portfolio, the smaller the impact of a single fund experiencing a catastrophic loss. Table 17.1 and Figure 17.3 illustrate the relationship between portfolio loss and the number of funds in a portfolio. For example, assuming equal weighting, having a single fund lose 30 percent would cause the portfolio to decline by nearly 4 percent when there are only eight funds, but by less than 1 percent when there are 32 funds. This mitigation of the impact of a single fund experiencing

Table 17.1 Idiosyncratic Risk: Single Fund Loss Impact versus Portfolio Size

Number of Funds	10%	20%	30%	40%	50%
8	1.3%	2.5%	3.8%	5.0%	6.3%
12	0.8%	1.7%	2.5%	3.3%	4.2%
16	0.6%	1.3%	1.9%	2.5%	3.1%
20	0.5%	1.0%	1.5%	2.0%	2.5%
24	0.4%	0.8%	1.3%	1.7%	2.1%
28	0.4%	0.7%	1.1%	1.4%	1.8%
32	0.3%	0.6%	0.9%	1.3%	1.6%

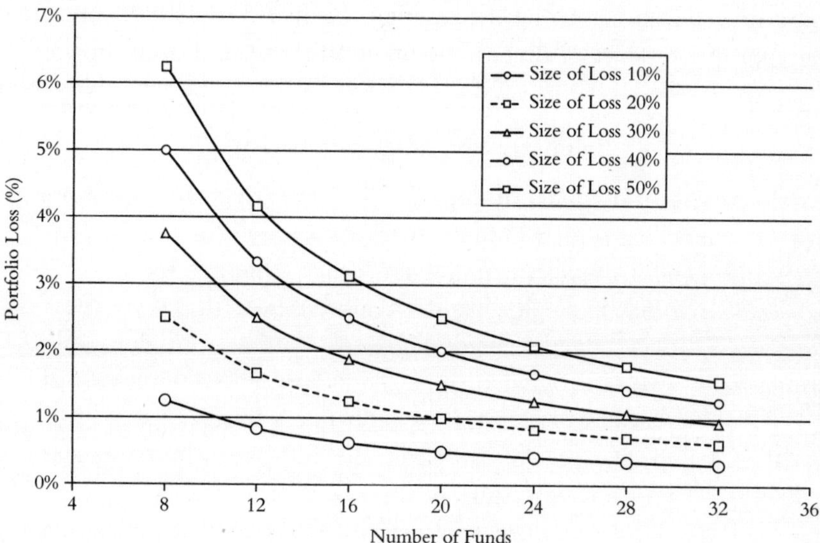

Figure 17.3 Idiosyncratic Risk: Single Fund Loss Impact versus Portfolio Size

a large loss is perhaps the most critical benefit of diversification and is a factor that remains important well beyond 10 funds.

A Qualification

The analysis in this chapter and the argument in favor of diversification assume that added investments are as attractive as existing investments. If, however, diversification requires extending the portfolio to include less desirable investments, the net benefit of diversification can no longer be assumed. In this case, the investor must weigh the trade-off of including second-tier investments versus the benefit of reduced risk provided by diversification.

In fact, if carried to an extreme, diversification would guarantee mediocrity by leading to index-like performance. If an index return is desirable, then it can be achieved much more efficiently by investing directly in an index or a fund that benchmarks the index. It follows that insofar as a goal of any investment process is, presumably, to surpass index performance, then diversification must, by definition, be limited. Although diversification is beneficial, if not essential, beyond some point more diversification can be detrimental. Each investor must determine the appropriate level of diversification as an individual decision.

Investment Misconception

Investment Misconception 46: The diversification benefits beyond 10 holdings are minimal (even for heterogeneous investment universes such as hedge funds).

Reality: Research studies that conclude that diversification benefits beyond 10 are minimal are invariably based on what happens *on average* across thousands of portfolios rather than what happens in the *worst case* to a specific portfolio (that is, tail risk). Most investors and portfolio managers, however, are very much concerned about the worst-case risk for their portfolios, not what happens on average across all portfolios. For these investors, diversification well beyond 10 can provide substantial risk-reduction benefits. How many more beyond 10 will be case dependent, but generally speaking, 20 or more will be a better choice than 10 (as long as added investments are of equivalent quality and sufficiently diversified with other managers to reduce the average correlation of managers in the portfolio).

Investment Insights

Although, in terms of the average across a large sample of portfolios, the major portion of diversification benefits is realized by simply diversifying to 10, in terms of worst-case outcomes for any single portfolio, diversification beyond 10 can still provide large reductions in risk. Thus, while the average value of any risk statistic measured across all portfolios may not be significantly lower for 30-manager portfolios than for 10-manager portfolios, for any individual portfolio, increasing the number of managers from 10 to 30 can reduce maximum risk very substantially.

For an individual portfolio, diversification beyond 10 provides the following two important benefits:

1. It significantly reduces the probability of experiencing any specified large percentage of losers in the portfolio in a single month (randomness risk).
2. It dramatically reduces the impact of a single fund witnessing an unusually large loss (idiosyncratic risk).

In effect, both these influences serve to substantially reduce the worst-case situations, or equivalently, the potential worst maximum drawdown for the portfolio.

The key benefit of extra diversification is catastrophe insurance. This benefit remains very strong going from 10 to 20 funds and remains very significant even beyond 20 funds. Confusing when one should be concerned with the worst case instead of the average can have devastating results. Incredibly, when the Army Corps of Engineers designed the New Orleans levee system, they built a system that was adequate based on the *average* soil strength instead of the *weakest* soil strength.

Chapter 18

Diversification: When More Is Less

Fred, a research analyst at a fund of funds firm, is given the task of constructing a portfolio of futures, global macro, and foreign exchange (FX) managers. After some research, he reports back to his boss, Sam, with a suggested five-manager portfolio shown in Table 18.1. The five managers have an average annualized return of 10.57 percent and an average annualized standard deviation of 15.74 percent. The average maximum drawdown of the five managers is 23.64 percent. Because of the benefits of diversification, the portfolio statistics are far better: an annualized return of 11.54 percent with a standard deviation of only 8.01 percent and a much reduced maximum drawdown of 6.56 percent.

Sam reviews the suggested portfolio and then calls Fred into his office. "The managers you picked appear to be an interesting mix," he says, "but I am troubled that there are only five managers in the

Table 18.1 Five-Manager Portfolio Statistics, January 2001 to June 2010

Manager	Average Annual Compounded Return (%)	Annualized Standard Deviation (%)	Maximum Drawdown (%)	Return/ Standard Deviation Ratio	Return/ Maximum Drawdown Ratio
Argonaut	15.17	13.02	12.23	1.17	1.24
Conquest	11.81	17.62	22.64	0.67	0.52
QFS Currency	5.71	14.32	18.83	0.40	0.30
Mapleridge (2.5×)	10.28	14.21	29.85	0.72	0.34
Forecast	9.86	19.52	34.6	0.51	0.28
Average	**10.57**	**15.74**	**23.64**	**0.69**	**0.54**
Portfolio	**11.54**	**8.01**	**6.56**	**1.44**	**1.76**

portfolio. We need to have much more diversification. I would like to add these 10 managers I have been looking at." He hands Fred the list of managers in Table 18.2.

Sam continues, "Interestingly, the average return of my 10 managers is almost identical to the average return of your five managers (10.50 percent versus 10.57 percent), and the risk statistics are virtually equivalent—the average standard deviation is slightly higher (16.68 percent versus 15.74 percent), but the average maximum drawdown is slightly lower (22.03 percent versus 23.64 percent). So this group of managers appears almost exactly equivalent to your managers in terms of performance, but adding them will triple the number of managers in the portfolio and give us the diversification we need. Run the statistics on this combined 15-manager portfolio and get back to me."

Fred does the analysis. He is surprised to discover that tripling the number of managers in the portfolio significantly increases the portfolio risk, even though, on average, the added managers had equivalent risk statistics to the original managers. The results are shown in Table 18.3. The portfolio average annual return does not change much—it falls slightly from 11.5 percent to 11.3 percent—but the risk statistics deteriorate significantly: The portfolio standard deviation increases by more than a third from 8.0 percent to 10.9 percent, and the maximum drawdown nearly doubles from 6.6 percent to 12.0 percent.

Table 18.2 Ten Added Manager Statistics, January 2001 to June 2010

Manager	Average Annual Compounded Return (%)	Annualized Standard Deviation (%)	Maximum Drawdown (%)	Return/ Standard Deviation Ratio	Return/ Maximum Drawdown Ratio
Transtrend	13.47	11.9	15.15	1.13	0.89
FTC	7.27	22.48	33.77	0.32	0.22
Aspect	9.69	17.42	21.52	0.56	0.45
Rabar	7.05	16.3	24.42	0.43	0.29
Millburn Diversified	6.79	15.42	22.79	0.44	0.30
Graham K4	15.19	20.96	29.84	0.72	0.51
Lynx	14.67	13.96	11.96	1.05	1.23
DKR	8.5	9.88	9.78	0.86	0.87
Eagle	11.74	22.34	32.08	0.53	0.37
Sunrise	10.67	16.09	18.95	0.66	0.56
Average	**10.50**	**16.68**	**22.03**	**0.67**	**0.57**

Table 18.3 Fifteen-Manager versus Five-Manager Portfolio Statistics

	Five-Manager Portfolio	15-Manager Portfolio
Average annual compounded return (%)	11.54	11.31
Annualized standard deviation (%)	8.01	10.86
Maximum drawdown (%)	6.56	12.04
Return/standard deviation ratio	1.44	1.04
Return/maximum drawdown ratio	1.76	0.94

What is going on? Why does adding more managers with equivalent performance cause the portfolio volatility to increase—the exact opposite effect sought by the additional diversification? The answer is that diversification depends not only on the number of managers, but also on the degree of correlation among the managers (versus each other and the total portfolio). Fred's original five-manager portfolio consisted of managers that were almost completely uncorrelated with each other: an average pair correlation of 0.07. In contrast, Sam's list of 10 managers all employed a similar methodology—systematic trend following—and therefore were highly correlated with each other (an average pair correlation of 0.69). As a result, rather than reducing risk through diversification, adding these managers was roughly equivalent to adding one grossly oversized position to the portfolio. If Sam had instead suggested adding a single manager to the original five, but at 10 times the allocation size of the other managers, we would intuitively expect the risk to increase. The situation is not much different when instead of adding one manager with 10 times the allocation size of other managers, we instead add 10 highly correlated managers.

The diversification of Fred's original five-manager portfolio would still be unsatisfactory due to its exposure to the randomness and idiosyncratic risks detailed in the previous chapter, but it would nonetheless be better diversified than the 15-manager portfolio. The critical point is that for diversification to work, the investments added to the portfolio must have a low average correlation to the existing investments and to each other.

The lesson to investors is that you can't judge the diversification of a multimanager portfolio by the number of managers. Some types of portfolios may be particularly prone to unsatisfactory diversification, even if the number of managers appears more than sufficient. One example is commodity trading advisor (CTA) portfolios, similar to the one we described in our illustration. Since the majority of CTAs utilize systematic trend-following techniques and most such approaches are highly correlated with each other, CTA portfolios can often be poorly diversified, even if they contain a large number of managers. As another example, long/short equity hedge portfolios are vulnerable to insufficient diversification because the majority of managers in this trading strategy style are significantly correlated to the equity market. In fact, for some strategies (e.g., convertible arbitrage), it would be virtually impossible to create a well-diversified portfolio, because manager performance is often more dependent on the investment environment for the strategy than on the manager's own individual methodology.

How can an investor judge whether a portfolio is insufficiently diversified? A simple gauge and an easily obtainable statistic is the average pair correlation—that is, the average of all manager pair correlations in the portfolio. For example, in a 20-manager portfolio, there would be 190 possible manager pairs and therefore 190 pair correlations. The average of these correlations provides an indicator of the degree of diversification in a portfolio. Any portfolio manager should be able to easily provide the investor with the average pair correlation for the portfolio. Although there are no clear-cut definitions of what constitutes adequate or inadequate diversification, I would suggest the following broad guidelines for the portfolio average pair correlation: A value greater than 0.50 reflects inadequate diversification; a value between 0.30 and 0.50 suggests that diversification is somewhat inadequate; a value less than 0.20 indicates that the managers are very well diversified. There are, however, circumstances when unsatisfactory diversification may be entirely acceptable. Specifically, if a portfolio is being considered as a component of a broader mix of investments, the fact that it is not adequately diversified as a standalone investment may not be a problem if it is well diversified with the other holdings in the investor's total portfolio.

Investment Misconception

Investment Misconception 47: Increasing the number of investments in a portfolio will increase diversification and reduce risk (assuming added investments are equivalent to existing investments in return and risk terms).

Reality: Increasing the number of investments can actually increase portfolio risk if the added investments are highly correlated to other portfolio holdings or each other.

Investment Insights

Increasing the number of investments in a portfolio can sometimes lead to less diversification rather than more. Diversification is a function of both the number of holdings and, even more importantly, the degree to which they are uncorrelated. A portfolio with a small number of uncorrelated holdings is effectively more diversified than a portfolio with a large number of significantly correlated assets.

Chapter 19

Robin Hood Investing

Many years ago, I worked for a brokerage firm where in addition to being the research director, I was also the department expert on the quantitative evaluation of commodity trading advisors (CTAs). This job responsibility got me thinking about better methods for constructing multimanager funds. At one point, it became apparent to me that if all the managers had equivalent expected future performance, the return/risk ratio would be increased if the total equity were rebalanced monthly, bringing the managers back to an equal percentage allocation.[1]

The assumption that all managers would have equivalent future performance did not mean that such an outcome was expected literally, but rather that one could not predict anything about the relative ranking order of the *future* performance of the selected managers. (Although the

[1]If the managers have disparate risk levels, it would make more sense to define equal allocation in risk-adjusted terms (rather than equal dollar terms)—a concept discussed in Chapter 21. Doing so would not alter the conclusions of this chapter.

past ranking order was certainly known, my implicit assumption was that the past ranking was a very poor indicator of the future ranking.)

The following analogy occurred to me: The assumption of equivalent performance could be thought of as monthly performance results being represented by a series of cards—each card representing one month—with each manager's set of results corresponding to a different shuffle of the same cards. Since all managers are assumed to have the same set of monthly results (that is, the same set of cards in a different order), and since reduced variability implies increased return (see Chapter 5), it seemed that the return/risk ratio based on the average of cards in each month—the mathematical equivalent of a monthly rebalancing—would have to be equal to or higher than the return of any individual set of cards (that is, the performance of each manager). In other words, if one had no a priori reason to believe that any manager in the selected group would perform better in the future than the other managers, a monthly rebalancing of equity would yield an equal or higher end return than a static one-time allocation.

As a very simple example to provide a feel of the preceding conclusion, assume a two-manager fund with a two-month performance period, in which Manager A makes 10 percent in the first month and loses 5 percent in the second, while Manager B witnesses the reverse order of monthly results. The respective net asset values (NAVs) would then be:

$$\begin{aligned}
\text{Manager A NAV} &= 1{,}000 \times 1.10 \times 0.95 = 1{,}045 \\
\text{Manager B NAV} &= 1{,}000 \times 0.95 \times 1.10 = 1{,}045 \\
\text{Fund with rebalancing} &= 1{,}000 \times 1.025 \times 1.025 = 1{,}050.6 \\
\text{Fund without rebalancing} &= (1{,}045 + 1{,}045)/2 = 1{,}045
\end{aligned}$$

In each month, one manager gains 10% on half the assets (or 5% on total assets), while the other manager loses 5% on the other half of assets (or 2.5% on total assets). Therefore in each month, there is a net gain of 5% – 2.5% = 2.5%.

Note in this simple example that the monthly rebalancing fund realizes a higher return than the fund that does not rebalance assets.

To check whether the idea of monthly rebalancing held up in the real world, I conducted the following empirical experiment. I selected 30 groups of six managers each from the available database. For each group I calculated the NAV over a three-year period for the following two situations:

1. An equal allocation of equity to start, with no further reallocations.
2. Monthly rebalancing (back to equal allocations), augmented by a 1.25 leverage factor (since monthly rebalancing reduced risk, part of the benefit was put back on the return side by using increased leverage).

I found that the leveraged/rebalanced fund almost invariably outperformed the fund without rebalancing. Even more striking, however, was the observation that the return of the leveraged/rebalanced fund was usually about in line with the best or second-best manager in the group, while the maximum drawdown and standard deviation (measures of risk) were about in line with the lowest or second-lowest figures among the group of managers. In other words, by employing a monthly rebalancing strategy with leverage, it was possible to approximate the return of the best return managers in the group and the risk of the best (lowest) risk managers in the group. In effect, rebalancing with leverage was a means of optimizing the *future* performance—achieving return/risk characteristics in line with those managers in a selected group who would perform best in the *future*.

I was very excited about my discovery. I next tried to convince management at my company of the logic and attractiveness of a multimanager fund that would be structured around the concept of monthly rebalancing and leverage. A number of meetings ensued, but I felt my idea was going nowhere. Then I struck upon the idea of applying my rebalancing/leverage strategy to a hypothetical fund consisting of the firm's five single-manager funds, most of which had disappointing track records and therefore, not surprisingly, were regarded with less than enthusiasm by management. As it turned out, the theoretical multimanager fund I constructed using my strategy had a performance profile that was only slightly inferior to the best manager in the group and far superior to the four other managers. Since the best manager could only have been selected with hindsight, the potential advantage of my approach seemed both obvious and compelling.

"This should clinch it," I thought. I made some color charts illustrating these performance comparisons and set up another meeting with the division manager whose approval was vital. After I completed my 15-minute presentation, I leaned back, waiting for the division head to extol the wisdom of my proposal.

Instead he exclaimed, "You mean you want to take from the winners and give to the losers!" in a tone that suggested I had just proposed the virtues of matricide.

"No," I replied, "you're missing the point. The assumption is that we believe all the managers in the fund are winners—that's presumably why we picked them in the first place. What we are doing is taking from winners during their winning periods and giving it to other winners during their losing periods." But all the logic in the world could not prevail. The division head simply could not get beyond the "shocking" nature of my proposal. My idea never went anywhere.

A New Test

In reconsidering this episode for this book, I realized my original analysis was flawed. The database I used to draw my samples contained only active managers (that is, surviving managers). I could not pick managers who had gone out of business—a group more likely to exhibit poor performance. If I had drawn samples that included defunct managers, perhaps monthly rebalancing, which effectively was equivalent to taking from the winners and giving to the losers, would not have been beneficial. Possibly, it might even have been detrimental. In short, my original analysis was subject to survivorship bias. There was no way of telling whether the apparent large benefit I found in rebalancing in my original analysis was sufficient to overcome this bias.

To test the rebalancing concept in a new analysis that avoided survivorship bias, I obtained the complete CTA database from Stark & Company (www.starkresearch.com)—a data set that included both existing and defunct managers. I randomly selected 10 portfolios of 10 managers each from this complete list,[2] assuming equal allocations and a

[2]I used the Excel function Randbetween to generate 100 random numbers (10 portfolios times 10 managers) with a top threshold set equal to the total number of all active and defunct managers in the database.

January 1, 2005, start date. I then compared the total period (2005 to 2010) portfolio results obtained assuming no further allocation adjustments with the results obtained by rebalancing the portfolios to equal allocations each month.

The rules for handling managers who went out of business were simple:

- **No-rebalancing portfolio.** The remaining assets at the time the CTA stopped operating were assumed placed in Treasury bills for the remainder of the test period.
- **Rebalanced portfolio.** The defunct CTA was replaced by a T-bill investment, which continued to be rebalanced to an equal allocation with the other investments each month (10 percent allocation). If, for example, three CTAs had terminated operations as of a certain month, 30 percent of the portfolio's allocation each month would be placed in T-bills.

Table 19.1 compares the portfolio rank versus the underlying CTAs in each portfolio in terms of return (average annual compounded), standard deviation (a risk proxy),[3] and the return/risk ratio. Since there are 11 items being ranked in each case (the portfolio and its 10 component investments), the median rank is six. The best performance ranking is "1" and the worst "11." For the standard deviation, lower values are defined as better ranking (that is, lower rank number). Both sets of portfolios (with and without rebalancing) rank significantly better than the median levels in terms of return, standard deviation, and the return/risk ratio, a clear demonstration of the benefits of diversification. The average rank for return is the same for both portfolios with and without rebalancing, but the portfolios with rebalancing generate better ranks for both risk and return/risk.

Table 19.2 compares the no-rebalancing and rebalancing portfolios in terms of return/risk—the key measure. (A portfolio with higher return/risk but lower return than another portfolio can be made to generate a higher return with equal or lower risk by using leverage.) The rebalanced

[3]For CTAs who trade highly liquid futures, hidden risk (as detailed in Chapter 4) is not usually a problem, and the standard deviation (a volatility measure) is a reasonable proxy for risk.

Table 19.1 Ranks of Portfolios versus CTAs in Portfolios

	Return		**Standard Deviation**		**Return/ SD Ratio**	
Portfolio	**No Rebalancing**	**Rebalancing**	**No Rebalancing**	**Rebalancing**	**No Rebalancing**	**Rebalancing**
1	5	3	5	5	5	4
2	4	5	2	2	1	1
3	5	5	4	4	3	3
4	3	5	4	3	2	1
5	5	5	5	4	3	2
6	4	5	1	1	1	1
7	4	4	3	3	4	4
8	5	5	4	4	6	6
9	6	4	4	4	4	2
10	5	5	7	6	3	3
Average	**4.6**	**4.6**	**3.9**	**3.6**	**3.2**	**2.7**

Table 19.2 Portfolio Return/Risk Comparison

Portfolio	No Rebalancing	Rebalancing	Rebalancing as Percentage of No Rebalancing
1	0.49	0.63	1.29%
2	1.57	1.64	1.04
3	0.62	0.75	1.20
4	2.03	2.44	1.20
5	0.86	1.01	1.17
6	2.38	2.37	0.99
7	0.41	0.46	1.12
8	0.18	0.29	1.60
9	0.85	0.99	1.16
10	1.28	1.27	0.99
		Average	**1.18%**

Table 19.3 Percentage of Portfolios for Which Rebalancing Outperforms No Rebalancing

	Rebalancing	Rebalancing with 10% Leverage
Return	50%	80%
Standard deviation	80%	70%
Return/SD ratio	80%	80%

portfolio generated a higher return/risk ratio in eight of the 10 portfolios, and the two exceptions were only marginally lower. On average, the rebalanced portfolios had an 18 percent higher return/risk ratio.

Table 19.3 shows the percentage of the portfolios for which rebalancing resulted in better performance for each of three metrics: return, standard deviation (proxy for risk), and return/standard deviation ratio. Rebalancing resulted in lower risk and higher return/risk in 80 percent of the portfolios, but provided a higher return only half the time. Since rebalancing reduces volatility in most of the portfolios, Table 19.3 also looks at the same comparison for a portfolio with rebalancing and a modest 10 percent leverage. This slight modification resulted in 80 percent of the portfolios with rebalancing outperforming the portfolios without rebalancing in terms of both return and return/risk, with 70 percent of the portfolios still having lower risk.

As Tables 19.2 and 19.3 illustrate, in our trial, which fully eliminated survivorship bias, rebalancing still seemed to provide significant performance improvement. These results offer empirical evidence that supports the hypothesis that rebalancing—routinely "taking from the winners and giving to the losers"—will tend to improve performance, but it by no means proves this contention. A more conclusive test would have required repeating the experiment for far more than 10 randomly selected portfolios—a requirement that exceeded both my patience in repeating Excel spreadsheet calculation steps and my programming ability, which is nil. Readers, however, can duplicate the same comparison between rebalancing and no rebalancing on the past returns of their own portfolios. Although some readers who conduct this experiment will find that rebalancing actually would have been detrimental, I believe most will discover that it would have been beneficial. The comparison should be made in terms of return/risk, not return, since rebalancing will tend to lower risk, a benefit that, if desired, can be translated into higher return through leverage.

Why Rebalancing Works

If the managers in a portfolio had identical performance (defined as identical monthly returns in different orders), it would be a mathematical certainty that rebalancing would improve performance. This point was demonstrated in nonrigorous fashion at the start of this chapter using the card shuffling analogy. Therefore, if there is no strong reason to expect one or more of the selected managers in a portfolio to outperform the other managers in the *future*, rebalancing would provide a mathematical edge.

At different times, market conditions will be favorable for different strategies. A strategy that works particularly well during one period may perform very poorly in another period. For example, if markets are generally experiencing choppy trading-range conditions, countertrend strategies are likely to do very well, while trend-following approaches get whipsawed. If market conditions then change so that there are many prevalent trends, trend-following methods will be very profitable, while countertrend traders will suffer losses. Rebalancing keeps the asset allocation among the different market strategies represented by different managers constant. Without rebalancing, assets would be more heavily concentrated in the strategies that worked best in the past. If market conditions then change, the largest asset allocations would be in the strategies that are most vulnerable. In effect, rebalancing helps mitigate the negative impact of the inevitable shifts in market conditions, which can result in being overweight, an outperforming strategy when that strategy has run its course and is about to turn negative; and being underweight, a strategy that is about to have a huge run.

Another way of understanding why rebalancing works is that it effectively forces profit taking when a manager witnesses an upside excursion and increases investment when a manager experiences a drawdown. Therefore, when a manager witnesses the inevitable retracement following an especially profitable run, the investment with that manager will be smaller than it would have been without rebalancing. Conversely, when a manager experiences a rebound after a drawdown, the investment with that manager will be greater than it would have been without rebalancing.

A Clarification

For simplicity of exposition, in this chapter we have assumed that rebalancing means a return to equal allocations each month. Rebalancing, however, neither requires nor implies equal allocation. Frequently, there will be good reason to use unequal allocations among managers. For example, it would be entirely reasonable, if not preferable, to give smaller allocations to higher-risk managers. If allocations are unequal, rebalancing would simply mean returning to the target allocations each month. For example, if a portfolio manager decides that because of higher risk, Manager A should get half the allocation of other managers, rebalancing would adjust the allocations to maintain this ratio in subsequent months.

Investment Misconception

Investment Misconception 48: In a multimanager portfolio, performance can be improved by increasing the allocations to managers who are doing well and reducing the allocations to those who are underperforming.

Reality: More often than not, doing the exact opposite, as is implicit in routinely rebalancing the portfolio, will provide a better outcome. Of course, a portfolio manager may decide to redeem a manager for any number of reasons, which is an entirely different matter. But as long as a manager is retained in the portfolio, increasing allocations after underperformance periods and decreasing allocations after outperformance periods is usually a better strategy.

Investment Insights

Theoretical arguments and empirical evidence suggest that monthly rebalancing of equity provides a means of enhancing the expected return/risk characteristics of multimanager portfolios. This does not mean that the use of rebalancing would improve the performance (that is, increase the return/risk ratio) of every multimanager fund; it does, however, mean that rebalancing would probably improve the performance of a majority of such funds. In other words, for any given multimanager fund, the odds favor that the use of rebalancing would enhance performance. Portfolio managers and investors can test rebalancing on their own portfolios by comparing their actual results with the results that would have been obtained if allocations were rebalanced to their initial allocation percentages each month.[4]

---

[4]Such a test would be complicated by the addition or redemption of holdings, as is likely to occur over time. One simplifying assumption for handling such situations is to rebalance monthly to the same percentage allocations that prevailed in the last month in which there was a portfolio change. In effect, the percentage allocation targets used for rebalancing would change each time there was a portfolio addition or redemption.

Given the apparent advantage of rebalancing, why is this method typically unused? The answer to this question is simple: human nature. The idea of shifting assets from traders who have just performed best in a given portfolio to those who performed worst goes against natural human instincts. Following these instincts, however, will usually lead to incorrect market decisions. One of the requirements for success in the markets is the ability to make decisions based on evidence, not based on what feels comfortable.

Chapter 20

Is High Volatility Always Bad?

It is widely assumed that when two funds have similar returns and are equivalent in all other respects (e.g., exposure to event risk, quality of personnel and operations, etc.), the fund with lower volatility is the better investment. On the face of it, the assumption that higher volatility is a negative attribute certainly seems reasonable. Although this assumption is true in most circumstances, its actual validity is dependent on a factor that is often overlooked. Sometimes, higher volatility doesn't matter or can even be beneficial.

On one occasion, I went to interview managers of a fund that was located in an off-the-beaten-path location. After I was done, I went to visit a fund of funds manager I knew who was located in the same region. At one point, our conversation turned to the fund I had just visited. I naturally assumed he knew the fund since there were few hedge funds in the area. It turned out that he not only knew the fund, but had worked with one of the managers for 12 years at another firm. His comments about the manager were favorable.

"Are you invested in his fund?" I asked.

"No," he replied.

"Can I ask why not?"

"Well, they have a Sharpe ratio of only about 0.4," he replied.

"I know," I said, "but that is because they have high volatility and since they are inversely correlated to everything else, high volatility is not a relevant factor. In fact, for an inversely correlated fund, high volatility may actually be beneficial. So a measure such as the Sharpe ratio, which penalizes volatility, is not meaningful here."

He seemed skeptical, to say the least. He seemed convinced that as long as a fund's return-to-volatility ratio was relatively low, it was not worth considering as a portfolio addition. The flaw in this line of thinking is that an investment must be viewed not only for its stand-alone characteristics, but also for its impact on the portfolio. For funds that are correlated to the portfolio for which they are being considered as an addition, a stand-alone evaluation may be sufficient to make a judgment regarding the fund's relative attractiveness. If, however, a fund is inversely correlated to a portfolio, its addition may improve the portfolio's return/risk characteristics even if the fund itself may not rate high as a single investment. Moreover, in regard to volatility, higher volatility for an inversely correlated fund could even result in lower volatility for the portfolio. Why? Because if a fund is inversely correlated to a portfolio, it will tend to be profitable when the portfolio witnesses a loss, thereby reducing the portfolio loss. This loss-reducing effect may well be greater if the fund's volatility is higher.

To illustrate these points, we will consider the simple example of adding an investment in the fund I had visited, which is a fund that pursues a short bias strategy but with positive net returns, to a portfolio represented by the S&P 500 index. In order to gauge the impact of volatility, we create a hypothetical fund with a return series that has the following characteristics:

- Same average monthly return as the fund.
- Same pattern of monthly returns as the fund (e.g., same best month, same second-best month, etc.).

- Double the volatility of the fund (as measured by the standard deviation).

Such a series can be generated by the following simple two-step transformation of the original returns:

1. Multiply the original returns by 2.
2. Subtract the average monthly return of the original series from each monthly return generated by step 1.

The resulting series will have the same average monthly return, same pattern of returns, and double the standard deviation.

In analogous fashion, we also generate a return series for another hypothetical fund with the same average monthly return and pattern of monthly returns as the fund, but half the volatility. In Table 20.1, we compare the performance characteristics of the fund to its low- and high-volatility counterparts. As can be seen, the three series have identical average monthly returns, but differ in their volatility levels, with the standard deviation ranging by a factor of 4:1 from the high-volatility series to the low-volatility series. The annual compounded returns differ, despite the equal average monthly returns, because higher volatility hurts returns (see Chapter 5). It would appear that the low-volatility series demonstrates far better performance than the high-volatility series, since its return/risk measure (return/standard deviation) is nearly eight times as high (0.95 versus 0.12). Although this conclusion is quite sound if we are evaluating performance from the perspective of a stand-alone investment, consider what happens when these alternative investments are combined with an S&P portfolio to which they are inversely correlated.

Table 20.1 The Stand-Alone Impact of Volatility on Return/Risk

	Fund	**High-Volatility Counterpart**	**Low-Volatility Counterpart**
Average monthly return	0.47%	0.47%	0.47%
Annual compounded return	5.11%	2.93%	5.66%
Annualized standard deviation	11.90%	23.81%	5.95%
Annualized return/SD ratio	0.43	0.12	0.95

Table 20.2 shows the results for portfolios created by combining an 80 percent investment in the S&P with a 20 percent investment in the fund or its high-volatility or low-volatility counterpart. (These combined portfolios have a lower return than the fund because the period used for the calculation—that is, the period of the fund's track record, January 2000 to January 2012—corresponded with a period in which the S&P's annual compounded return was a minuscule 0.7 percent.) The high-volatility series, which appeared so inferior to the low-volatility series when viewed as a stand-alone investment, now results in a combined portfolio with a slightly higher annual compounded return and a slightly lower volatility than the portfolio formed by using the low-volatility series. The highly negative impact of volatility on return/risk when viewed from the perspective of a stand-alone investment disappears at the portfolio level. This example illustrates the point that if an investment is significantly inversely correlated to the portfolio to which it is being added, then high volatility is not a negative factor and could even be helpful.

As an aside, readers might well question the plausibility of our example. Why would investors ever even consider a portfolio with a return of only 2 percent and a 12 percent standard deviation? The answer is that the past performance is often not indicative of future performance. Eighty percent of the portfolio in our example consisted of the S&P 500 index, which was up less than 1 percent per annum for the period surveyed. It is entirely reasonable for an investor to expect a significantly higher average return going forward. In fact, as the analysis in Chapter 3

Table 20.2 The Negative Impact of Volatility May Disappear for Inversely Related Investments

	80% S&P + 20% Fund	**80% S&P + 20% High-Volatility Counterpart**	**80% S&P + 20% Low-Volatility Counterpart**
Annual compounded return	2.11%	2.18%	2.05%
Annualized standard deviation	12.02%	11.45%	12.47%
Annualized return/SD ratio	0.18	0.19	0.16

showed, after a prior period of extended low returns, the S&P 500 is actually more likely to experience above-average future performance.

Investment Misconceptions

Investment Misconception 49: If two funds have similar returns (and are similar in other characteristics), the lower-volatility fund will *always* be preferred.

Reality: Although lower volatility is usually preferable, *if a fund is inversely correlated to the portfolio to which it is being added*, all bets are off. In this case, as was illustrated in the foregoing example, it is entirely possible that higher volatility could be net beneficial. (If the assets being combined are inversely correlated, higher volatility may be beneficial, detrimental, or neutral, depending on the series being combined.)

Investment Misconception 50: A higher return/volatility ratio is always preferred for equivalent funds.

Reality: *For investments that are inversely correlated to the portfolio to which they are being added*, the return/risk ratio breaks down as a meaningful measurement for the individual investment and has meaning only when applied to the combined portfolio.

Investment Insights

Portfolio considerations change everything in fund evaluation. When evaluating a fund for addition to a portfolio, there are two critical considerations:

1. The performance and qualitative assessment of the fund.
2. The correlation of the fund to the rest of the portfolio.

Sometimes, inverse correlation can make a fund with poorer standalone statistics the better choice as a portfolio addition. The moral is: If investing in a portfolio, think from a portfolio perspective.

Chapter 21

Portfolio Construction Principles

The Problem with Portfolio Optimization

Portfolio construction would seem to be a simple task given the availability of portfolio optimization software, which requires the input of only the returns for the holdings in the portfolio and provides the optimal allocations based on this input. The software will provide an efficient frontier curve, which consists of the portfolios (that is, allocation mixes) that result in the highest return for any target level of volatility. (Two efficient frontier curves—one including only stocks and bonds and the other adding alternatives to the mix—are illustrated in Figure 21.1.) If the investor decides an 8 percent annualized volatility is the desired target risk level for the portfolio, the portfolio corresponding

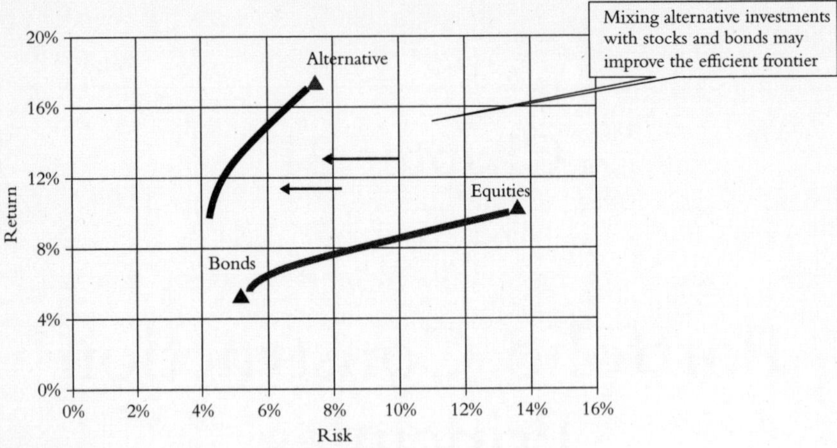

Figure 21.1 Portfolio Optimization
SOURCE: EDHEC-Risk Institute. Reproduced with kind permission.

to an 8 percent volatility on the efficient frontier curve will be the mix of assets that provides the highest return for an 8 percent volatility. So it would seem that all the investor has to do is choose the list of investments and the desired portfolio volatility level and, presto, the software would provide the mathematically derived optimal percentage allocation for each holding. Not much decision making or heavy lifting required here.

Although portfolio optimization provides an easy and seemingly scientific approach to portfolio allocation, it is based on two critically flawed implicit assumptions:

1. Past returns, volatilities, and correlations are representative of future returns, volatilities, and correlations.

One very common problem is that the length of available track records for funds in the portfolio are too short to be representative of varied market conditions. This problem is compounded by the practical consideration that a portfolio optimization analysis is constrained to the shortest-length track record included. Insofar as a portfolio includes funds with track records as short as a few years, the choice is between restricting the portfolio analysis to a short past period that includes all (or nearly all) funds or restricting the analysis to only a portion of the portfolio (that is, those funds with track records exceeding a certain minimum length).

Because of track-record-based limitations of available data, portfolio optimizations are prone to overfit allocations to the most recent market cycle. In effect, the so-called optimal allocation will be the one that performed best in recent years. When there are market transitions, however, the investments that worked best in recent years may well be among the worst future performers. In these instances, portfolio optimization will not merely be useless, but will actually lead to worse-than-random results. For example, at the start of 2000, because of their stellar performance in the recent preceding years, long-biased equity strategies, particularly those focused on technology, would have been assigned much larger than normal allocations in an optimization—exactly at the time they were about to become among the worst-performing assets. Similarly, a portfolio optimization run at the start of 2008 would have assigned heavier weights to those strategies that proved to be most exposed to the financial meltdown later in the year (e.g., long exposure to credit risk, illiquid securities, emerging markets, etc.).

Limitations in available data will also make correlation calculations less reliable. In many instances, correlations between assets can vary widely over time, and the correlation for an insufficient-length period may reflect only part of the normal range. Also, over shorter periods, there is a significant likelihood that even unrelated funds might appear correlated simply due to chance (e.g., both witnessing large gains or losses in the same month or two for unrelated reasons).

Even when there is extensive data available, the implicit assumption that this past data can be used as a proxy for future expectations is a highly tenuous one. For example, as of 2012, Treasury bonds had been in a bull market for over 30 years, a fact that would increase their optimized weighting in any portfolio in which they were an asset. Yet, ironically, the fact that T-bonds had been in such a long-term advance made their prospects for future returns less favorable, not more favorable, since the resulting low interest rate levels suggested far more limited scope for a further decline in interest rates (that is, rise in bond prices). See Chapter 6 for a more detailed discussion of this example.

The question must always be asked: Are the factors responsible for past returns still likely to be valid for the future? If they are not, portfolio optimization would yield, at best, meaningless and, at worst, misleading results.

2. Volatility is a good proxy for risk.

This inherent premise of portfolio optimization is often entirely unfounded because major risks are frequently not manifested in the track record. Also, higher volatility may sometimes be due to outsized returns that do not imply symmetrical risk. See Chapter 4 for a detailed discussion of the confusion between risk and volatility. The use of volatility as a proxy is most appropriate for highly liquid strategies, such as futures and foreign exchange (FX) trading, where event risk is not a factor, as it is for many hedge fund strategies.

Portfolio optimization provides a mathematically precise answer to the wrong question. The question it answers is: What is the optimal allocation mix for a portfolio, assuming future returns, volatilities, and correlations look like the past? The question we would like to answer is: What is the optimal allocation mix given our best assessment of prospective returns, risks, and proclivity to simultaneous losses for the investments in the portfolio? These two questions are most definitely not the same. Frequently, past returns are unrepresentative of potential future returns, past track records do not reflect known major risks, and correlations may not accurately represent tendencies toward simultaneous losses. Portfolio optimization provides an exact solution to the problem of allocating in the theoretical world. Unfortunately, we invest in the real world, and the two are often strikingly different. Consequently, a manual approach that takes into consideration key factors, including those not visible in past track records, is preferable to the easy-to-generate seeming precision of a portfolio optimization. It is better to get an approximate answer for the appropriate assumptions than an exact answer for the wrong assumptions.[1]

[1]The foregoing discussion of portfolio optimization refers to its application using past data as the assumed representative data for the various investments. Portfolio optimization, however, does provide a useful tool for determining optimal allocations implied by given assumptions. But, of course, in this latter case, the results are only as good as the assumptions.

Eight Principles of Portfolio Construction

Some of the principles that underlie sound portfolio construction have already been discussed in detail in earlier chapters. Where this is the case, we simply summarize these concepts here as they pertain to portfolio allocation and indicate the reference chapter.

1. Focus on return/risk, not return (Chapter 8).

Investors often focus most on returns without taking into account that risk exposure will directly impact returns. A manager who doubles position sizes will double returns, but will also double risk. It would be absurd to consider such a doubling of return as representing much better performance. A focus on return/risk will avoid such nonsensical comparison biases. What if a higher-return/risk manager has a lower than desired return level? In this case, the return can be increased by leverage, while still maintaining risk at a lower level than for a lower-return/risk manager with an acceptable return level. If equivalent in qualitative terms and in terms of diversification with other portfolio holdings, a higher-return/risk manager would always be preferred.

2. Focus on risk, not volatility (Chapter 4).

Volatility is only one type of risk and, in some cases, may not even represent a risk as viewed from the investor's perspective of risk, which is based on the probability and magnitude of loss. Many of the most important risks may not be reflected in the track record. The one exception where the use of volatility as a proxy for risk is roughly appropriate (although not in all cases) is for highly liquid strategies (e.g., futures and FX trading).

3. Don't confuse manager skill with a bull market. Understand the reasons for past performance (Chapter 6).

Frequently, managers may compile impressive performance records by taking substantial market exposure in a benign market environment. If widely varying market exposure is part of the investment process, then good performance in a bull market can be considered skill. If, however, the manager has consistently assumed substantial market exposure and the track record coincides with a rising market, then past returns may reflect the market more than manager skill.

4. Diversify well beyond 10 (Chapter 17).

Although, *on average*, the benefits of diversification are often only moderate beyond 10 diversified holdings, this view misses the point that the main value of greater diversification is mitigating *worst-case* outcomes ("tail risk" in the industry vernacular). Substantially greater diversification is therefore still beneficial, *provided that added investments are considered of equivalent quality and are not more correlated to other holdings.*

5. Favor bottom-up (manager-based) rather than top-down (category-based) allocation.

Many fund of fund managers follow a top-down philosophy to achieve diversification: They decide how much to allocate to each hedge fund category (e.g., long/short equity, event driven, global macro, etc.) and then select the individual managers within each strategy category. There are numerous logical inconsistencies with a top-down approach:

- Strategy category labels are not well defined, as is evident by the wide differences in the number of strategy categories among different hedge fund database providers.
- Some hedge funds fit into multiple strategy categories.
- Some hedge funds don't fit well into any strategy category.
- Hedge funds in the same category can be uncorrelated.
- Hedge funds in different categories may be highly correlated.

Category labels are inconsistent and potentially misleading as indicators of differentiation. If the goal is to select well-diversified managers, it makes much more sense to focus on the individual investment statistics (e.g., correlation, beta) and qualitative comparisons of strategies than on category labels, which are unavoidably arbitrary and inconsistent.

6. Correlation to other managers is critical. Target a low average pair correlation and a low coincidence of losing months between managers.

Selecting managers for a portfolio is different from selecting managers as stand-alone investments. The portfolio impact of adding a manager depends on both the manager's individual performance and the manager's correlation to other portfolio holdings. A manager who has a low or inverse correlation to other managers may be preferable as a portfolio addition to a qualitatively equivalent manager with a higher return/risk ratio. As another example, an inversely correlated manager with very high volatility may well reduce rather than increase portfolio volatility (see Chapter 20).

As a general guideline, a fund of funds portfolio manager or a multimanager investor should target a low average pair correlation. A pair correlation is the correlation between any two investments in the portfolio. The number of pairs in a portfolio is equal to $N \times (N-1)/2$, where N equals the total number of investments. For example, if there are 20 managers in a fund of funds portfolio, there would be $(20 \times 19)/2 = 190$ pair correlations. The *correlation matrix* detailed in the next section provides a convenient way to look at all of the portfolio's pair correlations.

It is also instructive to look directly at the coincidence of losses between different funds in a portfolio. A tool for detecting patterns of simultaneous losses in a portfolio is described later in this chapter in the section "Going Beyond Correlation." The fund of funds manager should seek to minimize the number of funds in a portfolio that exhibit a strong tendency to lose money at the same time.

7. Employ a risk-adjusted allocation process, instead of an equal allocation approach, to reduce portfolio risk.

Assume that all the managers in a portfolio are deemed to be of approximately equal quality and all are equivalently diversified versus the other managers. How should the assets be allocated? Given the foregoing simplified example, it might appear that equal allocation would be the logical choice. Actually, equal allocation can be folly, even assuming investments of equivalent merit. The absurdity of an equal allocation approach is illustrated by the following fictitious tale of two partners who co-manage a fund but have a basic disagreement on how the fund should be traded.

Carol and Andrew are partners as managers of a fund that employs a systematic futures trading strategy. Both are happy with the trading system they have developed, but they have a problem. They are currently trading their system using a 14 percent margin-to-equity ratio, a middle-of-the-road exposure level for commodity trading advisors (CTAs). Carol is very conservative and is most concerned about keeping equity drawdowns small. Andrew, however, feels they are being too cautious and should increase exposure.

One day, Carol says, "Investors are more concerned about equity drawdowns than return, and, frankly, so am I. I think we should cut our exposure in half to 7 percent margin to equity."

"Are you crazy?" Andrew shoots back. "We are already trading at too low an exposure level. Our worst drawdown so far has only been 10 percent. I think we should double our margin-to-equity level. We will double our returns, and most investors will still be fine with a maximum drawdown of 20 percent."

Carol is so exasperated that she almost can't decide where to begin. "Who says our future worst drawdown will be only as large as our past maximum drawdown? What if it is twice as large? Then with your suggestion, we would be down 40 percent and out of business!"

They decide to keep the status quo, but neither partner is satisfied. They have the same argument repeatedly over the ensuing weeks, but neither partner can budge the other. Finally, they decide to split apart, with each maintaining rights to use the system they co-developed.

Carol and Andrew each start their own funds. Both continue to use the exact same system without any alteration. The only difference is that Carol trades the system with 7 percent margin to equity, while Andrew uses 28 percent margin to equity.

Now consider a fund of funds manager who uses an equal allocation approach and adds Carol's or Andrew's fund to the portfolio. Both funds represent the exact same strategy and both will experience near identical return/risk performance. While equal allocation may sound like a neutral approach, it would result in sizing the same investment four times as large if Andrew's fund is chosen instead of Carol's. By any logic, an allocation to Andrew should be one-quarter the size of an allocation to Carol, in which case both return and risk would be equalized for what are equivalent investments.

The risk level at which a fund is run is based on the manager's subjective preferences. There is no reason why an investor needs to buy into the same risk levels. If different investments have different risk levels, then allocation levels should be adjusted accordingly. If two funds are deemed to be equivalently attractive as holdings and one has twice the risk of the other (with risk measured in whatever way is deemed most appropriate), then it should receive half the allocation. The key point is that the starting baseline allocation should be based on equal risk, not equal assets. Of course, other factors, such as relative quantitative and qualitative assessments, as well as diversification with other holdings, should also influence the allocation size. But all else being equal, higher-risk investments should get proportionally smaller allocations.

An equal allocation fund will tend to be more volatile as higher-risk holdings exert a disproportionate impact. In contrast, a risk-based allocation approach will mitigate portfolio volatility by holding proportionally smaller allocations in higher-risk investments.

8. Target a majority of positive months during negative equity months.

If a fund of funds portfolio is intended to be used as a diversifier to traditional investments rather than just as a stand-alone investment, it should seek to be net profitable in the majority of bear market months. To enhance the likelihood of achieving this goal, seek managers who have been net profitable across the down market months that occurred during their track records.

Correlation Matrix

In comparing a portfolio of investments, it is highly useful to view correlations between the investments as a group rather than one pair at a time. A correlation matrix summarizes all pair correlations between a set of investments (or any other data). An illustration of a correlation matrix is shown in Figure 21.2. Note that both the horizontal and vertical labels are the same. To find a correlation between any given pair of investments, simply look at the cell that is the intersection of those two investments. For example, to check the correlation between Fund C and

Fund Name	A	B	C	D	E	F	G	H	I	J
Fund A		−0.06	0.17	0.00	0.17	0.30	0.00	0.06	0.19	0.43
Fund B	−0.06		0.17	0.00	−0.14	0.15	0.07	−0.14	−0.17	0.17
Fund C	0.17	0.17		0.00	0.09	−0.07	0.00	0.13	0.45	0.21
Fund D	0.00	0.00	0.00		0.12	0.00	0.30	−0.09	0.87	0.03
Fund E	0.17	−0.14	0.09	0.12		−0.04	0.37	0.21	−0.21	0.32
Fund F	0.30	0.15	−0.07	0.00	−0.04		0.84	0.03	0.12	0.47
Fund G	0.00	0.07	0.00	0.30	0.37	0.84		0.87	0.55	0.17
Fund H	0.06	−0.14	0.13	−0.09	0.21	0.03	0.87		−0.07	0.22
Fund I	0.19	−0.17	0.45	0.87	−0.21	0.12	0.55	−0.07		0.38
Fund J	0.43	0.17	0.21	0.03	0.32	0.47	0.17	0.22	0.38	

Figure 21.2 Correlation Matrix

Fund E, look at the intersection of the row for Fund C and the column for row E, or equivalently, the intersection of the row for Fund E and the column for row C. Both show a correlation of 0.09. The upper diagonal half of the correlation matrix duplicates the data of the lower half of the matrix. For this reason, frequently only the lower diagonal half of the correlation matrix is shown. The diagonal values of the correlation matrix would always be 1.0, as each cell in the diagonal is the intersection of a fund and itself. Since this is a trivial case, these cells are frequently left blank. It may be useful to highlight correlation values above some threshold. For example, Figure 21.2 shades all correlation values greater than 0.7. The average of all the correlation pairs in the correlation matrix provides a good summary indication of the degree of diversification in the portfolio. The lower the average pair correlation, the better.

Going Beyond Correlation

Although correlation is a useful tool for flagging investments that may be prone to witness simultaneous losses, for reasons detailed in Chapter 9, moderate or even high correlation between two funds does not necessarily imply that they will experience losses at the same time, nor does low correlation assure that this is not the case. Examining how each fund behaves when the other funds in the portfolio experience decline provides a more focused analysis than correlation in directly addressing the key concern: simultaneous losses.

The *coincident negative return* (CNR) matrix provides a convenient format for assessing the degree to which investments in the portfolio are vulnerable to losses when other portfolio holdings experience a decline. The CNR matrix would look similar to the conventional correlation matrix, but would differ in the following two essential ways:

1. Instead of showing the correlation between two investments, the value of each cell would show the percentage of time the investment in that row was down, given that the column investment was down. For example, the number in the cell at the intersection between row Fund E and column Fund C would indicate the percentage of the time Fund E was down when Fund C was down. If Fund C was down in 20 percent of all months and in 60 percent of those same months Fund E was also down, then the value in row E/column C would be 60 percent. Any time period could be used to calculate the CNR matrix, and monthly data was assumed in the preceding example. If available, however, daily (or even weekly) data would offer statistically more meaningful results in indicating which investments are most likely to experience simultaneous losses.
2. In contrast to the standard correlation matrix, the CNR matrix is nonsymmetrical—that is, the segment above the diagonal is not a duplicate of the segment below the diagonal. The reason for this asymmetry is that the percentage of time the row investment is down given that the column investment is down is not the same as the percentage of time the column investment is down given that the row investment is down.

There would be one parameter input required to calculate the CNR matrix: the minimum loss threshold (T) to define a losing period (month for monthly data). The default value for T would be zero; that is, any loss would represent a losing month. There is, however, a good reason to use a higher threshold: It may be more pertinent to focus on significant simultaneous losses rather than all simultaneous losses. For example, we may not care whether Fund E declined in months when Fund C was down a minimal amount. If T were set to a value of 0.5 percent, then the CNR matrix would show the percentage of times the row managers lost at least 0.5 percent when the column managers lost at least 0.5 percent.

The significance of what percentage of the time a manager loses when another manager loses depends on whether this percentage is more or less than the manager's average percentage of losses. Thus, it may be more meaningful to use a normalized version of the CNR matrix, wherein each percentage is divided by a manager's average percentage of losses worse than the threshold (T). For example, if Manager A is down in 30 percent of all months but in only 20 percent of the months when Manager B is down (for simplicity of exposition we assume $T = 0$), then the *normalized* CNR statistic would be 66.7 percent (20%/30% = 0.667), indicating it is less likely for Manager A to lose when Manager B is down than in a randomly selected month. If, however, Manager A is down in 50 percent of the months when Manager B is down, then the *normalized* CNR statistic would be 166.7 percent (50%/30% = 1.667), indicating it is more likely for Manager A to lose when Manager B is down than in a randomly selected month.

Note: The CNR is my own invention and not available on any existing software. It will, however, be included in the Schwager Analytics Module currently being developed by Gate 39 Media as a module for their Clarity Portfolio Viewer system, an add-on scheduled for release in the second quarter of 2013. Interested readers can get more information at: www.gate39media.com/schwager-analytics. For the sake of disclosure, I have a financial interest in this product.

Investment Misconceptions

Investment Misconception 51: Portfolio optimization provides the best means for achieving the optimal return for any targeted volatility level.

Reality: The key implicit premise of portfolio optimization is that past returns, volatilities, and correlations provide reasonable estimates for expected future levels. This inherent assumption is not merely frequently invalid, but when there are major market turning points, optimized portfolios may well yield worse-than-random results. The exactness provided by portfolio optimization is a false precision because it is usually based on inaccurate assumptions.

Investment Misconception 52: Top-down allocation is a useful tool in assuring adequate diversification.

Reality: Category labels are unavoidably arbitrary and can be poor indicators of fund differentiation. If the objective is to achieve a well-diversified portfolio, it is far more effective to focus on selecting differentiated managers than to allocate specified percentages to different category buckets. A top-down approach can easily result in an overly correlated portfolio because managers in different categories can still end up being vulnerable to the same risk factors.

Investment Misconception 53: If managers are considered qualitatively equivalent, the manager with better return/risk potential would always be preferred.

Reality: What is true in selecting a stand-alone investment is not necessarily true in selecting an investment for a portfolio. A poorer-performing investment could well be more beneficial to portfolio performance than a superior-performing investment if it is also significantly inversely correlated to other portfolio holdings.

Investment Misconception 54: If the investments in a portfolio are judged to be of approximately equivalent merit, then an equal allocation approach is appropriate.

Reality: Equal risk provides a more logical neutral allocation guideline than equal assets and is also likely to be more effective in mitigating portfolio risk.

Investment Misconception 55: The portfolio correlation matrix provides a comprehensive tool for identifying funds that are likely to lose money in the same periods.

Reality: The correlation matrix is very useful in flagging funds that *may* be more likely to witness simultaneous losses, but because correlation is based on all months rather than losing months, it can sometimes be inadequate and even misleading in identifying funds that are prone to losses at the same time as other funds in the portfolio. The coincident negative return matrix provides a useful supplement to the correlation matrix in helping identify funds that are prone to simultaneous losses.

Investment Insights

Efficient portfolio allocation can dictate decisions that would be irrational for stand-alone investments. Lower return/risk managers might sometimes be preferred over higher return/risk managers for a portfolio allocation if they are inversely correlated to the portfolio. The key consideration is which manager will provide a *portfolio* with the highest expected return/risk characteristics, not which manager has the highest expected return/risk characteristics.

Portfolio optimization applies mathematical precision to the portfolio allocation process, but it is often based on faulty assumptions. The typical implicit assumption in portfolio optimization is that past returns, volatilities, and correlations are reasonable estimates for future expected levels. The problem is that this assumption is often deeply flawed, particularly in the case of returns. At major market transition points, portfolio optimization may often yield worse-than-random results.

Equal allocation is often viewed as the default neutral portfolio allocation. In reality, however, because managers often differ widely in the risk they assume, an equal allocation portfolio will inadvertently allocate far more risk to some managers than others. A more sensible neutral approach is to allocate in terms of equal risk, which ironically will imply that some managers will get much larger allocations than others.

Epilogue

32 Investment Observations

1. Listening to the experts may be detrimental to your financial health.
2. The market is not always right. The best opportunities arise when the market is most wrong.
3. Big price moves begin on fundamentals but end on emotion.
4. The price move often causes the news rather than the other way around.
5. Past returns are not future returns. Past returns can be very misleading if there are reasons to believe that future market conditions are likely to be significantly different from those that shaped past returns.
6. At major fundamental or psychological transition points, the best past performers often become among the worst future performers.
7. The best time to initiate long-term investments in equities is after extended periods of underperformance.
8. Faulty risk measurement is worse than no risk measurement at all because it will lull investors into unwarranted complacency.

9. Volatility is frequently a poor proxy for risk. Many low-volatility investments have high risk, while some high-volatility investments have well-controlled risk. Typically, volatility is a good measure of risk for only highly liquid investments.
10. The real risks are often invisible in the track record.
11. Volatility is detrimental to return.
12. Leveraged exchange-traded funds (ETFs) can drastically underperform equivalently leveraged investments in the underlying market—sometimes even losing when they get the market direction right.
13. High past returns sometimes reflect excessive risk taking in a favorable market environment rather than manager skill. Understanding the source of returns is critical to evaluating their implications and relevance.
14. Comparisons between managers should be made only for coincident periods.
15. Pro forma results that are hindsight dependent can be extremely misleading. However, pro forma results that only adjust for differences between current and past fees and commissions can be more representative than actual results. It is critical to differentiate between these two radically different applications of the same term: pro forma.
16. Return alone is a meaningless statistic because return can be increased by increasing risk. The return/risk ratio should be the primary performance metric.
17. Although the Sharpe ratio is by far the most widely used return/risk measure, return/risk measures based on downside risk come much closer to reflecting risk as it is perceived by most investors.
18. Conventional arithmetic-scale net asset value (NAV) charts provide a distorted picture, especially for longer-term track records that traverse a wide range of NAV levels. A log scale should be used for long-term NAV charts.
19. The correlation of an investment to an index (e.g., S&P 500) only measures the degree to which its returns will tend to be higher when the index is stronger and lower when the index is weaker. Correlation does not directly measure the degree to which down months in the index imply down months in the investment. It is

even entirely possible for an investment to be significantly correlated to an index and still be up a large majority of the time when the index is down. If investors are concerned about a fund doing poorly when the S&P is down, then the analysis should focus on the investment's performance during past down months.

20. The general perception is that hedge funds are a high-return/high-risk investment. The reality is that a well-diversified hedge fund portfolio provides a *conservative* investment with *moderate return* potential. The conventional wisdom that hedge funds are inappropriate for conservative investors is based on prejudice rather than fact. The statistical evidence indicates that the typical diversified hedge fund investment not only is less risky than a traditional portfolio, but also provides diversification benefits.

21. Never use hedge fund indexes based on single funds to represent hedge fund performance. These indexes contain many biases that will make hedge fund performance appear much better than it really is. Indexes based on funds of hedge funds provide a far more realistic representation of hedge fund performance.

22. Leverage alone tells you nothing about risk. Risk is a function of *both* the underlying portfolio and leverage. Leveraged portfolios can often have lower risk than unleveraged portfolios; it depends on the assets in the portfolio.

23. Increasing leverage does not necessarily imply increased risk. Leverage that is used for hedging will actually reduce risk.

24. Managed accounts provide a much safer investment vehicle for investors than the conventional fund structure. The best due diligence process in the world can't compete with the safeguards of direct investor ownership and transparency that are inherent in the managed account structure.

25. Research studies that conclude that diversification benefits beyond 10 are modest are invariably based on what happens *on average* across thousands of portfolios rather than what happens in the *worst case* to a specific portfolio. Portfolio managers who are concerned about tail risk should diversify well beyond 10 holdings (except when added assets are considered to be inferior to existing assets).

26. Increasing the number of holdings will not necessarily enhance diversification. The key is the degree to which added assets are uncorrelated to existing assets. Adding correlated holdings could even reduce diversification.

27. Portfolio rebalancing, which implies redistributing assets from better-performing managers during the recent period to inferior performers during the same period, will often lead to improved long-term performance (although the outcome is case dependent).

28. Although lower volatility is usually preferable, if a fund is inversely correlated to the portfolio to which it is being added, higher volatility may be an attribute (case dependent).

29. The exactness provided by portfolio optimization is a false precision because it is usually based on unrepresentative inputs. Portfolio optimization is appropriate only if past returns, volatilities, and correlations are considered reasonable estimates for the future. At major market turning points, optimized portfolios may well yield worse-than-random results.

30. Given the unavoidably arbitrary nature of hedge fund category labels, a bottom-up approach is often more effective than a top-down approach in achieving a diversified portfolio.

31. When selecting managers for a portfolio, it is important to evaluate managers not only on their stand-alone qualities, but also on their portfolio diversification characteristics. A poorer-performing manager that is qualitatively differentiated and relatively uncorrelated (or inversely correlated) with the other managers in the portfolio could well be more beneficial to portfolio performance than a superior-performing manager.

32. Equal risk provides a more logical neutral allocation guideline for a portfolio than equal assets and is also likely to be more effective in mitigating portfolio risk.

Appendix A

Options—Understanding the Basics*

There are two basic types of options: calls and puts. The purchase of a *call option* provides the buyer with the right—but not the obligation—to purchase the underlying item at a specified price, called the *strike* or *exercise* price, at any time up to and including the *expiration date*. A *put option* provides the buyer with the right—but not the obligation—to sell the underlying item at the strike price at any time prior to expiration. (Note, therefore, that buying a put is a *bearish* trade, whereas selling a put is a *bullish* trade.) The price of an option is called a *premium*. As an example of an option, an IBM April 210 call gives the purchaser the right to buy 100 shares of IBM at $210 per share at any time during the life of the option.

The buyer of a call seeks to profit from an anticipated price rise by locking in a specified purchase price. The call buyer's maximum possible loss will be equal to the dollar amount of the premium paid for

*This appendix is adapted from an appendix originally published in Jack D. Schwager, *Market Wizards* (New York: New York Institute of Finance, 1989).

the option. This maximum loss (the premium paid) would occur on an option held until expiration if the strike price was above the prevailing market price. For example, if IBM was trading at $205 when the 210 option expired, the option would expire worthless. If at expiration, however, the price of the underlying market was above the strike price, the option would have some value and would hence be exercised. However, if the difference between the market price and the strike price was less than the premium paid for the option, the net result of the trade would still be a loss. In order for a call buyer to realize a net profit, the difference between the market price and the strike price would have to exceed the premium paid when the call was purchased (after adjusting for commission cost). The higher the market price, the greater the resulting profit.

The buyer of a put seeks to profit from an anticipated price decline by locking in a sales price. Like the call buyer, the maximum possible loss is limited to the dollar amount of the premium paid for the option. In the case of a put held until expiration, the trade would show a net profit if the strike price exceeded the market price by an amount greater than the premium of the put at purchase (after adjusting for commission cost).

Whereas the buyer of a call or put has limited risk and unlimited potential gain, the reverse is true for the seller. The option seller (often called the *writer*) receives the dollar value of the premium in return for undertaking the obligation to assume an opposite position *at the strike price* if an option is exercised. For example, if a call is exercised, the seller must assume a short position in the underlying market at the strike price (since by exercising the call, the buyer assumes a long position at that price).

The seller of a call seeks to profit from an anticipated sideways to modestly declining market. In such a situation, the premium earned by selling a call provides the most attractive trading opportunity. However, if the trader expected a large price decline, he or she would usually be better off going short the underlying market or buying a put—trades with open-ended profit potential. In a similar fashion, the seller of a put seeks to profit from an anticipated sideways to modestly rising market.

Some novices have trouble understanding why a trader would not always prefer the buy side of the option (call or put, depending on market opinion), since such a trade has unlimited potential and limited risk. Such confusion reflects the failure to take probability into account. Although the option seller's theoretical risk is unlimited, the price levels that have the greatest probability of occurrence (i.e., prices in the vicinity of the market price when the option trade occurs) would result in a net gain to the option seller. Roughly speaking, the option buyer accepts a large probability of a small loss (the premium paid) in return for a small probability of a large gain, whereas the option seller accepts a small probability of a large loss in exchange for a large probability of a small gain.

The option premium consists of two components: intrinsic value plus time value. The *intrinsic value* of a call option is the amount by which the current market price is above the strike price. (The intrinsic value of a put option is the amount by which the current market price is below the strike price.) In effect, the intrinsic value is that part of the premium that could be realized if the option were exercised at the current market price. The intrinsic value serves as a floor price for an option. Why? Because if the premium were less than the intrinsic value, a trader could buy and exercise the option and immediately offset the resulting market position, thereby realizing a net gain (assuming that the trader covers at least transaction costs).

Options that have intrinsic value (i.e., calls with strike prices below the market price and puts with strike prices above the market price) are said to be *in-the-money*. Options that have no intrinsic value are called *out-of-the-money* options. Options with a strike price closest to the market price are called *at-the-money* options.

An out-of-the-money option, which by definition has an intrinsic value equal to zero, will still have some value because of the possibility that the market price will move beyond the strike price prior to the expiration date. An in-the-money option will have a value greater than the intrinsic value because, if priced at the intrinsic value, a position in the option would always be preferred to a position in the underlying market. Why? Because both the option and the market position would then gain equally in the event of a favorable price movement, but the option's maximum loss would be limited. The portion of the premium that exceeds the intrinsic value is called the *time value*.

The three most important factors that influence an option's time value are:

1. *Relationship between the strike and market price*—Deeply out-of-the-money options will have little time value since it is unlikely that the market price will move to the strike price—or beyond—prior to expiration. Deeply in-the-money options have little time value, because these options offer positions very similar to the underlying market—both will gain and lose equivalent amounts for all but an extremely adverse price move. In other words, for a deeply in-the-money option, the fact that risk is limited is not worth very much, because the strike price is so far from the prevailing market price.

2. *Time remaining until expiration*—The more time remaining until expiration, the greater the value of the option. This is true because a longer life span increases the probability of the intrinsic value increasing by any specified amount prior to expiration.

3. *Volatility*—Time value will vary directly with the estimated *volatility* (a measure of the degree of price variability) of the underlying market for the remaining life span of the option. This relationship is a result of the fact that greater volatility raises the probability of the intrinsic value increasing by any specified amount prior to expiration. In other words, the greater the volatility, the greater the probable price range of the market.

Although volatility is an extremely important factor in the determination of option premium values, it should be stressed that the future volatility of a market is never precisely known until after the fact. (In contrast, the time remaining until expiration and the relationship between the current market price and the strike price can be exactly specified at any juncture.) Thus, volatility must always be estimated on the basis of *historical volatility* data. The future volatility estimate implied by market prices (i.e., option premiums), which may be higher or lower than the historical volatility, is called the *implied volatility*.

On average, there is a tendency for the implied volatility of options to be higher than the subsequent *realized volatility* of the market till the options' expiration. In other words, options tend to be priced a little high. The extra premium is necessary to induce option sellers to take the open-ended risk of providing price insurance to option buyers. This situation is entirely analogous to home insurance premiums being priced at levels that provide a profit margin to insurance companies—otherwise, they would have no incentive to assume the open-ended risk.

Appendix B

Formulas for Risk-Adjusted Return Measures

This appendix provides the formulas for the performance measures described in Chapter 8.

Sharpe Ratio

$$SR = \frac{AR - RF}{SD}$$

where:

SR = Sharpe ratio
AR = Average return (used as proxy for expected return)
RF = Risk-free interest rate (e.g., Treasury bill return)
SD = Standard deviation

The standard deviation is calculated as follows:

$$SD = \sqrt{\frac{\sum_{I}^{N}(X_i - \overline{X})^2}{N-1}}$$

where:

$\overline{X}$ = Mean
X_i = Individual returns
N = Number of returns

Assuming monthly data is used to calculate the Sharpe ratio, as is most common, the Sharpe ratio would be annualized by multiplying by the square root of 12. Note that the return is an arithmetic average return, not the compounded return.

Sortino Ratio

$$SR = \frac{ACR - MAR}{DD}$$

where:

SR = Sortino ratio
ACR = Annual compounded return
MAR = Minimum acceptable return (e.g., zero, risk-free, average)
DD = Downside deviation

where DD is defined as:

$$DD = \sqrt{\frac{\sum_{i}^{N}\left(MIN(X_i - MAR, 0)\right)^2}{N}}$$

where:

X_i = Individual returns
MAR = Minimum acceptable return (e.g., zero, risk-free, average)
N = Number of data values

For example, if we define $MAR = 0$, then DD calculations will include only deviations for months with negative returns (the other months will equal zero).

Symmetric Downside-Risk Sharpe Ratio

$$SDRSR = \frac{ACR - RF}{\sqrt{2} \times DD}$$

where:

$SDRSR$ = Symmetric downside-risk Sharpe ratio
ACR = Annual compounded return
RF = Risk-free interest rate (e.g., T-bill return)
DD = Downside deviation

where DD is defined as:

$$DD = \sqrt{\frac{\sum_{i}^{N} \left(MIN(X_i - \overline{X}, 0) \right)^2}{N - 1}}$$

where:

X_i = Individual returns
$\overline{X}$ = Benchmark return (e.g., mean, zero, risk free)

Since the SDR Sharpe ratio includes only the downside deviation, multiplying by the square root of 2 (a consequence of doubling the squared deviations) is equivalent to assuming the upside deviation is equal (i.e., symmetric) to the downside deviation. This proxy replacement of the upside deviation is what makes it possible to compare SDR Sharpe ratio values with Sharpe ratio values.

Gain-to-Pain Ratio (GPR)

$$GPR = \frac{\sum_{i=1}^{N} X_i}{\left|\sum_{i}^{N} MIN(X_i, 0)\right|}$$

where:

X_i = Individual returns

Tail Ratio

$$TR = \frac{\frac{\sum_{p=0}^{p=T} X_p}{N_{p<T}}}{\frac{\sum_{p=100-T}^{p=100} X_p}{N_{p>100-T}}}$$

where:

X_p = Return at percentile p

T = Threshold percentile to calculate numerator of tail ratio (Implicit assumption: Lower percentile rankings represent higher return. For example, the top 10% of returns would be all returns less than T, where T = 10.)

$N_{p<T}$ = Number of returns below percentile

$TN_{p>100-T}$ = Number of returns above percentile 100-T

MAR and Calmar Ratios

$$MAR = \frac{ACR}{1 - MIN\left(\frac{NAV_j}{NAV_i}\right)}$$

where:

ACR = Annual compounded return (expressed in decimal form)
NAV = Net asset value
$j > i$

Return Retracement Ratio

$$RRR = \frac{ACR - RF}{AMR}$$

where:

ACR = Annual compounded return
RF = Risk-free return
AMR = Average maximum retracement = MR_i/N

where:

N = Number of months
$MR_i = \max(MRPNH_i, MRSNL_i)$

where $MRPNH_i$ is the maximum retracement from prior NAV high, and is defined as:

$$MRPNH_i = (PNH_i - NAV_i)/PNH_i$$

where:

PNH_i = Prior NAV high (prior to month i)
NAV_i = NAV at end of month i

$MRSNL_i$ is the maximum retracement to a subsequent NAV low, and is defined as:

$$MRSNL_i = (NAV_i - SNL_i)/NAV_i$$

where SNL_i is the subsequent NAV low (subsequent to month i)

Acknowledgments

First and foremost I would like to thank Joel Greenblatt for writing the Foreword. His first book, *You Can Be a Stock Market Genius*, was both an instruction manual and an inspiration to many hedge fund managers. I am honored that Joel, an immensely successful manager and a writer with the gift of making the complex not only understandable but also entertaining, agreed to write the Foreword to this volume.

I would like to thank Peter V. Rajsingh for his careful review of the manuscript and for his thought-provoking comments and suggestions, which unquestionably helped improve the precision and clarity of the text. I would also like to thank Caren Bianco for her meticulous reading of the manuscript—I couldn't believe how many errors she spotted in what I thought was relatively clean copy. Her thoughtful comments and questions also inspired some revisions in the text.

I am grateful to Christopher Brodie for suggesting the market example I used in Chapter 2 to illustrate the nonsynchronous relationship between changes in fundamentals and market price response and for providing the accompanying charts.

I would like to thank Mark Hulbert for providing me with full access to his very comprehensive database on market newsletter returns as implied by their recommendations. The *Hulbert Financial Digest* is probably the only source for this data, and the relevant study in Chapter 1 would have been impossible without it. I would like to thank Daniel Stark for providing me access to Stark & Company's very comprehensive commodity trading advisor (CTA) database that, critically, also contains returns for defunct funds—data that is essential in conducting statistically unbiased analysis of the relationship between past and future returns.

About the Author

Jack D. Schwager is a recognized industry expert in futures and hedge funds and the author of a number of widely acclaimed financial books. He is currently the co–portfolio manager for the ADM Investor Services Diversified Strategies Fund, a portfolio of futures and foreign exchange (FX) managed accounts. He is also an adviser to Marketopper, an India-based quantitative trading firm, supervising a major project that will adapt that firm's trading technology to trade a global futures portfolio.

Previously, Mr. Schwager was a partner in the Fortune Group, a London-based hedge fund advisory firm acquired by the Close Brothers Group. His previous experience also includes 22 years as director of futures research for some of Wall Street's leading firms and 10 years as the co-principal of a CTA.

Mr. Schwager has written extensively on the futures industry and great traders in all financial markets. He is perhaps best known for his best-selling series of interviews with the greatest hedge fund managers of the past two decades: *Market Wizards* (1989, new edition 2012), *The New Market Wizards* (1992), *Stock Market Wizards* (2001), and *Hedge Fund Market Wizards* (2012). Mr. Schwager's first book, *A Complete*

Guide to the Futures Markets (1984), is considered to be one of the classic reference works in the field. He later revised and expanded this original work into the three-volume series, *Schwager on Futures*, consisting of *Fundamental Analysis* (1995), *Technical Analysis* (1996), and *Managed Trading: Myths & Truths* (1996). He is also the author of *Getting Started in Technical Analysis* (1999), part of John Wiley & Sons' popular "Getting Started" series.

Mr. Schwager is a frequent seminar speaker and has lectured on a range of analytical topics, including the characteristics of great traders, investment fallacies, hedge fund portfolios, managed accounts, technical analysis, and trading system evaluation. He holds a BA in economics from Brooklyn College (1970) and an MA in economics from Brown University (1971).

Index